image comics presents...

Nothing Lasts Forever

Other books by Sina Grace:

Not My Bag
&
Self-Obsessed

IMAGE COMICS, INC.
Robert Kirkman—Chief Operating Officer
Erik Larsen—Chief Financial Officer
Todd McFarlane—President
Marc Silvestri—Chief Executive Officer
Jim Valentino—Vice-President

Eric Stephenson—Publisher
Corey Murphy—Director of Sales
Jeff Boison—Director of Publishing Planning & Book Trade Sales
Chris Ross—Director of Digital Sales
Jeff Stang—Director of Specialty Sales
Kat Salazar—Director of PR & Marketing
Branwyn Bigglestone—Controller
Sue Korpela—Accounts Manager
Drew Gill—Art Director
Brett Warnock—Production Manager
Meredith Wallace—Print Manager
Tricia Ramos—Traffic Manager
Briah Skelly—Publicist
Aly Hoffman—Events & Conventions Coordinator
Sasha Head—Sales & Marketing Production Designer
David Brothers—Branding Manager
Melissa Gifford—Content Manager
Drew Fitzgerald—Publicity Assistant
Vincent Kukua—Production Artist
Erika Schnatz—Production Artist
Ryan Brewer—Production Artist
Shanna Matuszak—Production Artist
Carey Hall—Production Artist
Esther Kim—Direct Market Sales Representative
Emilio Bautista—Digital Sales Representative
Leanna Caunter—Accounting Assistant
Chloe Ramos-Peterson—Library Market Sales Representative
Maria Eizik—Administrative Assistant
IMAGECOMICS.COM

NOTHING LASTS FOREVER. First printing. June 2017. Published by Image Comics, Inc. Office of publication: 2701 NW Vaughn St., Suite 780, Portland, OR 97210.

Printed in the USA. For information regarding the CPSIA on this printed material call: 203-595-3636 and provide reference #RICH–738673. Representation: Law Offices of Harris M. Miller II, P.C. (rightsinquiries@gmail.com). ISBN: 978-1-5343-0183-2.

NOTHING LASTS FOREVER

FOREVER

WRITTEN & ILLUSTRATED BY

SINA GRACE

WITH ADDITIONAL COLOR WORK BY JENNY D. FINE

AN
IMAGE COMICS
GRAPHIC MEMOIR

for Chris

Journal

· a daily record of
events on business;
a private journal
is usually referred
to as a diary

About the format...

This book is comprised of journal entries and strips from when I was sick, and thus the new material and coloring were created to match the tone and vulnerability of the rougher content within.

TL;DR - this book is intentionally a bit rough. Sorry not sorry.

♡ Sina

" By the time I got your letter
I lost my mind
I was trippin'
When you're getting better
it's a jagged line
Nothing lasts forever when you
travel time ... "

— Jenny Lewis
" the Voyager "

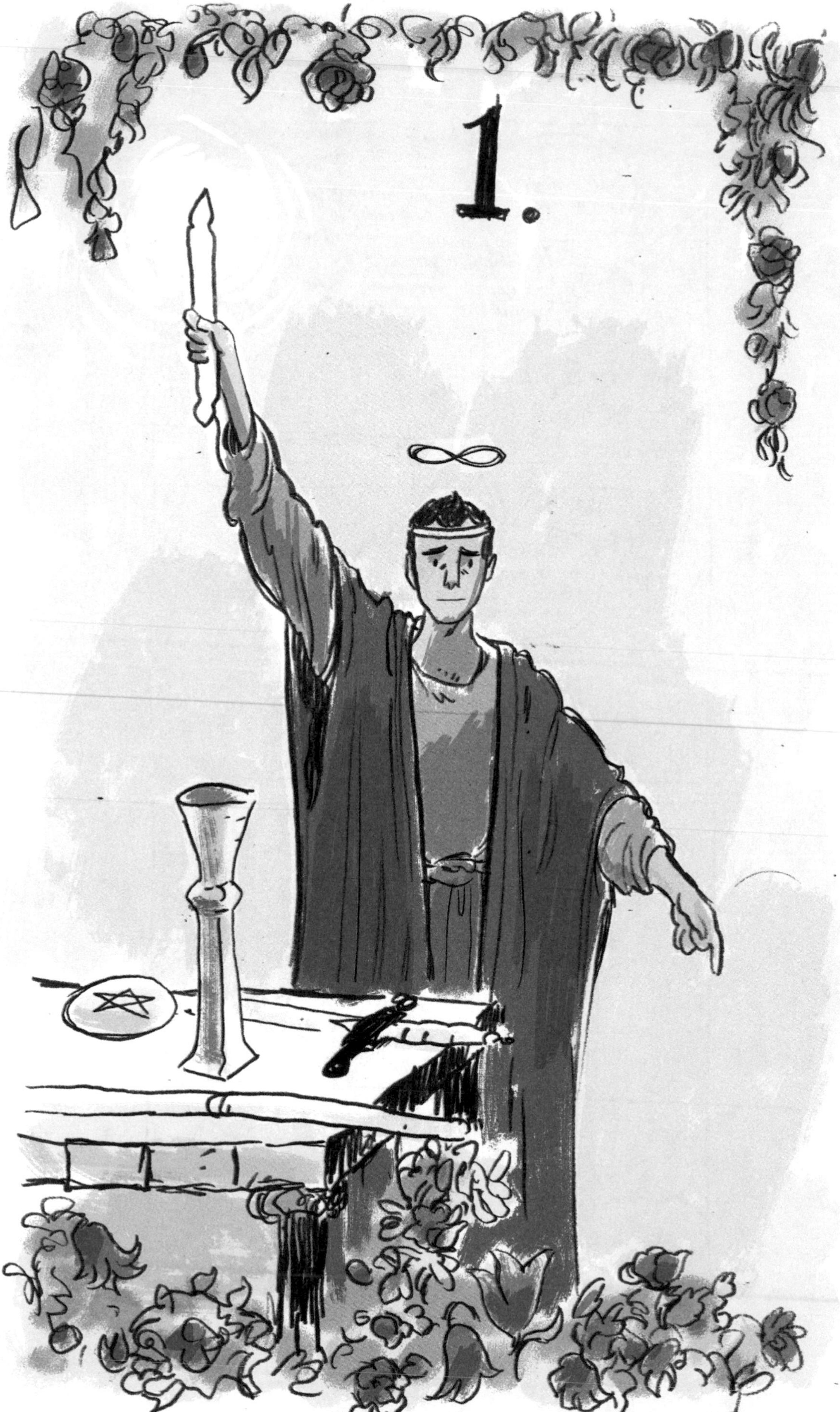
1.

a memory
(the day before my grandma died)

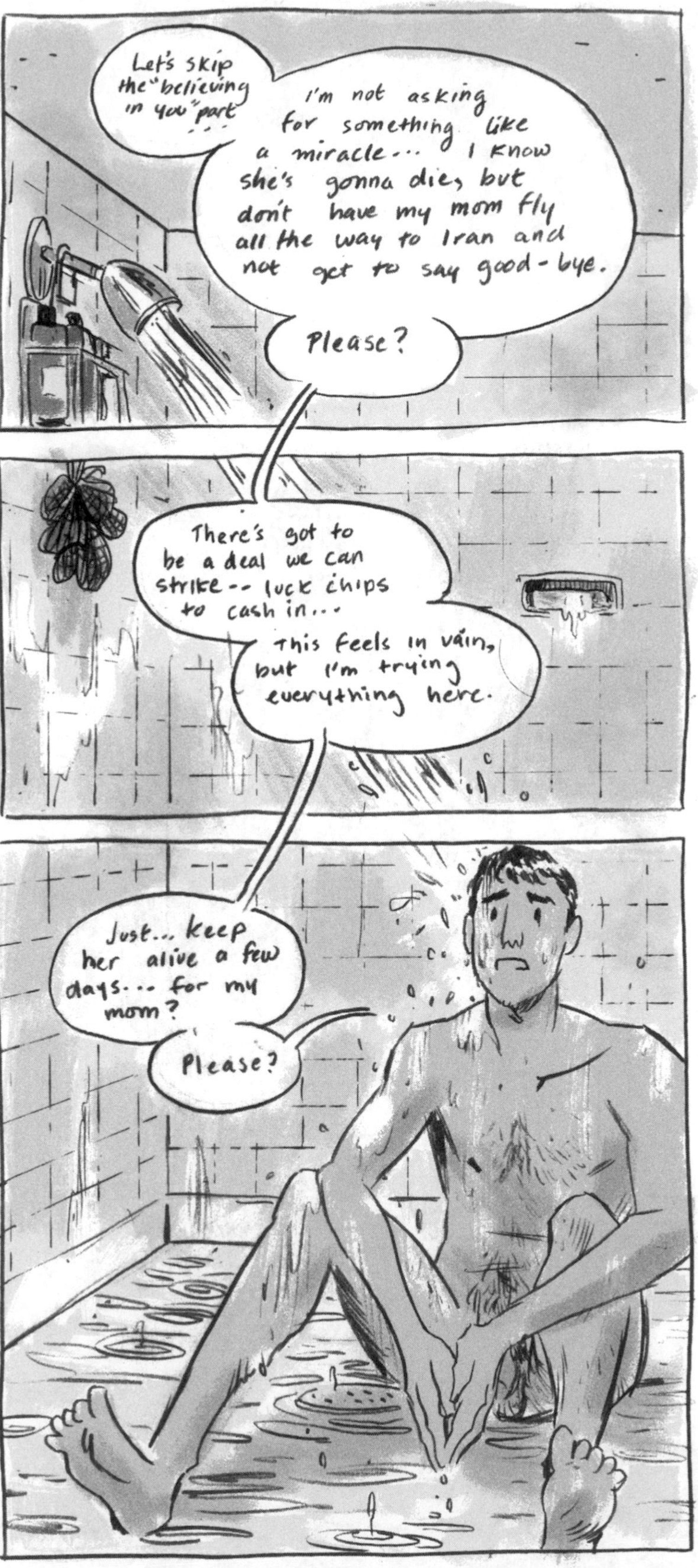

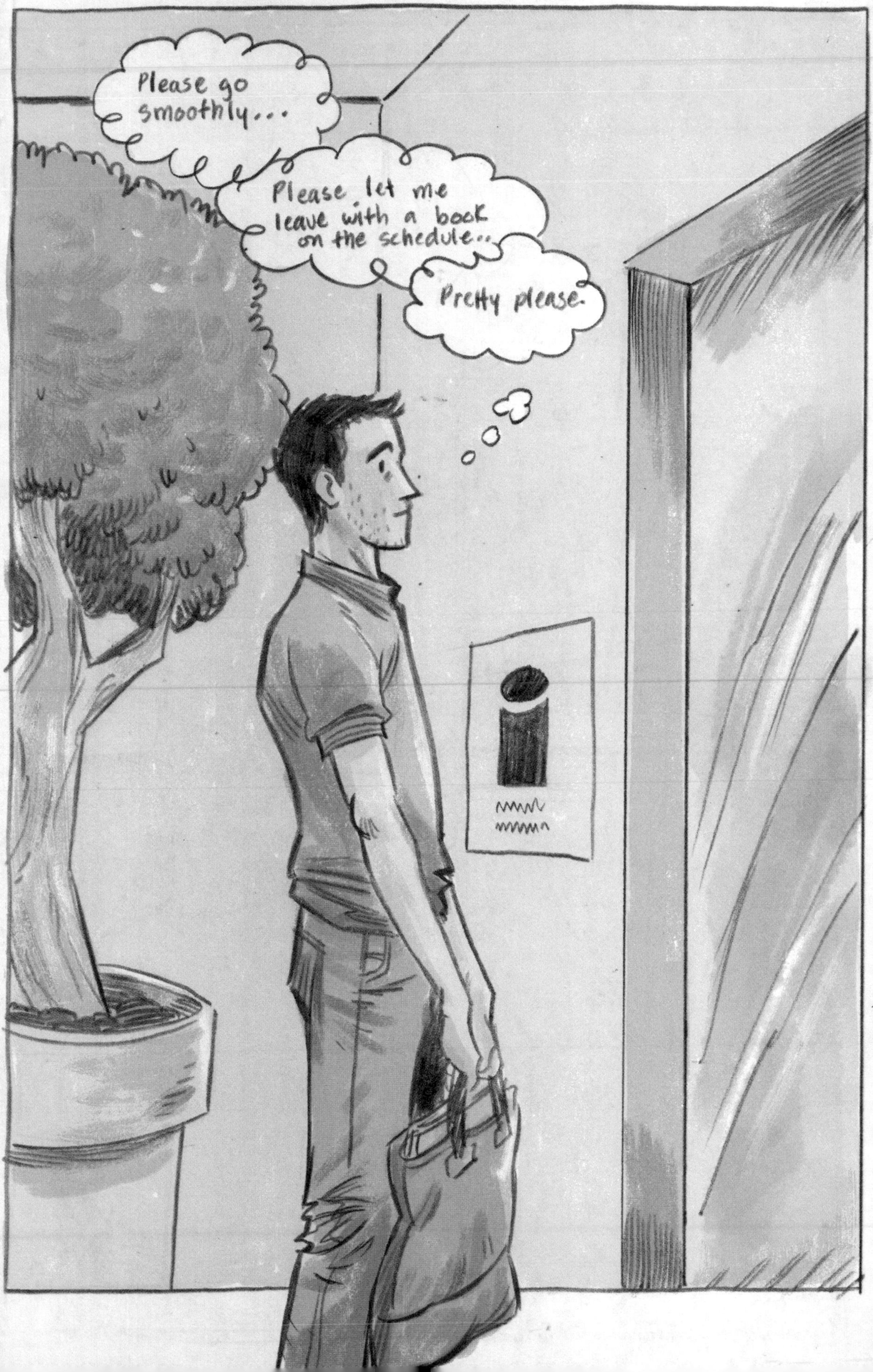
Please go smoothly...
Please let me leave with a book on the schedule...
Pretty please.

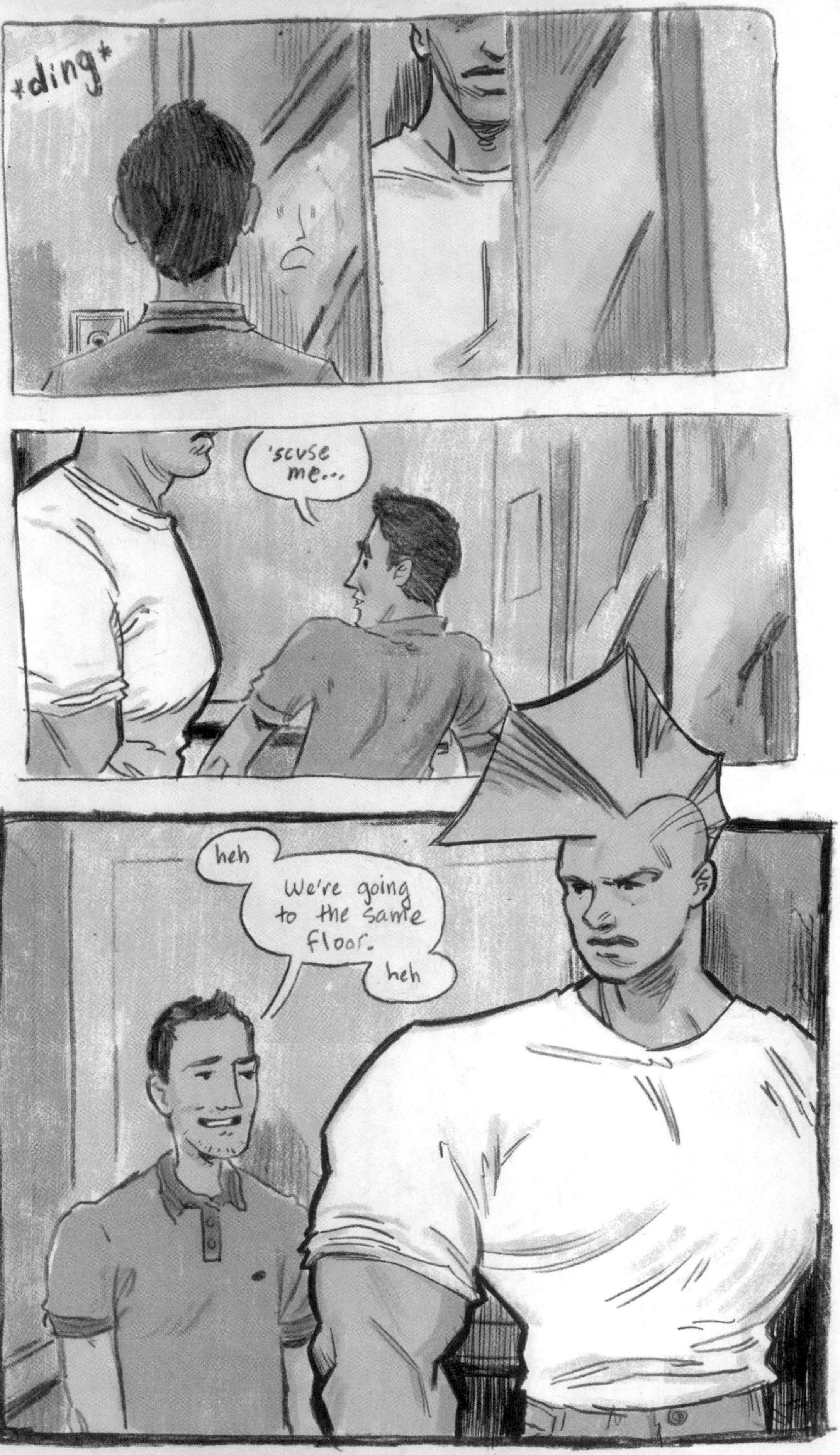
ding
'scuse me...
heh
We're going to the same floor.
heh

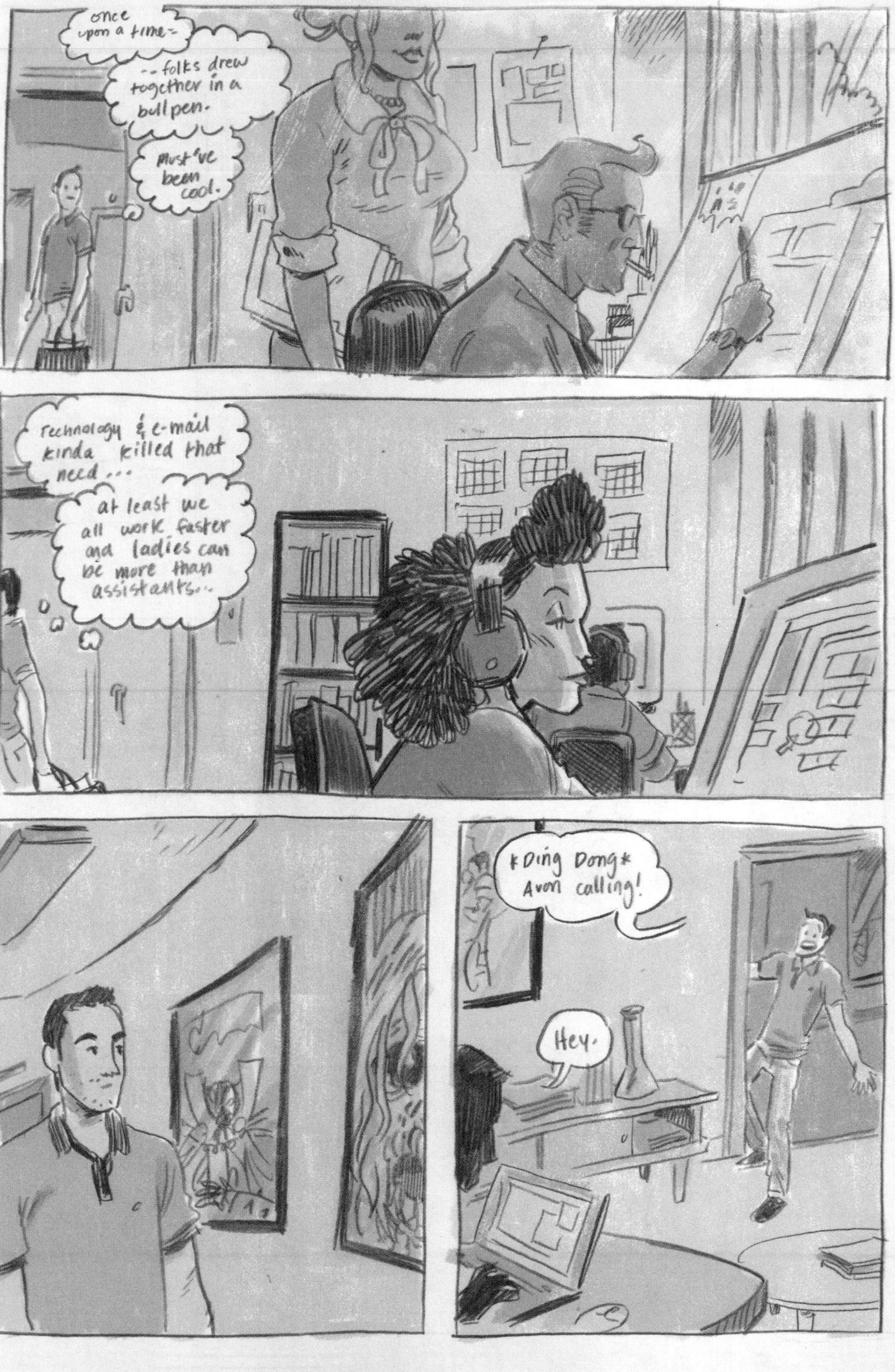
once upon a time-
-- folks drew together in a bullpen.
Must've been cool.
Technology & e-mail kinda killed that need...
at least we all work faster and ladies can be more than assistants...
Ding Dong Avon calling!
Hey.

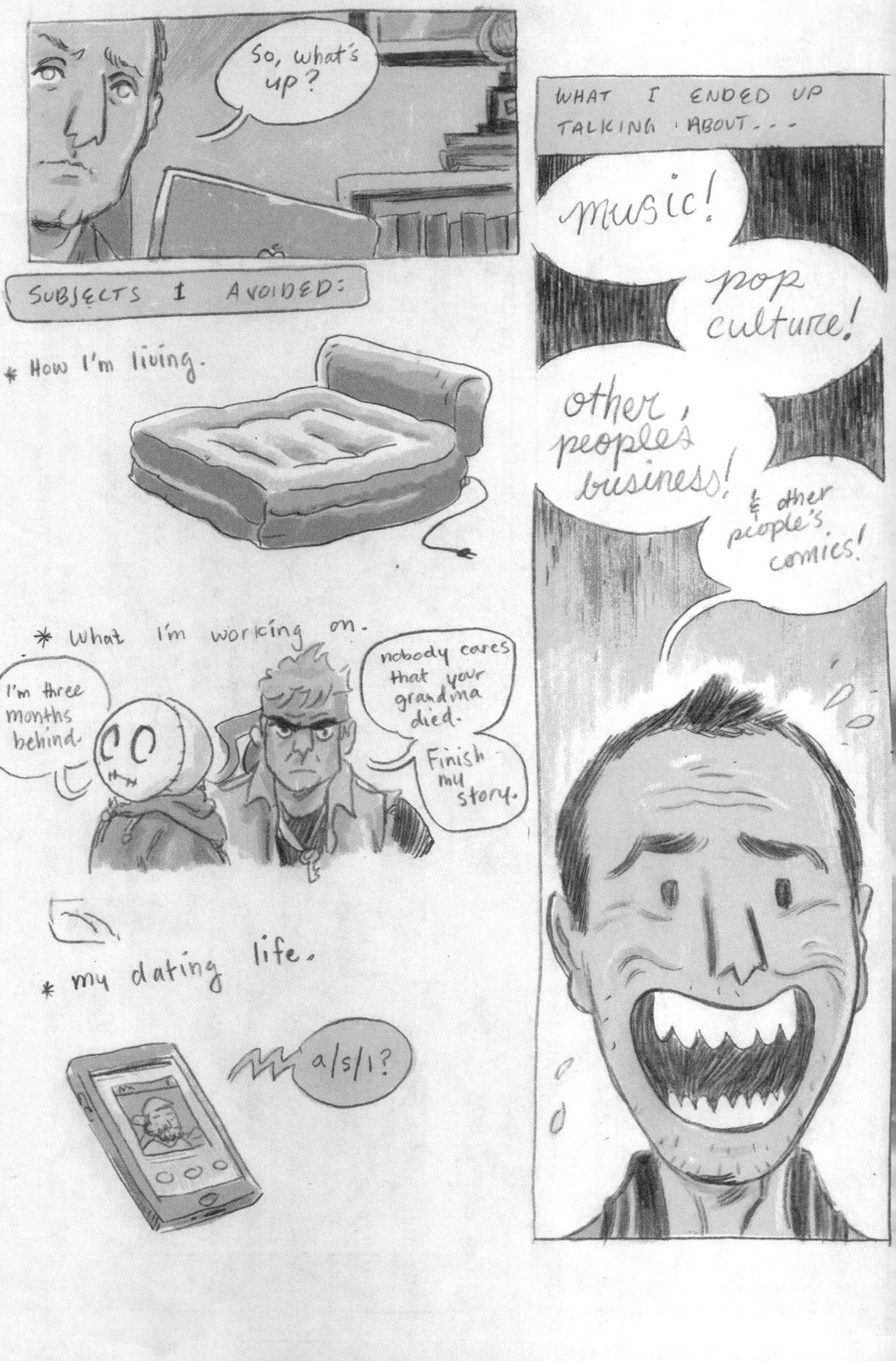
So, what's up?
SUBJECTS I AVOIDED:
* How I'm living.
* What I'm working on.
I'm three months behind.
nobody cares that your grandma died.
Finish my story.
* my dating life.
a/s/l?
WHAT I ENDED UP TALKING ABOUT...
music!
pop culture!
other people's business!
& other people's comics!

and as the visit with my publisher became more social, my nerve disappeared...

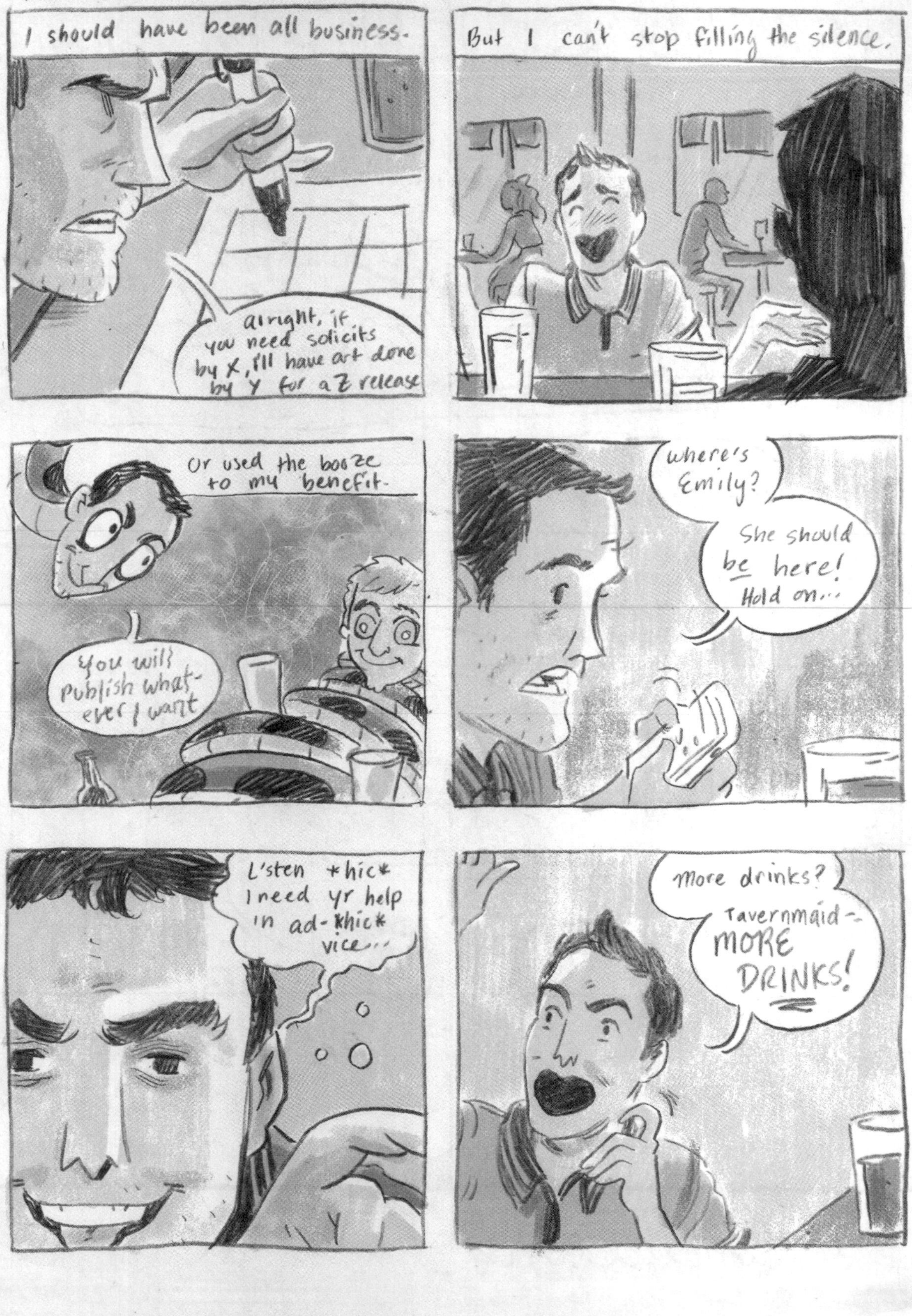
I should have been all business.
alright, if you need solicits by X, I'll have art done by Y for a Z release
But I can't stop filling the silence.
Or used the booze to my benefit.
You will publish what-ever I want
where's Emily?
She should be here! Hold on...
L'sten *hic* I need yr help in ad-*hic* vice...
More drinks?
Tavernmaid-- MORE DRINKS!

assumptions

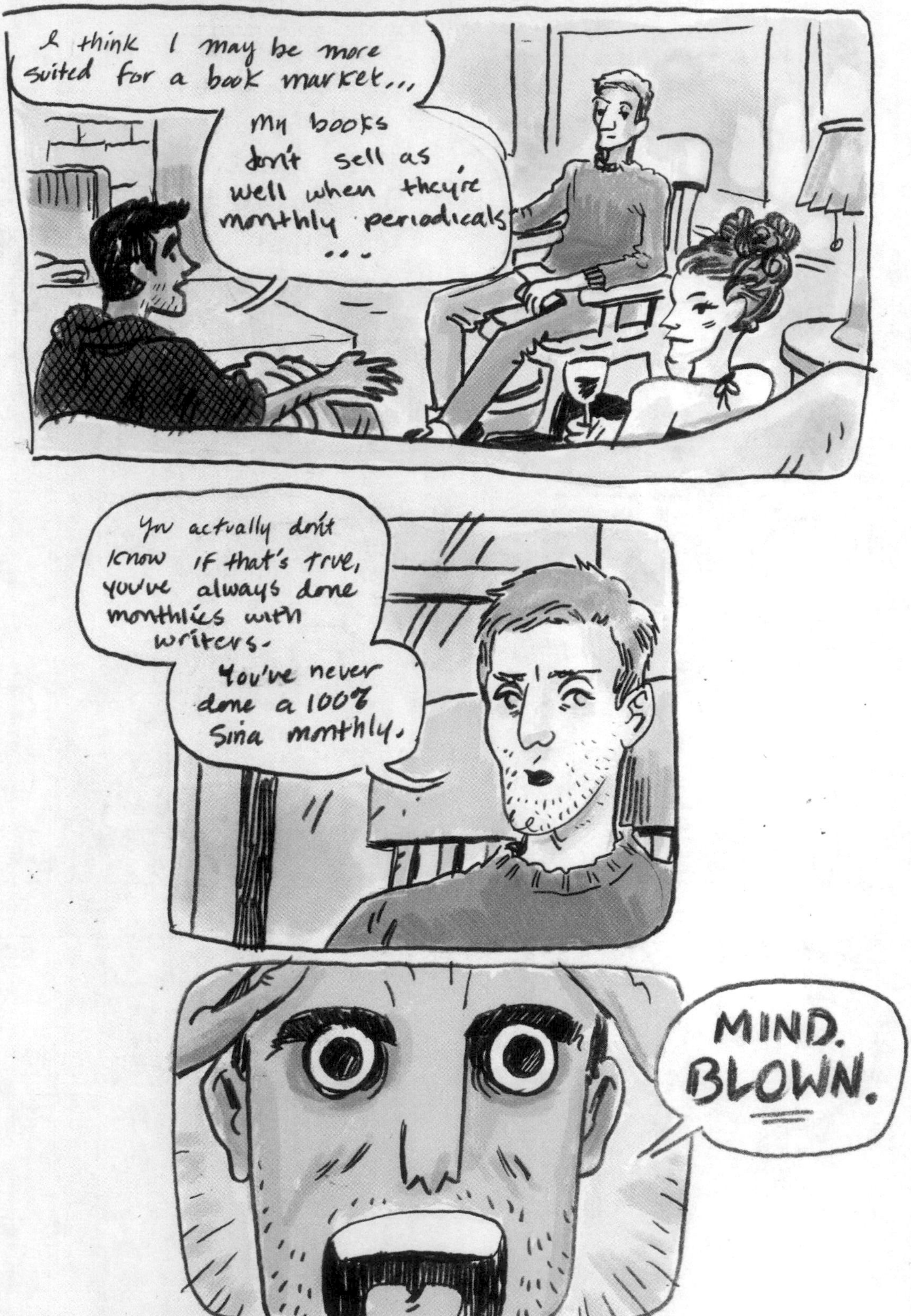

conclusions

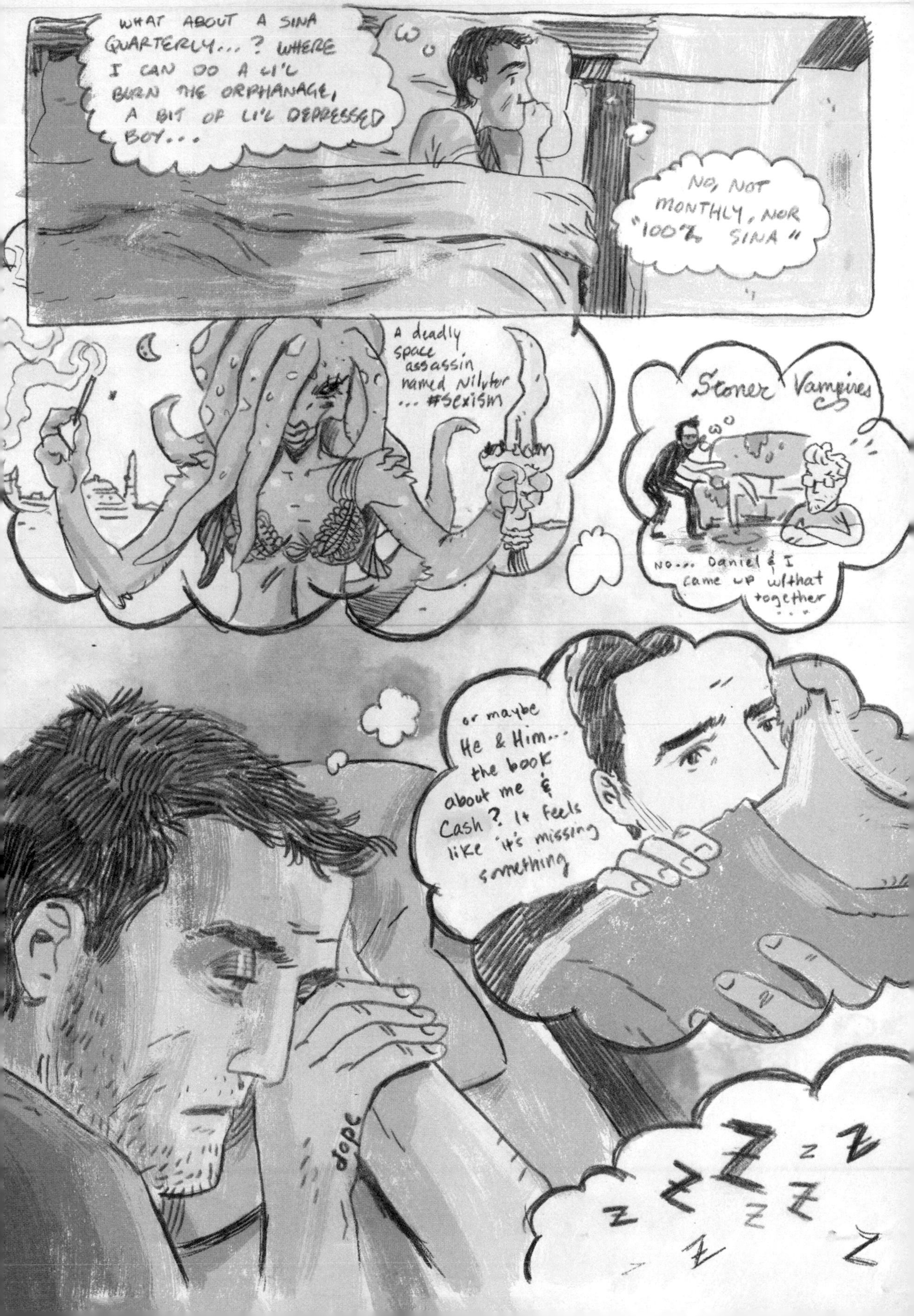
WHAT ABOUT A SINA QUARTERLY...? WHERE I CAN DO A LI'L BURN THE ORPHANAGE, A BIT OF LI'L DEPRESSED BOY...
NO, NOT MONTHLY, NOR "100% SINA"
A deadly space assassin named Nilvter ... #sexism
Stoner Vampires
No... Daniel & I came up w/that together...
or maybe He & Him... the book about me & Cash? It feels like it's missing something
dope
Z Z Z Z Z Z Z Z Z

in sleep, there are no visions for the next project-- no inspiration to wrap up old projects...

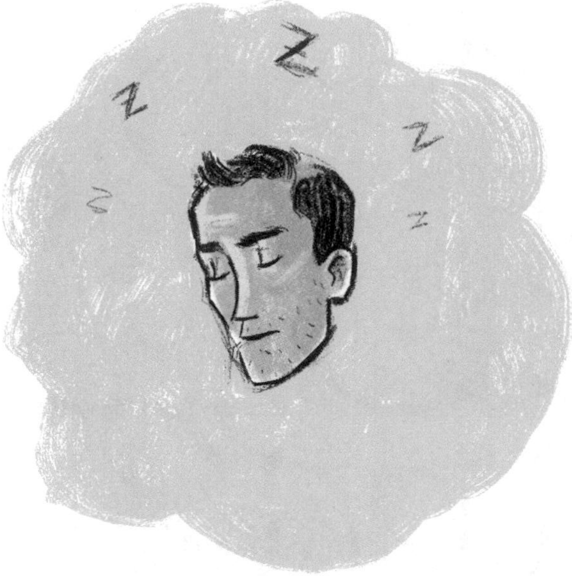
Z
Z
Z
Z
Z

... there's just drool.

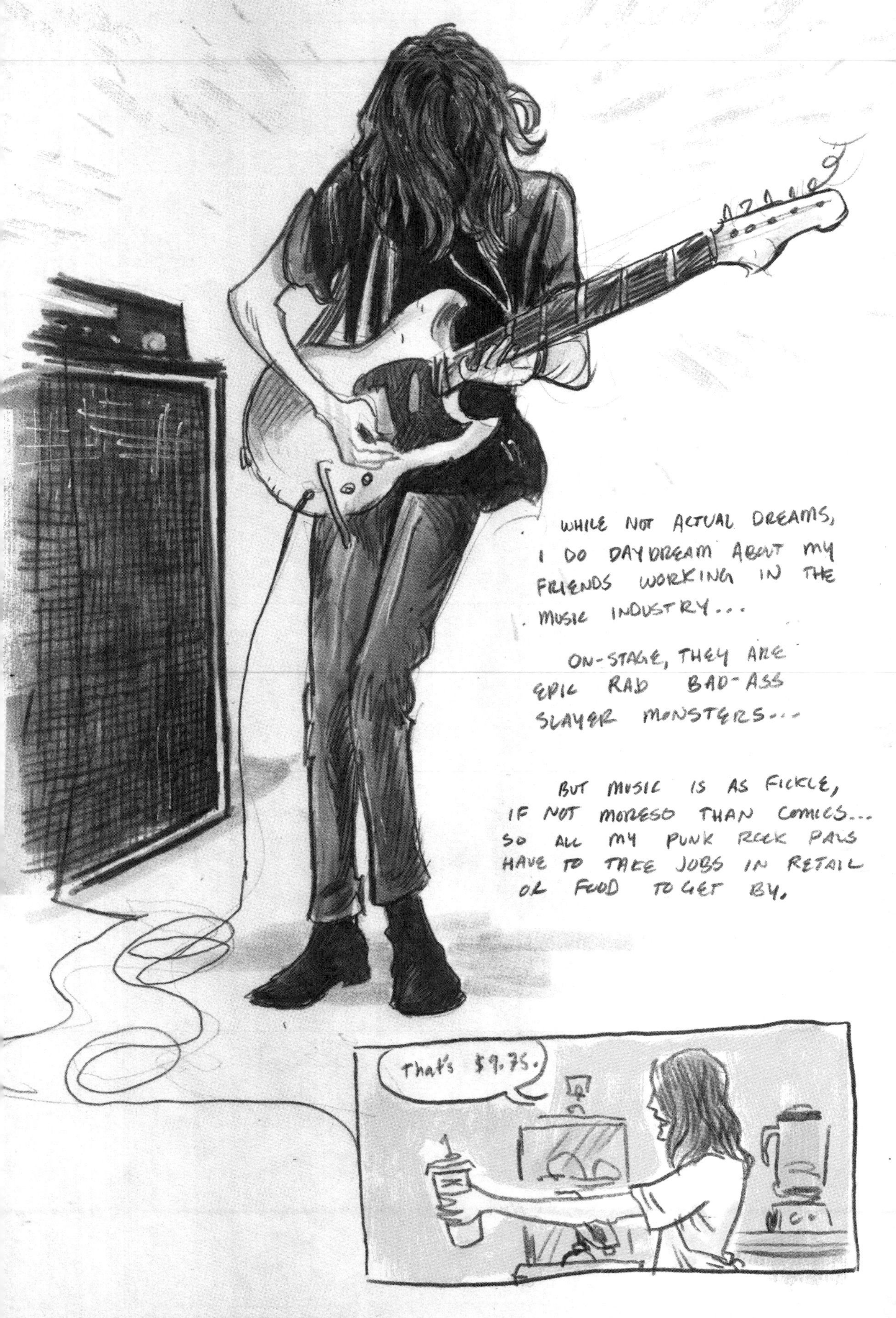
WHILE NOT ACTUAL DREAMS, I DO DAYDREAM ABOUT MY FRIENDS WORKING IN THE MUSIC INDUSTRY...
ON-STAGE, THEY ARE EPIC RAD BAD-ASS SLAYER MONSTERS...
BUT MUSIC IS AS FICKLE, IF NOT MORESO THAN COMICS... SO ALL MY PUNK ROCK PALS HAVE TO TAKE JOBS IN RETAIL OR FOOD TO GET BY.
That's $9.75.

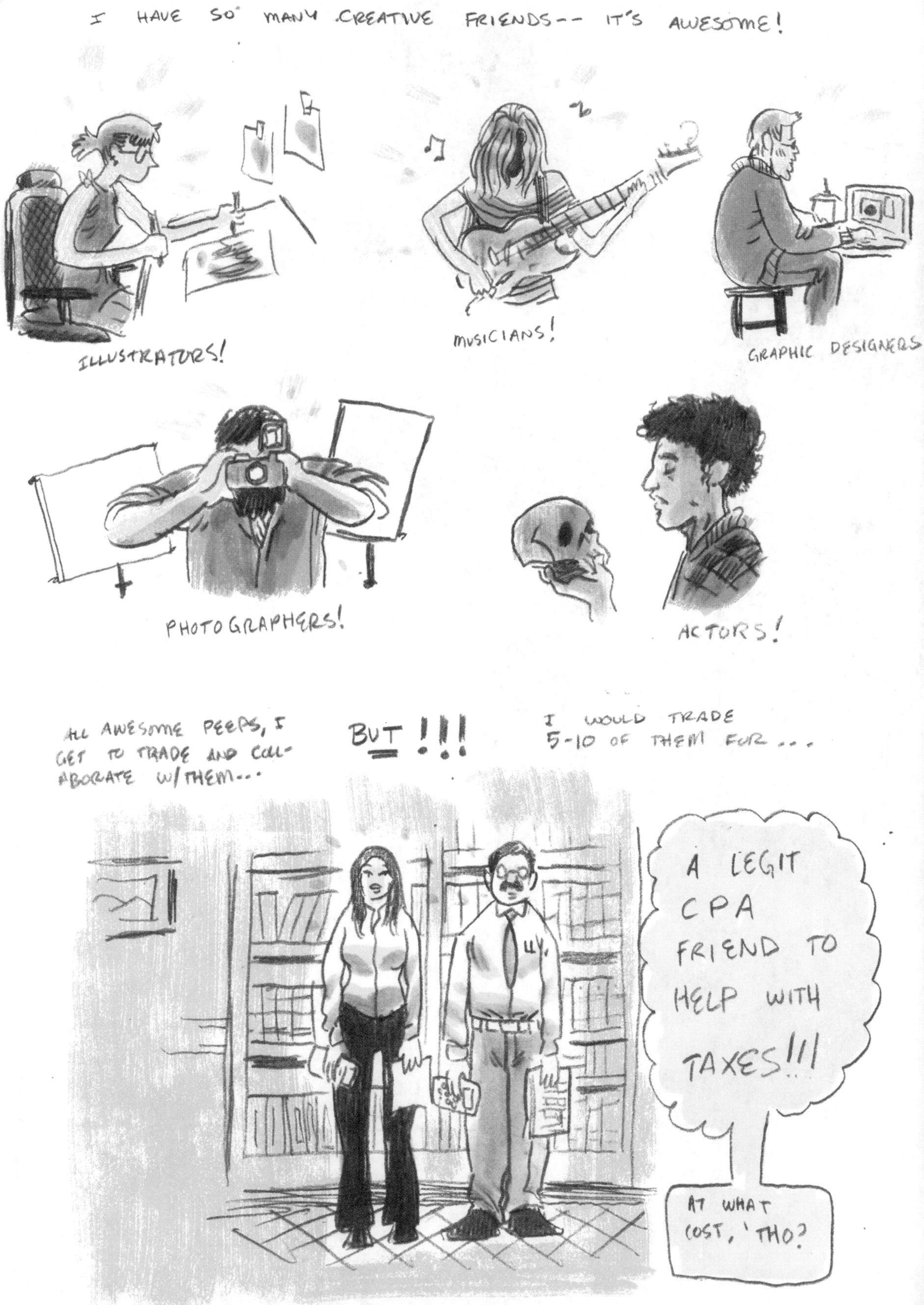
I HAVE SO MANY CREATIVE FRIENDS-- IT'S AWESOME!
ILLUSTRATORS!
MUSICIANS!
GRAPHIC DESIGNERS
PHOTOGRAPHERS!
ACTORS!
ALL AWESOME PEEPS, I GET TO TRADE AND COLLABORATE W/THEM...
BUT!!!
I WOULD TRADE 5-10 OF THEM FOR...
A LEGIT CPA FRIEND TO HELP WITH TAXES!!!
AT WHAT COST, 'THO?

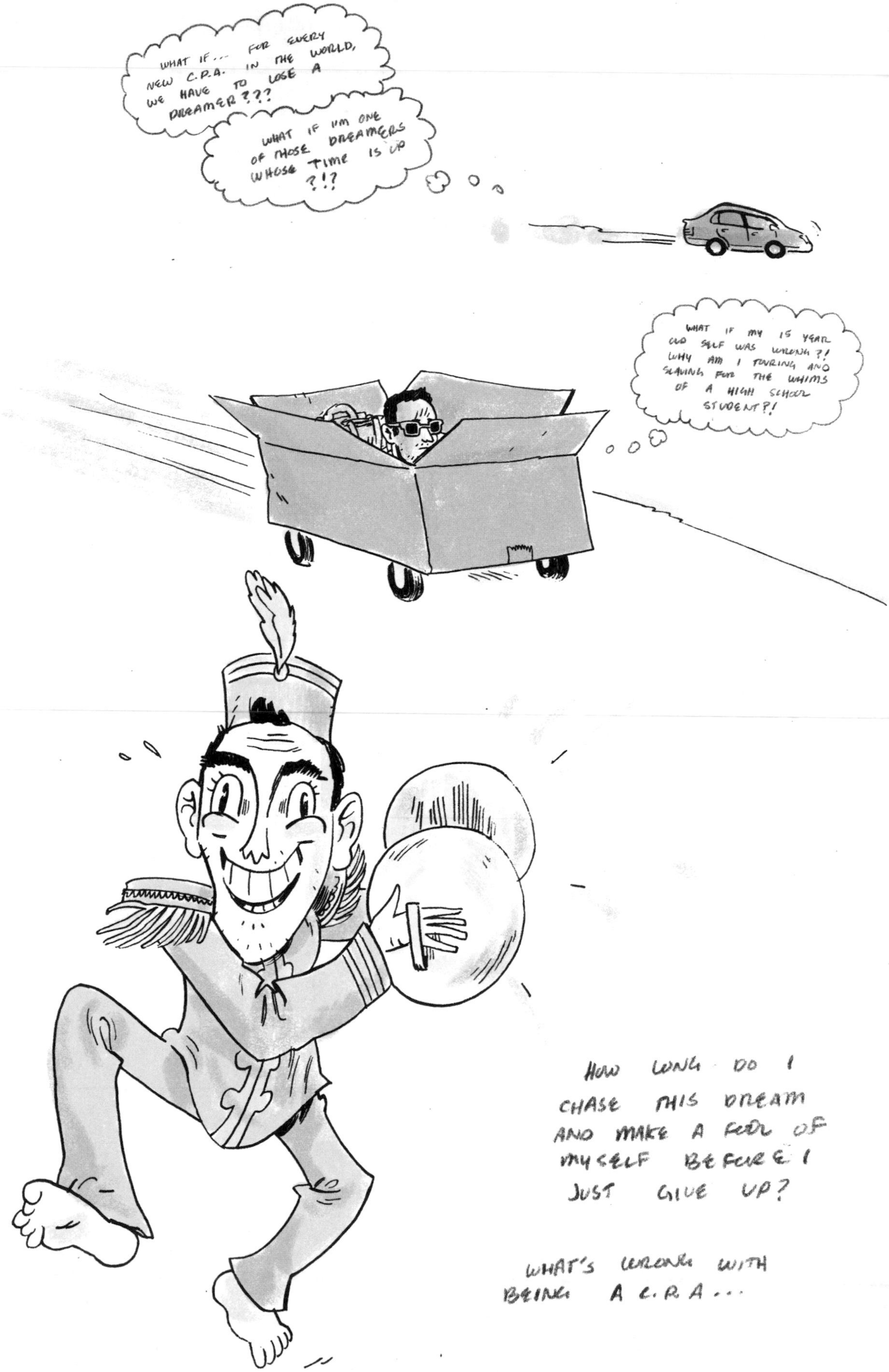
WHAT IF... FOR EVERY NEW C.P.A. IN THE WORLD, WE HAVE TO LOSE A DREAMER???
WHAT IF I'M ONE OF THOSE DREAMERS WHOSE TIME IS UP ?!?
WHAT IF MY 15 YEAR OLD SELF WAS WRONG?! WHY AM I TOURING AND SLAVING FOR THE WHIMS OF A HIGH SCHOOL STUDENT?!
HOW LONG DO I CHASE THIS DREAM AND MAKE A FOOL OF MYSELF BEFORE I JUST GIVE UP?
WHAT'S WRONG WITH BEING A C.P.A...

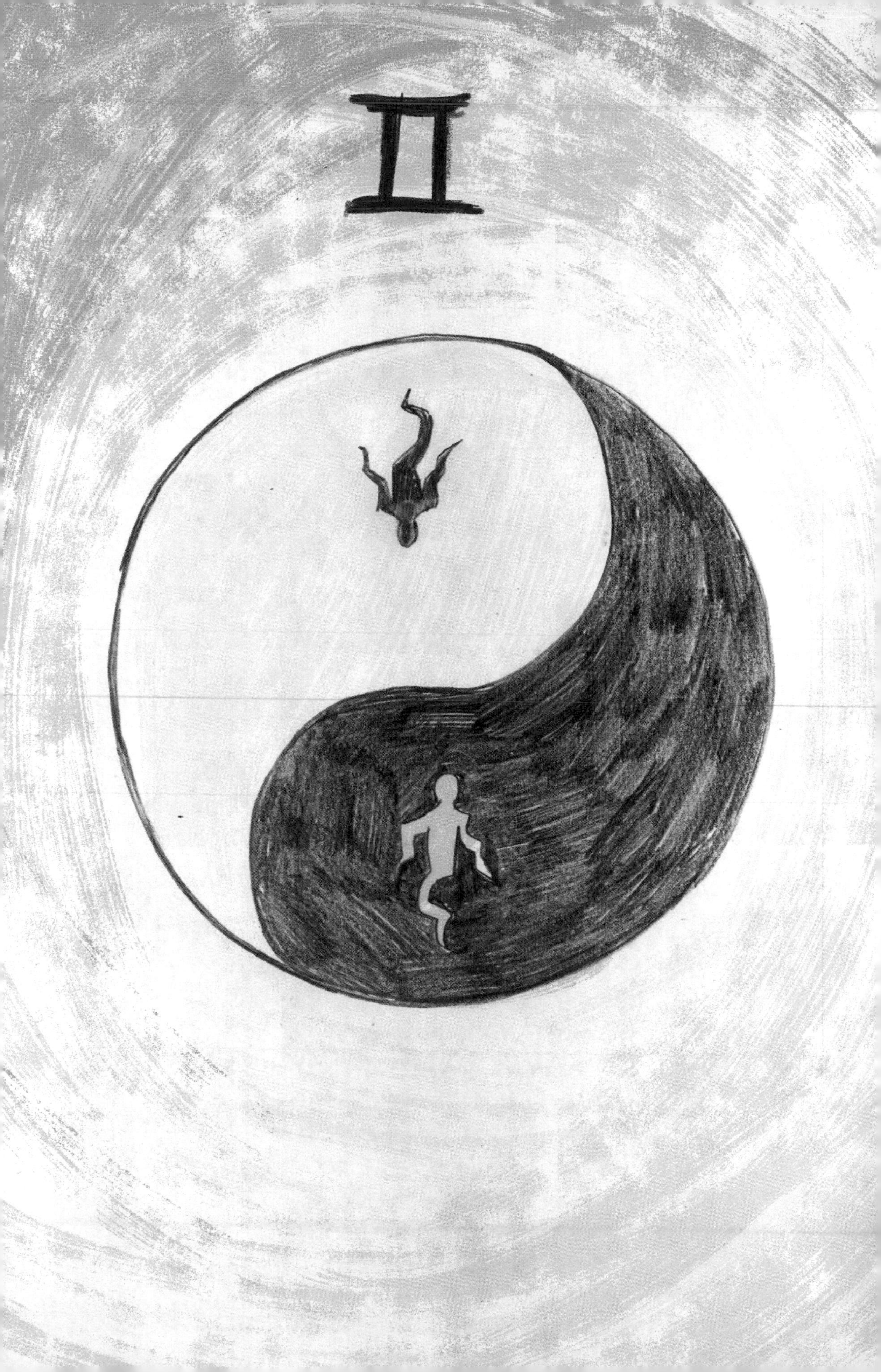

a memory

(drunk at a bar in Portland)

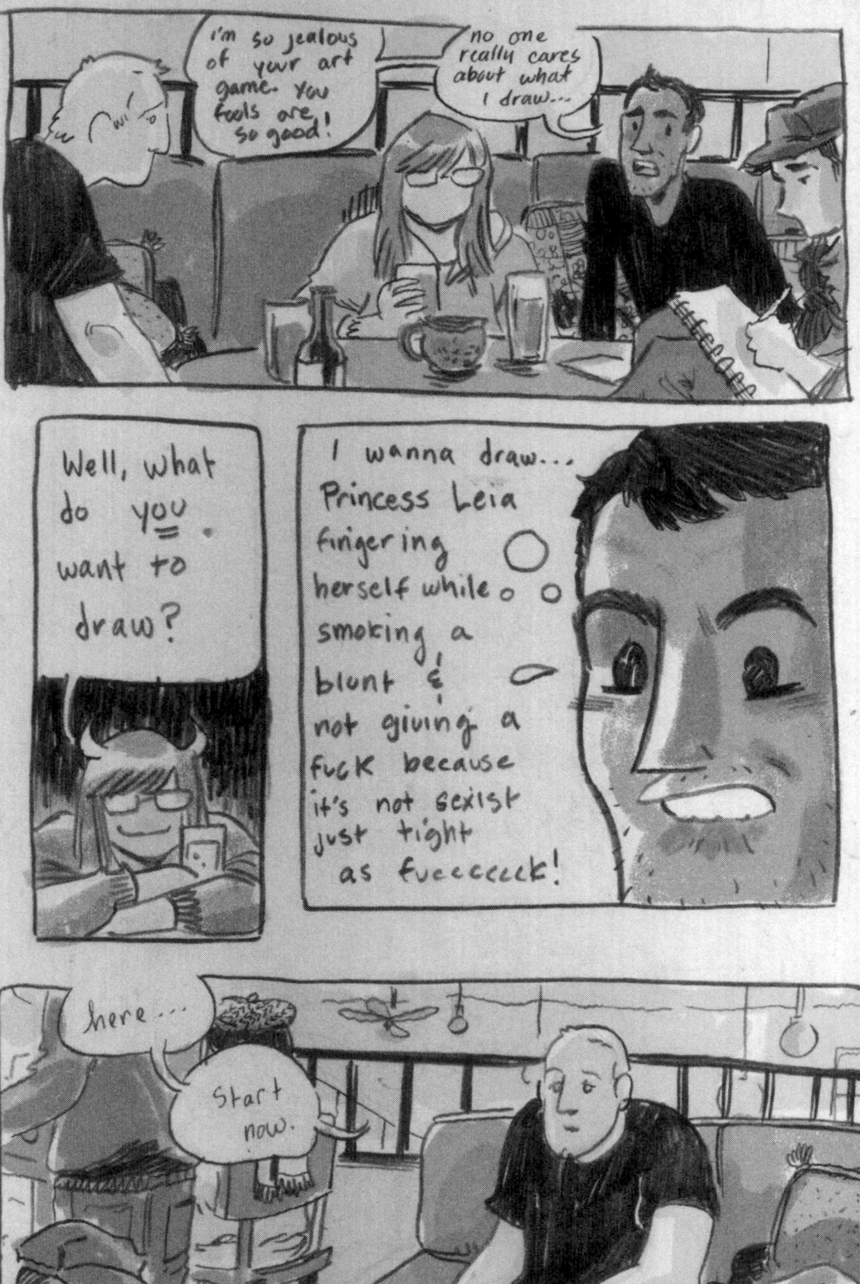

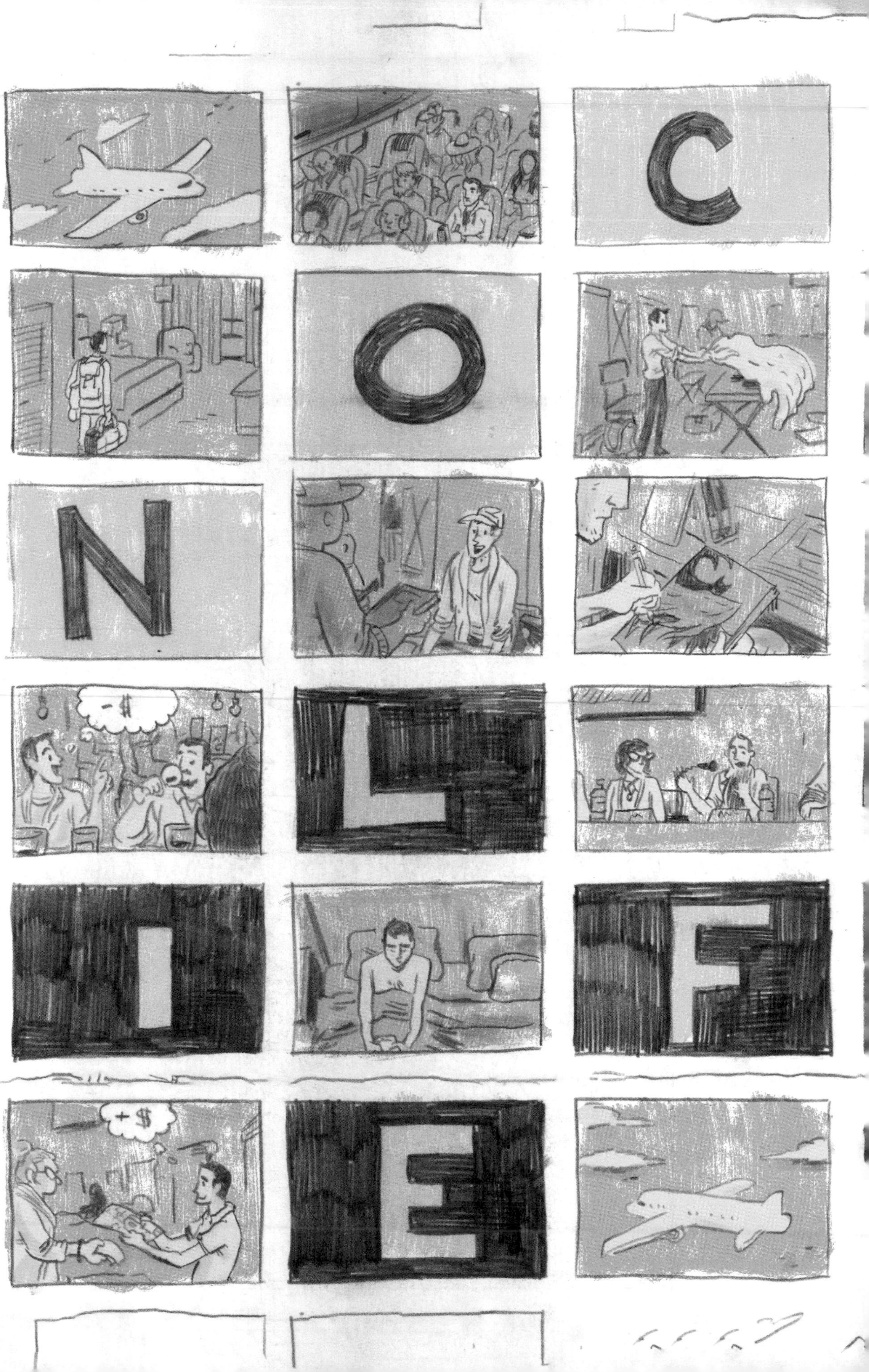
C
O
N
-$
L
I
F
+$
E

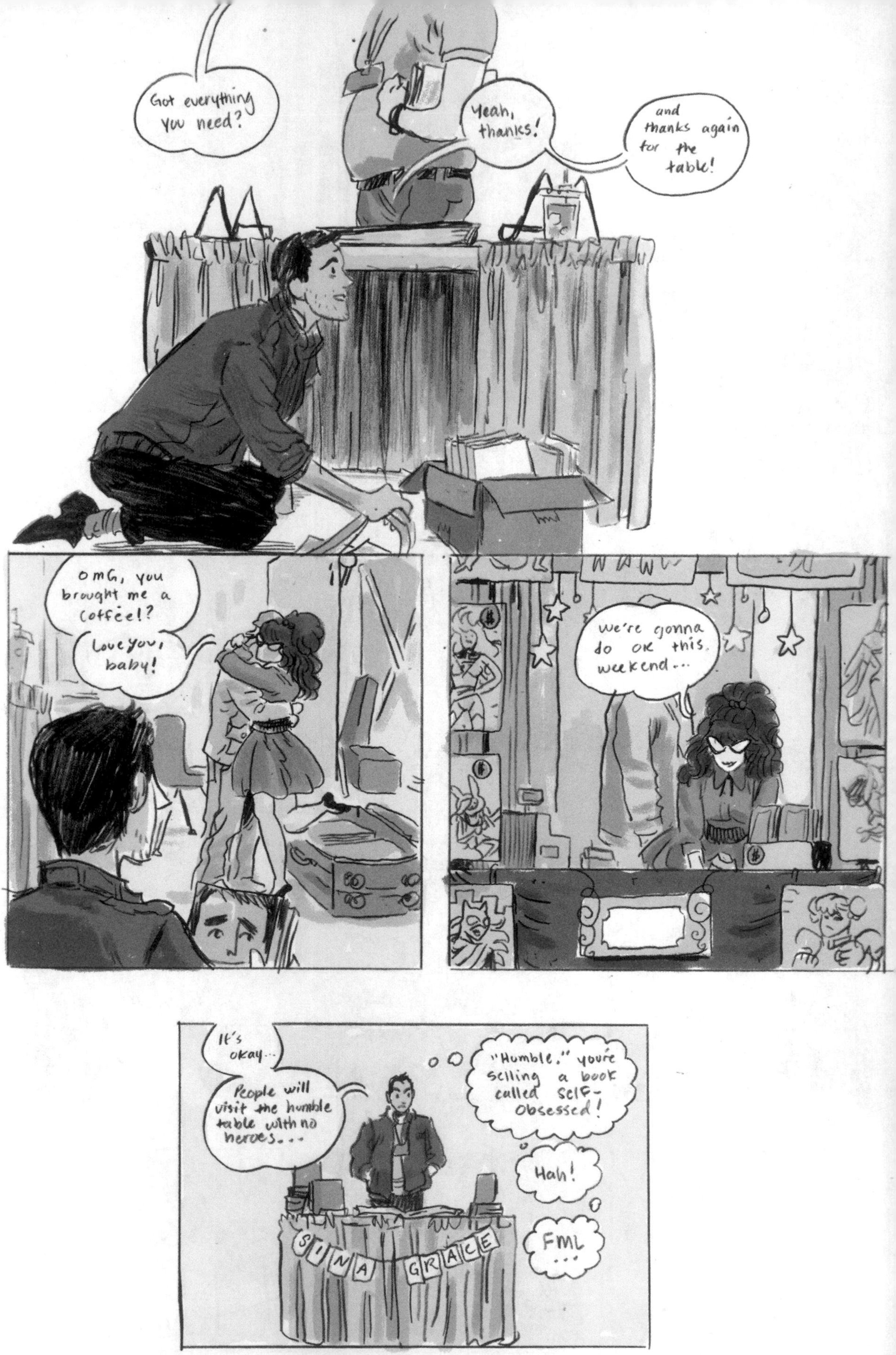

Got everything you need?
Yeah, thanks!
and thanks again for the table!
OMG, you brought me a coffee!?
Love you, baby!
We're gonna do OK this weekend...
It's okay...
People will visit the humble table with no heroes...
"Humble," you're selling a book called Self-Obsessed!
Hah!
FML...
SINA GRACE

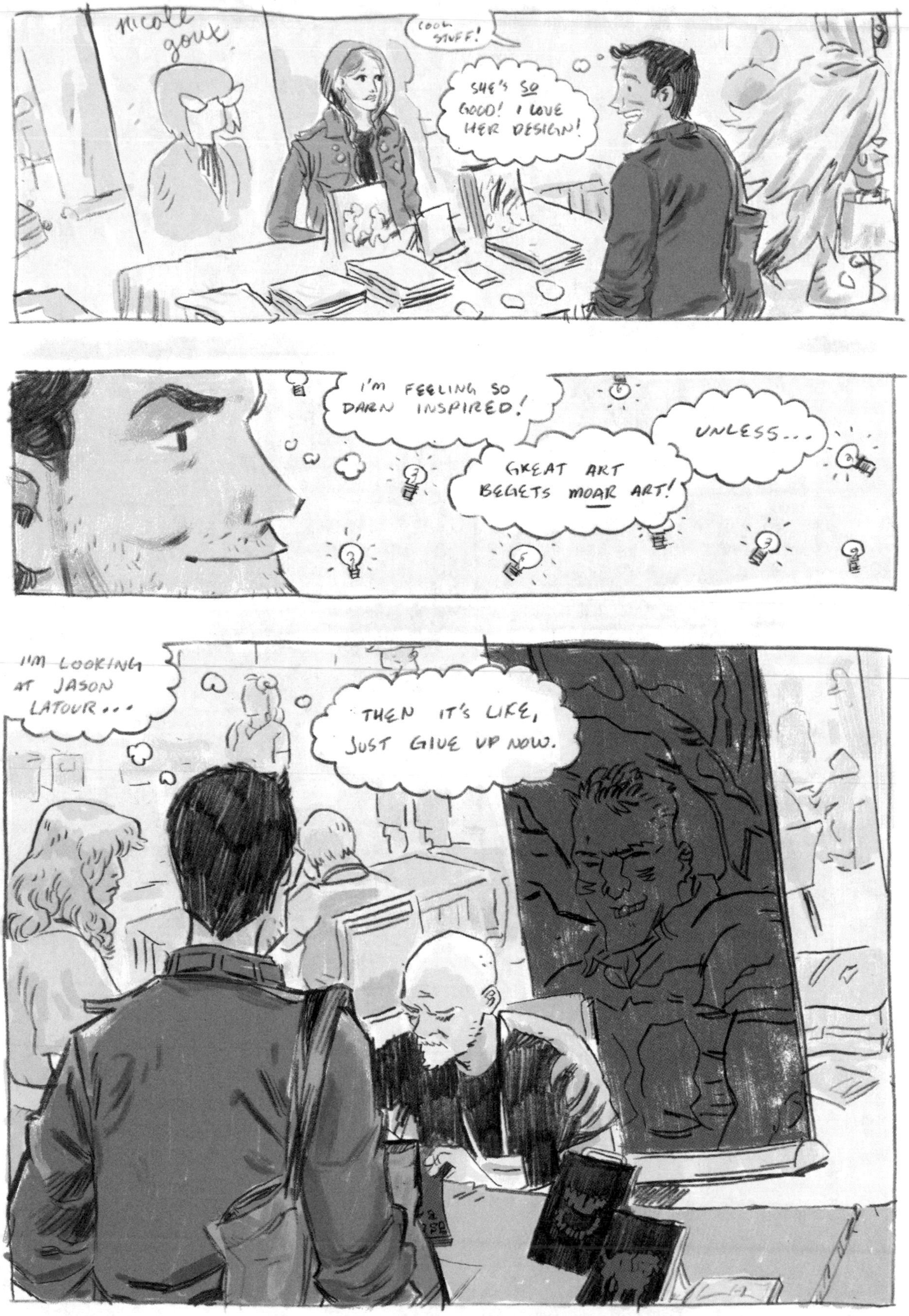
nicole goux
COOL STUFF!
SHE'S SO GOOD! I LOVE HER DESIGN!
I'M FEELING SO DARN INSPIRED!
GREAT ART BEGETS MOAR ART!
UNLESS...
I'M LOOKING AT JASON LATOUR...
THEN IT'S LIKE, JUST GIVE UP NOW.

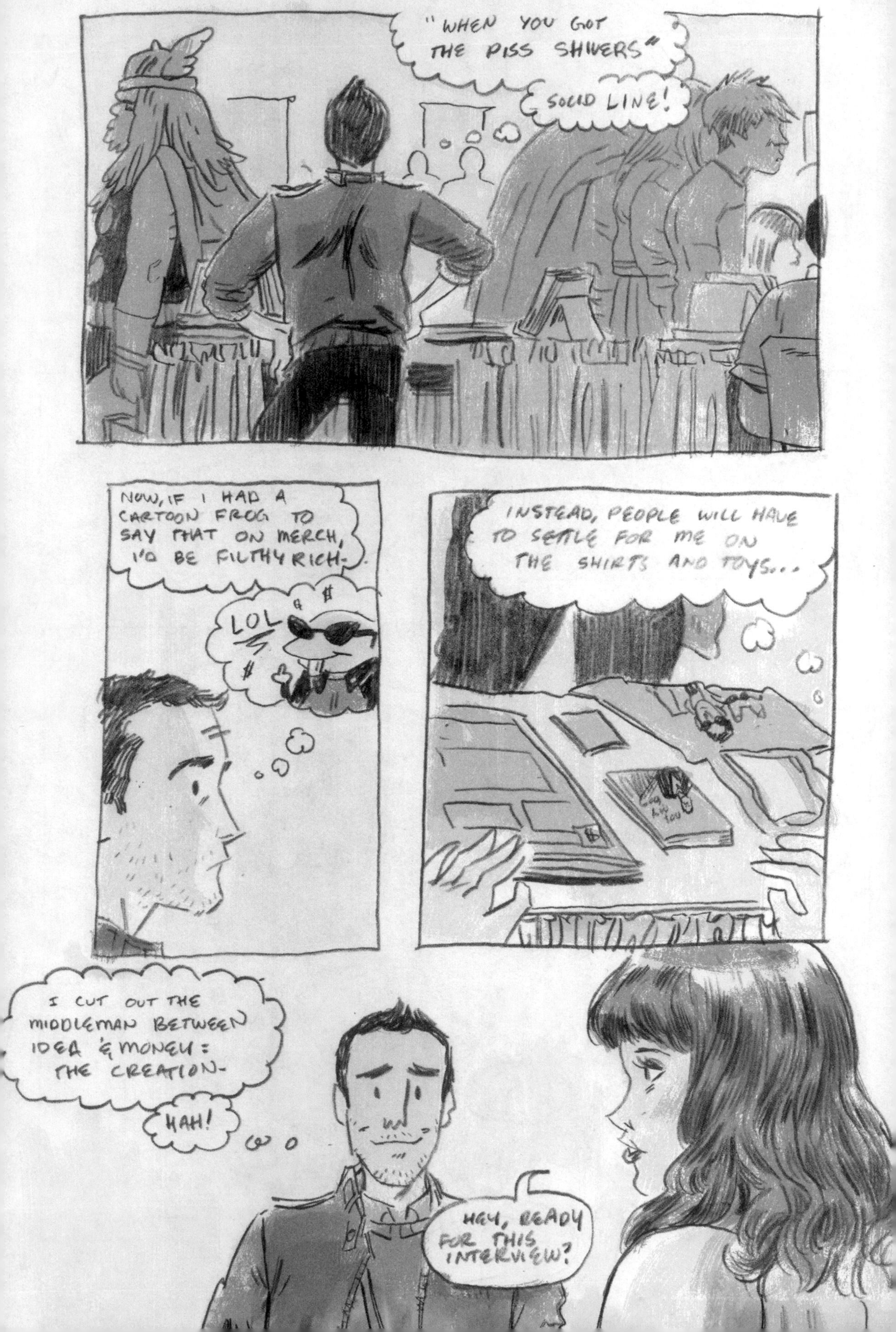
"WHEN YOU GOT THE PISS SHIVERS"
SOLID LINE!
NOW, IF I HAD A CARTOON FROG TO SAY THAT ON MERCH, I'D BE FILTHY RICH-
LOL
INSTEAD, PEOPLE WILL HAVE TO SETTLE FOR ME ON THE SHIRTS AND TOYS...
I CUT OUT THE MIDDLEMAN BETWEEN IDEA & MONEY: THE CREATION-
HAH!
HEY, READY FOR THIS INTERVIEW?

BLAH

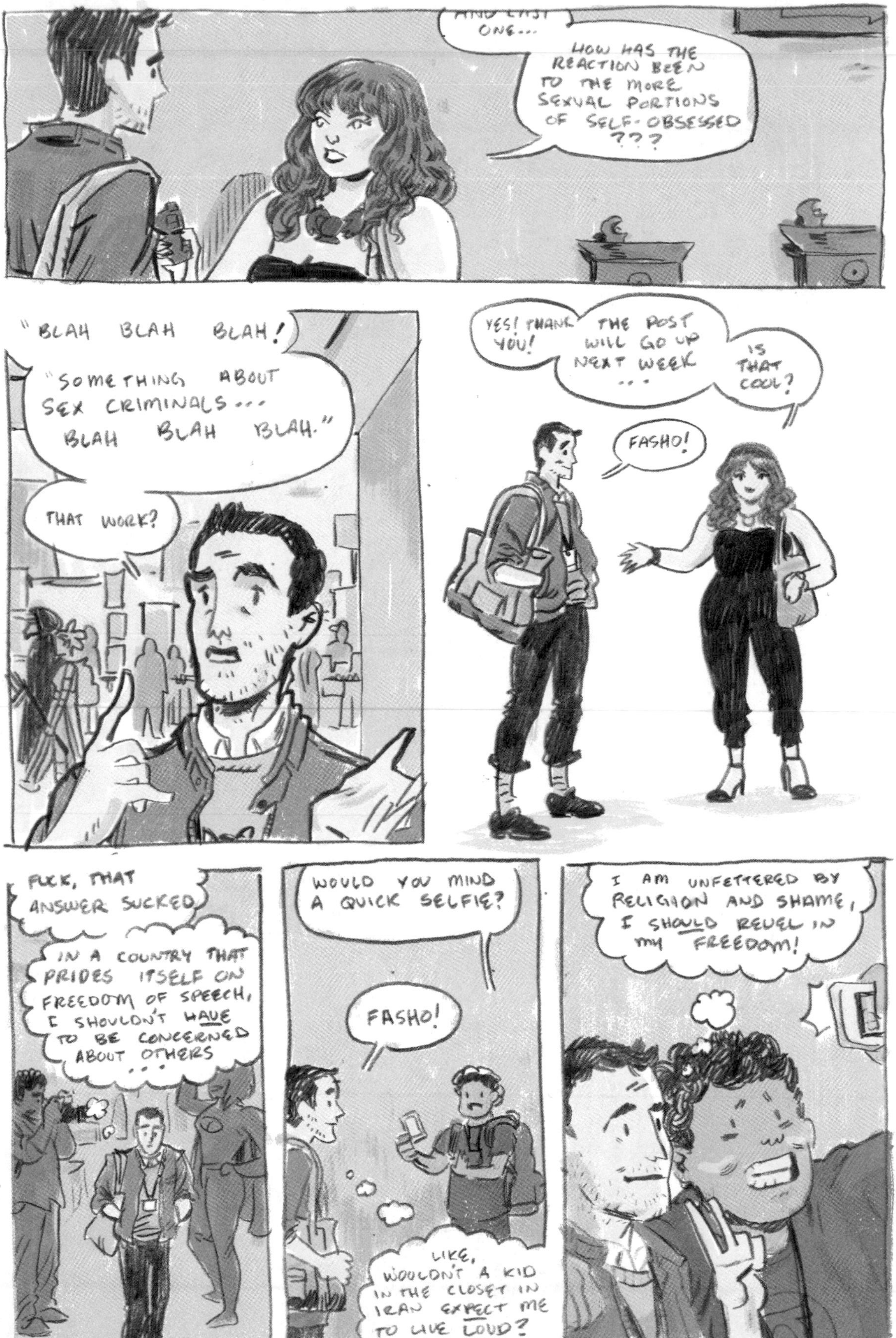

ONE...
HOW HAS THE REACTION BEEN TO THE MORE SEXUAL PORTIONS OF SELF-OBSESSED???
"BLAH BLAH BLAH!
"SOMETHING ABOUT SEX CRIMINALS... BLAH BLAH BLAH."
THAT WORK?
YES! THANK YOU!
THE POST WILL GO UP NEXT WEEK...
IS THAT COOL?
FASHO!
FUCK, THAT ANSWER SUCKED.
IN A COUNTRY THAT PRIDES ITSELF ON FREEDOM OF SPEECH, I SHOULDN'T HAVE TO BE CONCERNED ABOUT OTHERS...
WOULD YOU MIND A QUICK SELFIE?
FASHO!
LIKE, WOULDN'T A KID IN THE CLOSET IN IRAN EXPECT ME TO LIVE LOUD?
I AM UNFETTERED BY RELIGION AND SHAME, I SHOULD REVEL IN MY FREEDOM!

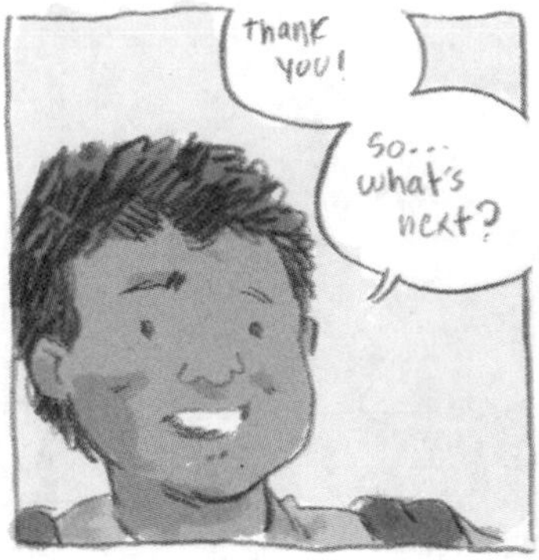
thank you!
so... what's next?

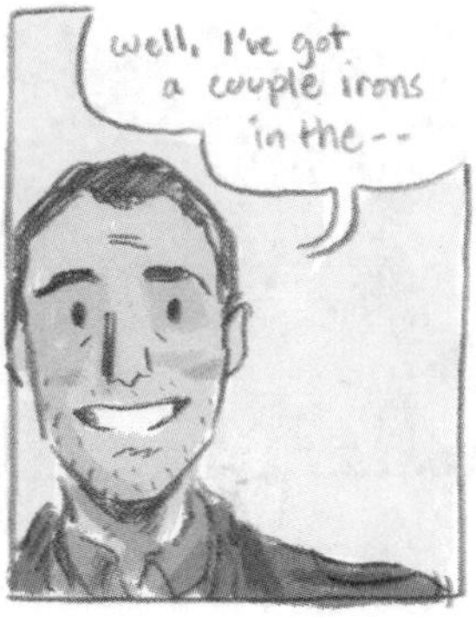
well, I've got a couple irons in the--

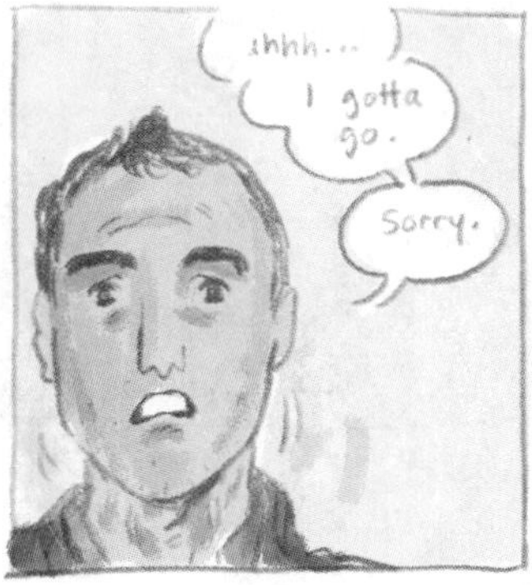
uhhh... I gotta go.
Sorry.

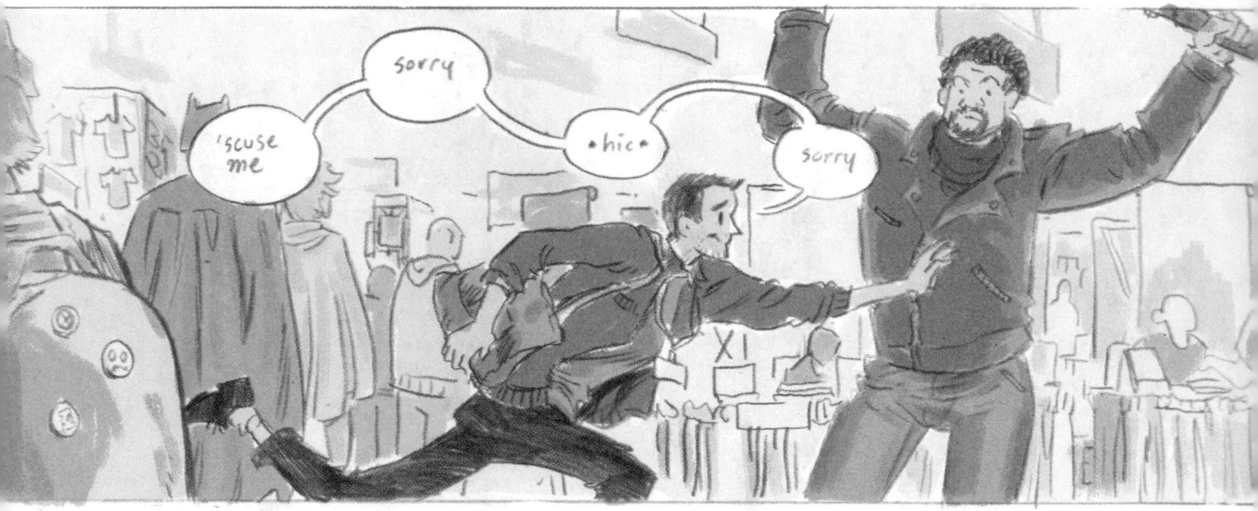
'scuse me
sorry
hic
sorry

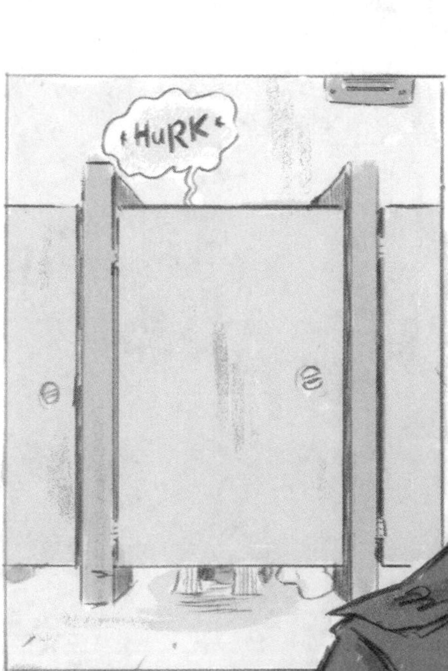
HURK

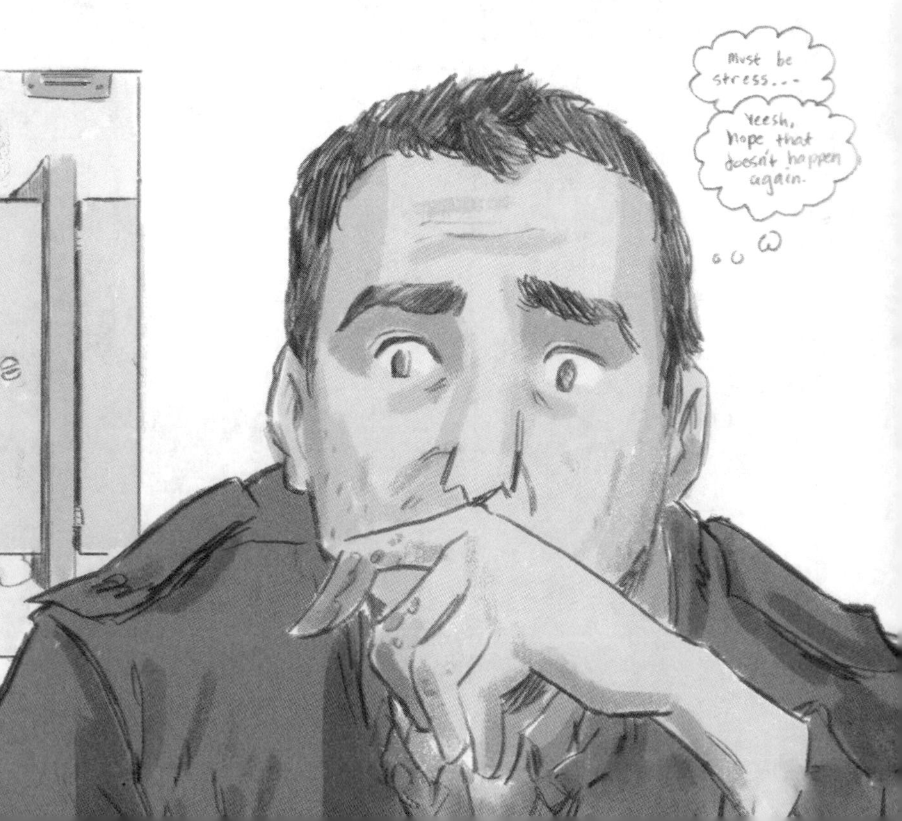
Must be stress...
Yeesh, hope that doesn't happen again.

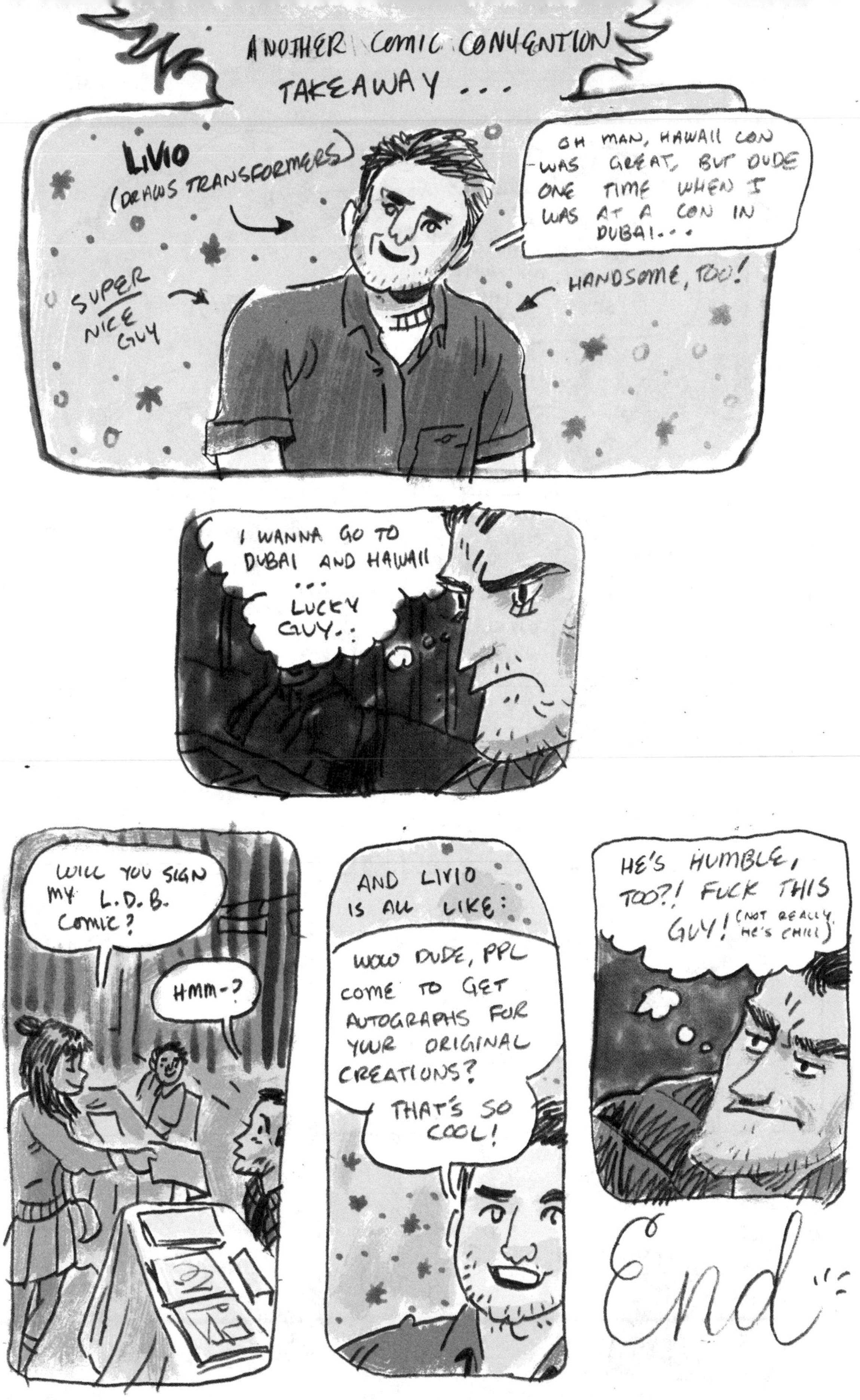
ANOTHER COMIC CONVENTION TAKEAWAY . . .
LIVIO (DRAWS TRANSFORMERS)
OH MAN, HAWAII CON WAS GREAT, BUT DUDE ONE TIME WHEN I WAS AT A CON IN DUBAI . . .
SUPER NICE GUY
HANDSOME, TOO!
I WANNA GO TO DUBAI AND HAWAII . . . LUCKY GUY. . .
WILL YOU SIGN MY L.D.B. COMIC?
HMM-?
AND LIVIO IS ALL LIKE:
WOW DUDE, PPL COME TO GET AUTOGRAPHS FOR YOUR ORIGINAL CREATIONS?
THAT'S SO COOL!
HE'S HUMBLE, TOO?! FUCK THIS GUY! (NOT REALLY, HE'S CHILL)
End

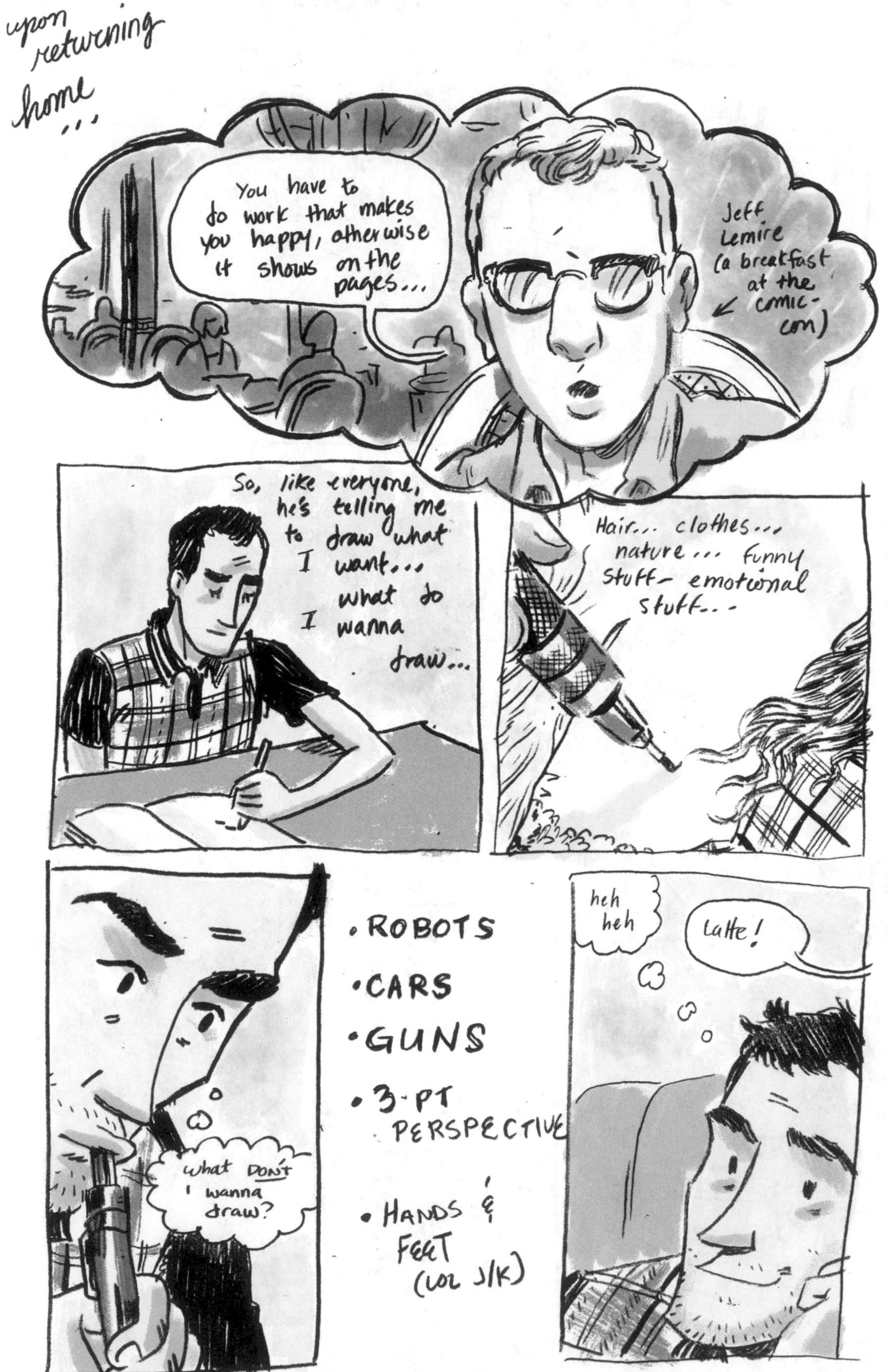
upon returning home...
You have to do work that makes you happy, otherwise it shows on the pages...
Jeff Lemire (a breakfast at the comic-con)
So, like everyone, he's telling me to draw what I want... what do I wanna draw...
Hair... clothes... nature... funny stuff- emotional stuff...
•ROBOTS
•CARS
•GUNS
•3-PT PERSPECTIVE
•HANDS & FEET (LOL J/K)
What DON'T I wanna draw?
heh heh
Latte!

COFFEE DATE W/AMBER

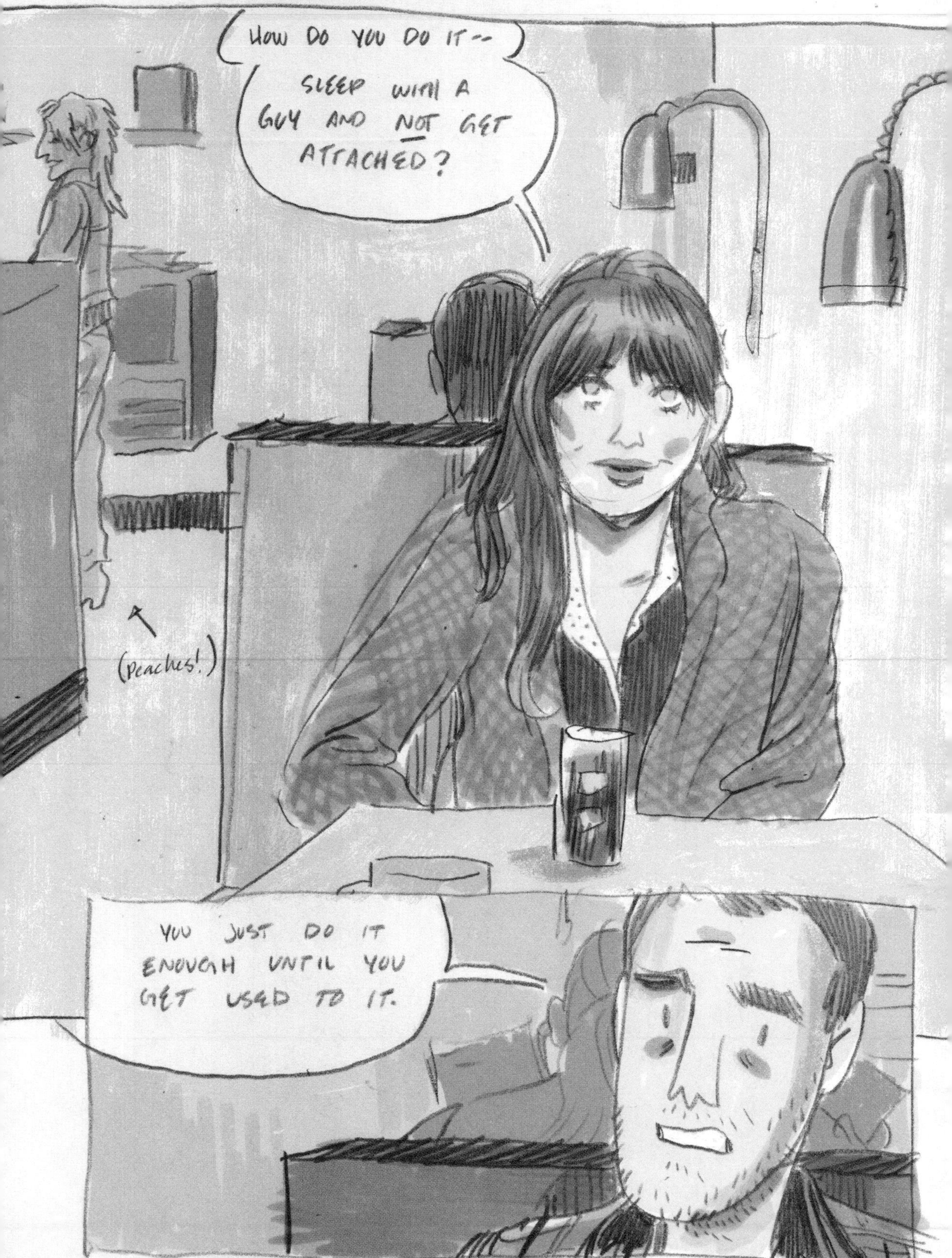
HOW DO YOU DO IT -- SLEEP WITH A GUY AND NOT GET ATTACHED?
(Peaches!)
YOU JUST DO IT ENOUGH UNTIL YOU GET USED TO IT.

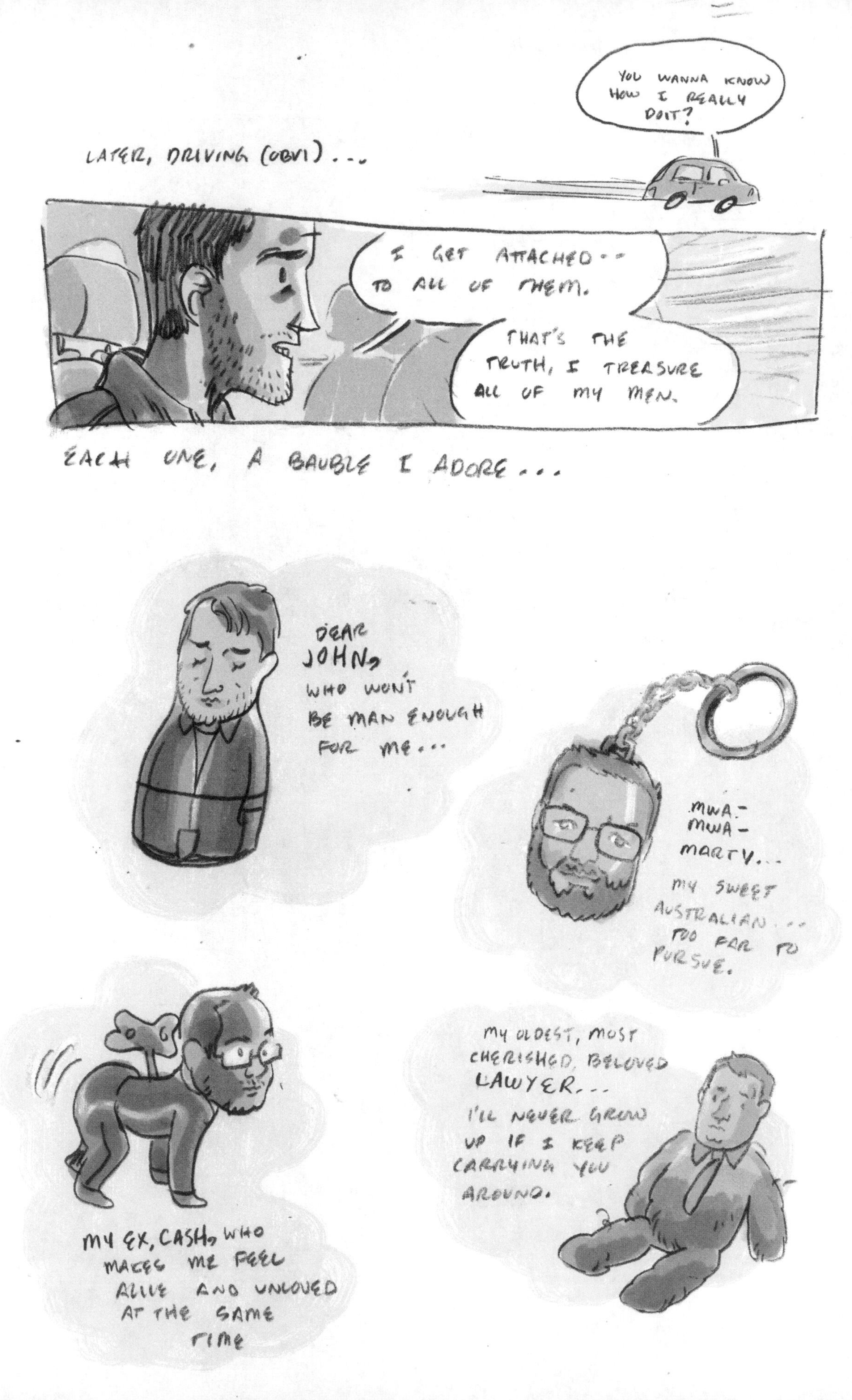
LATER, DRIVING (OBVI)...
YOU WANNA KNOW HOW I REALLY DO IT?
I GET ATTACHED-- TO ALL OF THEM.
THAT'S THE TRUTH, I TREASURE ALL OF MY MEN.
EACH ONE, A BAUBLE I ADORE...
DEAR JOHN, WHO WON'T BE MAN ENOUGH FOR ME...
MWA-MWA-MARTY... MY SWEET AUSTRALIAN... TOO FAR TO PURSUE.
MY EX, CASH, WHO MAKES ME FEEL ALIVE AND UNLOVED AT THE SAME TIME
MY OLDEST, MOST CHERISHED, BELOVED LAWYER... I'LL NEVER GROW UP IF I KEEP CARRYING YOU AROUND.

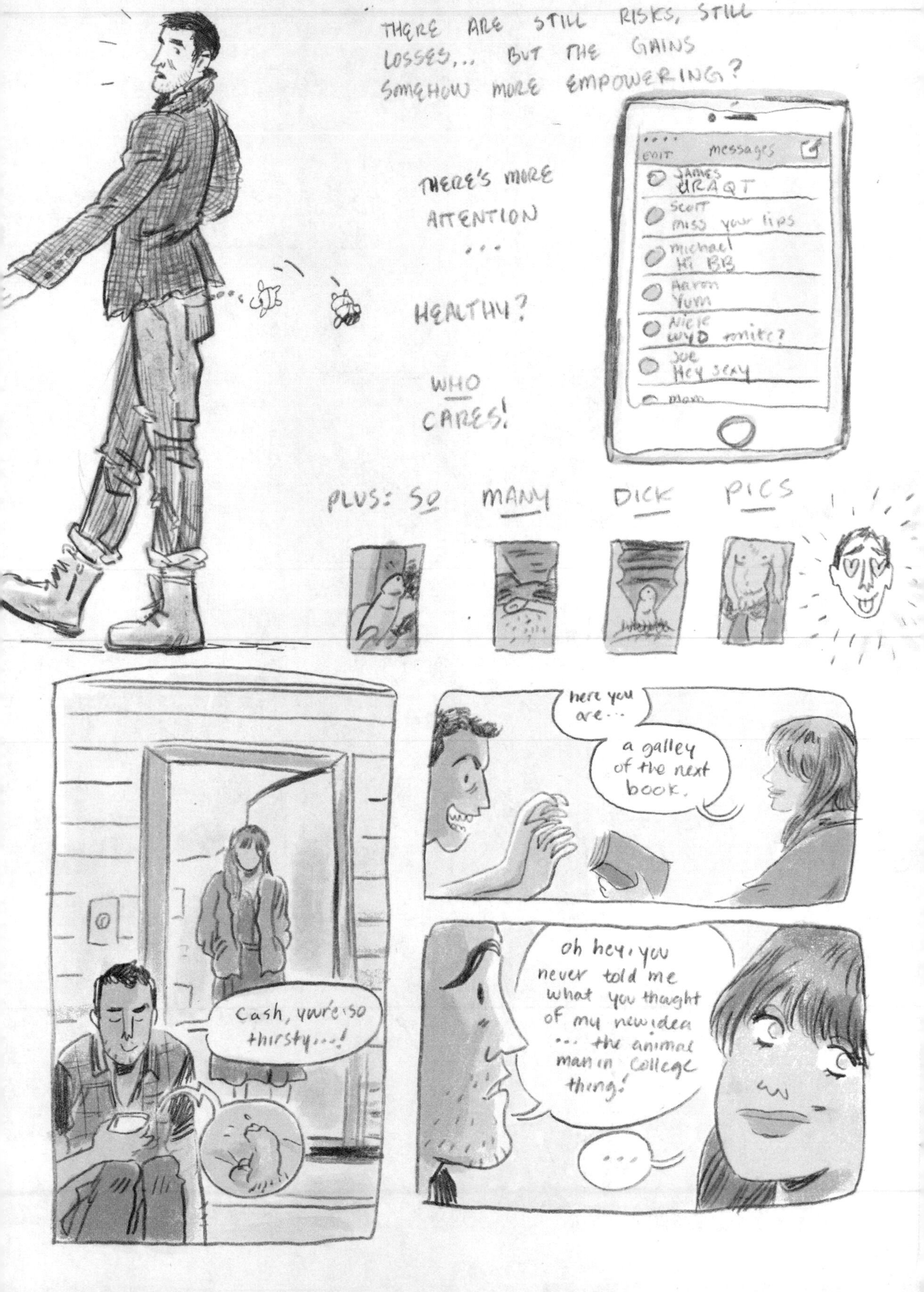
THERE ARE STILL RISKS, STILL LOSSES... BUT THE GAINS SOMEHOW MORE EMPOWERING?
EDIT
messages
James
URAQT
Scott
miss your lips
michael
Hi BB
Aaron
Yum
Nick
WYD tonite?
Joe
Hey sexy
THERE'S MORE ATTENTION
...
HEALTHY?
WHO CARES!
PLUS: SO MANY DICK PICS
Cash, you're so thirsty...!
here you are...
a galley of the next book.
oh hey, you never told me what you thought of my new idea ... the animal man in college thing!
...

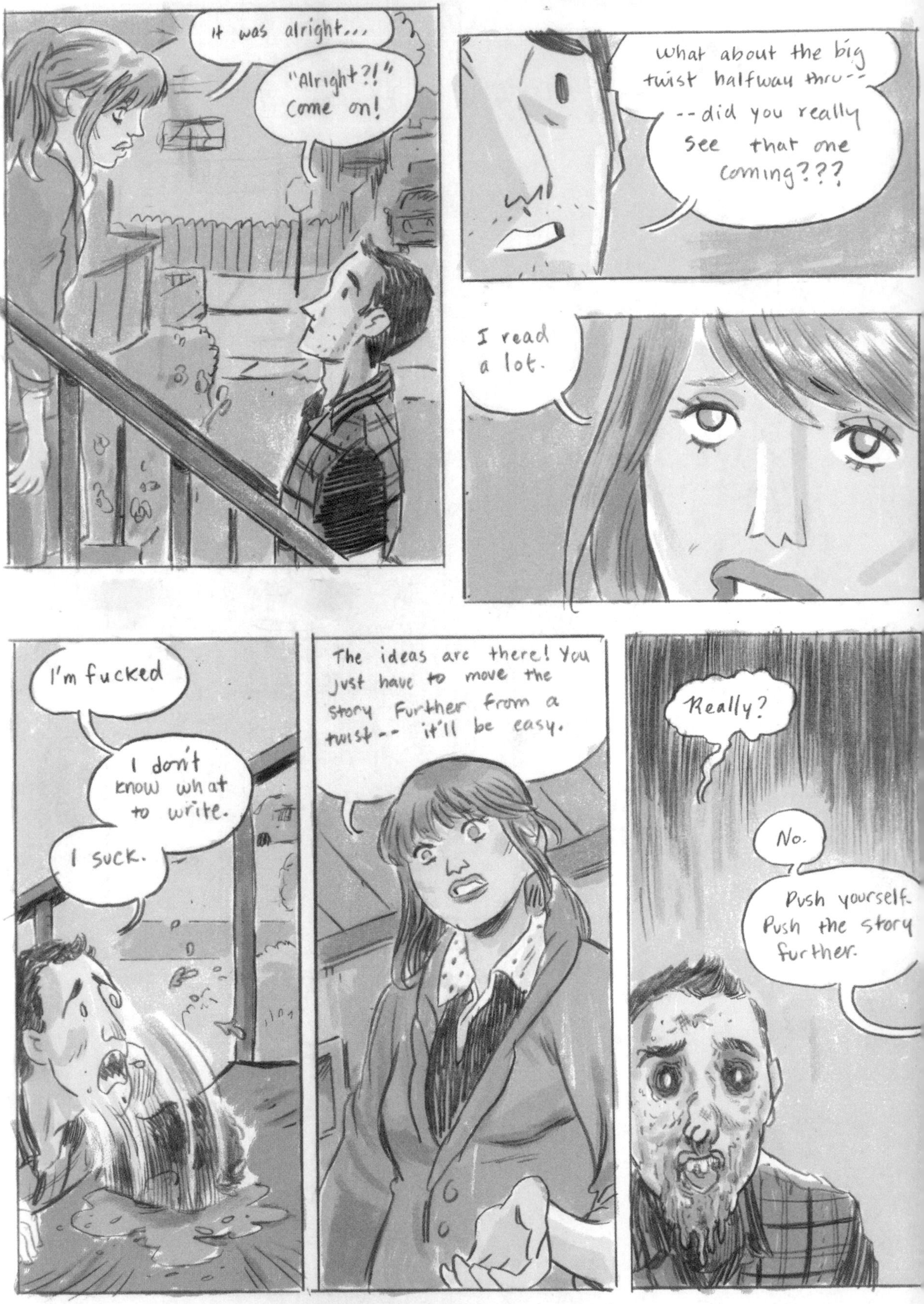
It was alright...
"Alright?!" Come on!
What about the big twist halfway thru--
--did you really see that one coming???
I read a lot.
I'm fucked
I don't know what to write.
I suck.
The ideas are there! You just have to move the story further from a twist-- it'll be easy.
Really?
No.
Push yourself. Push the story further.

all the times Amber was right...

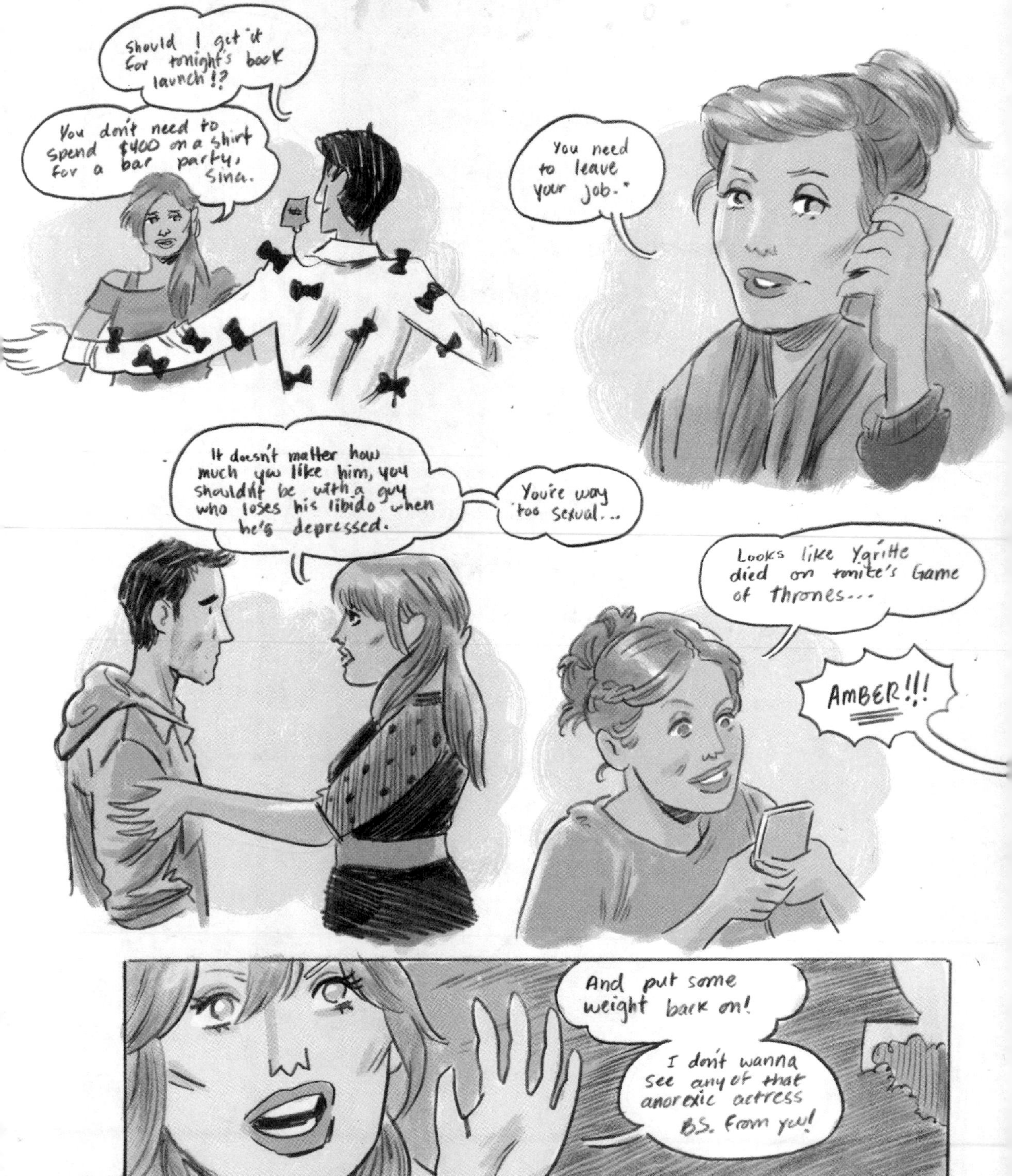
Should I get it for tonight's book launch!?
You don't need to spend $400 on a shirt for a bar party, Sina.
You need to leave your job.*
It doesn't matter how much you like him, you shouldn't be with a guy who loses his libido when he's depressed.
You're way too sexual...
Looks like Ygritte died on tonite's Game of Thrones...
AMBER!!!
And put some weight back on!
I don't wanna see any of that anorexic actress B.S. from you!

* see "Self-Obsessed" for more deets.

I always trust Amber's judgment
because I respect her own journey

She's accomplished, surrounded by
love, and treats everyone with respect.

I almost always go
to her with my problems.

Almost.

III

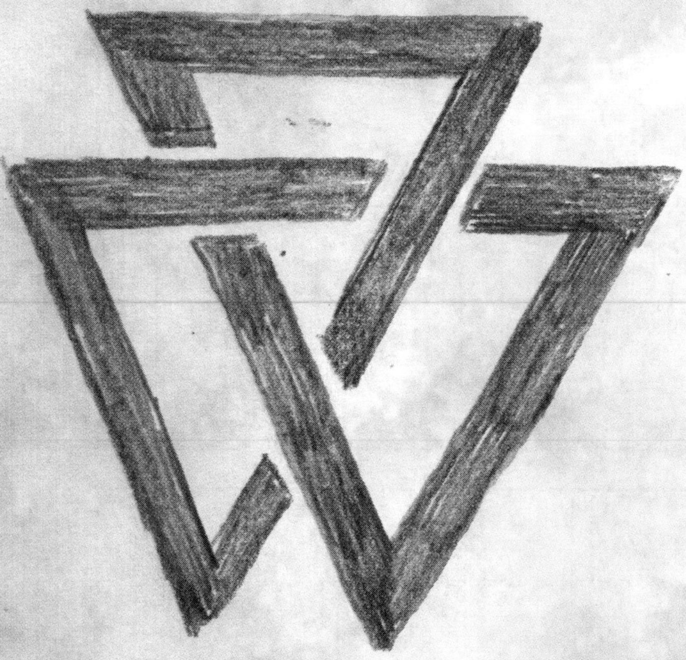

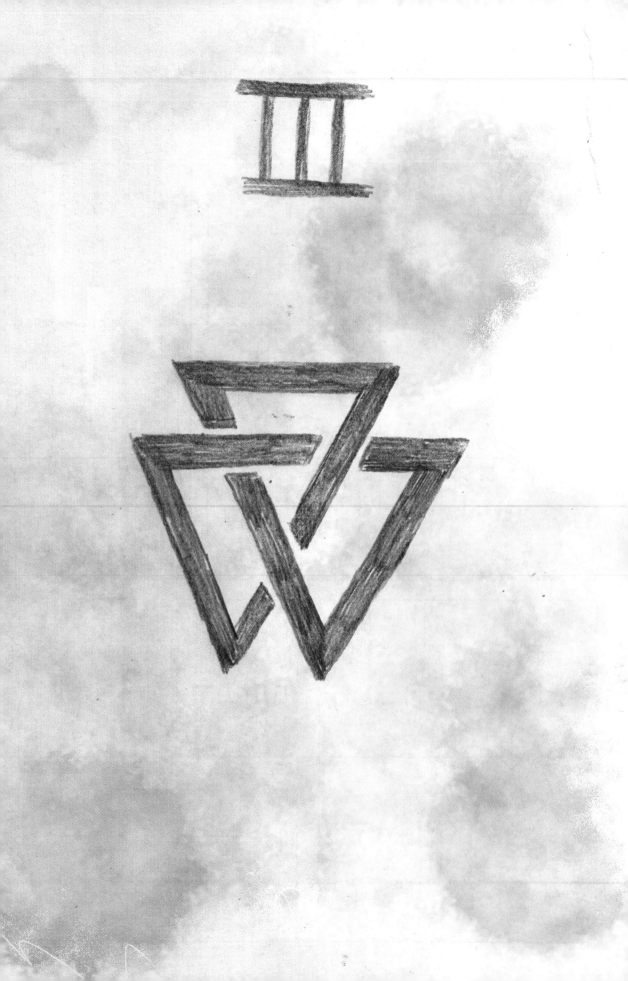

a memory
(a party between break-ups)

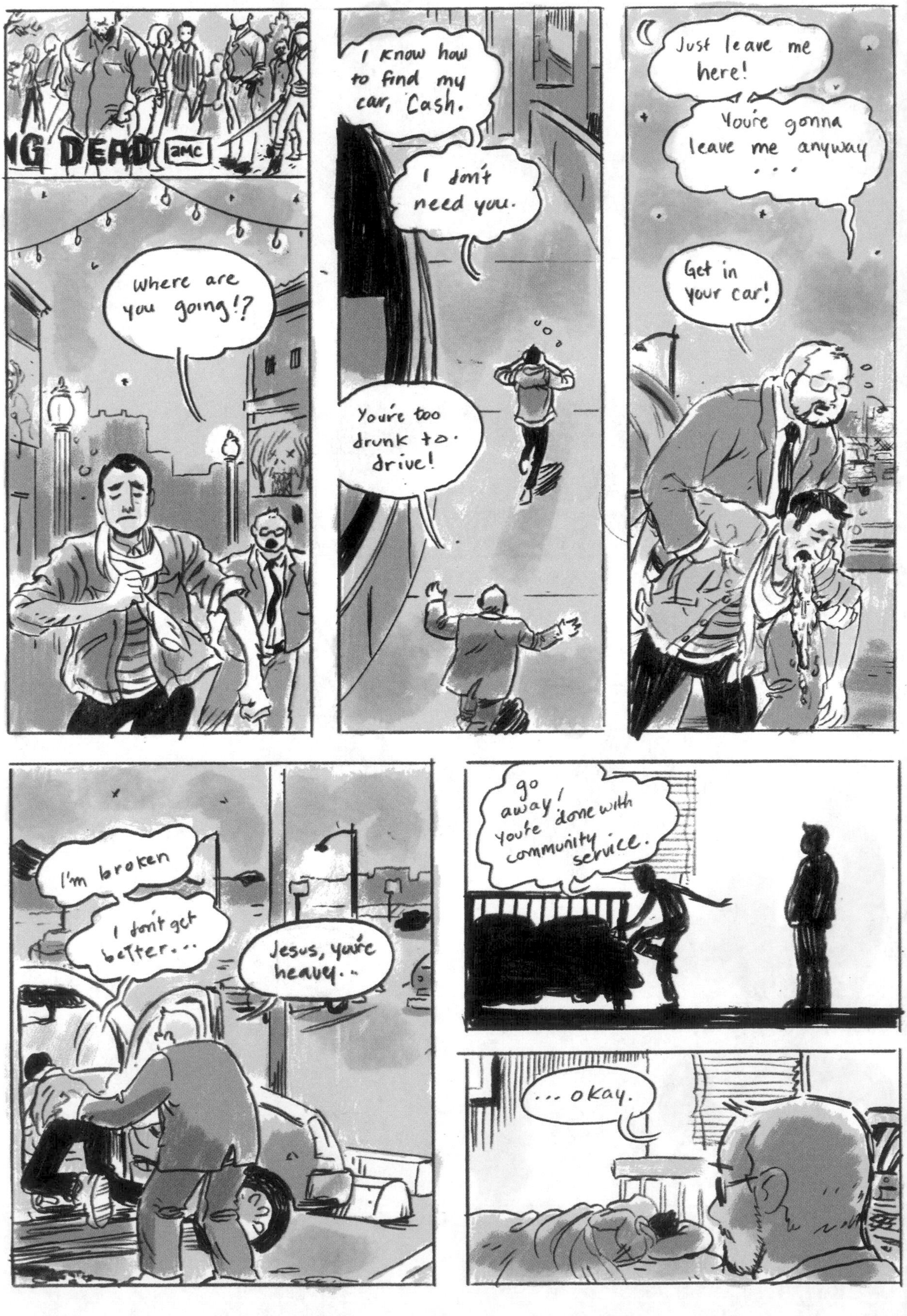
NG DEAD
AMC
Where are you going!?
I know how to find my car, Cash.
I don't need you.
You're too drunk to drive!
Just leave me here!
You're gonna leave me anyway . . .
Get in your car!
I'm broken
I don't get better...
Jesus, you're heavy..
go away! You're done with community service.
...okay.

He and Him really seemed like the golden idea...

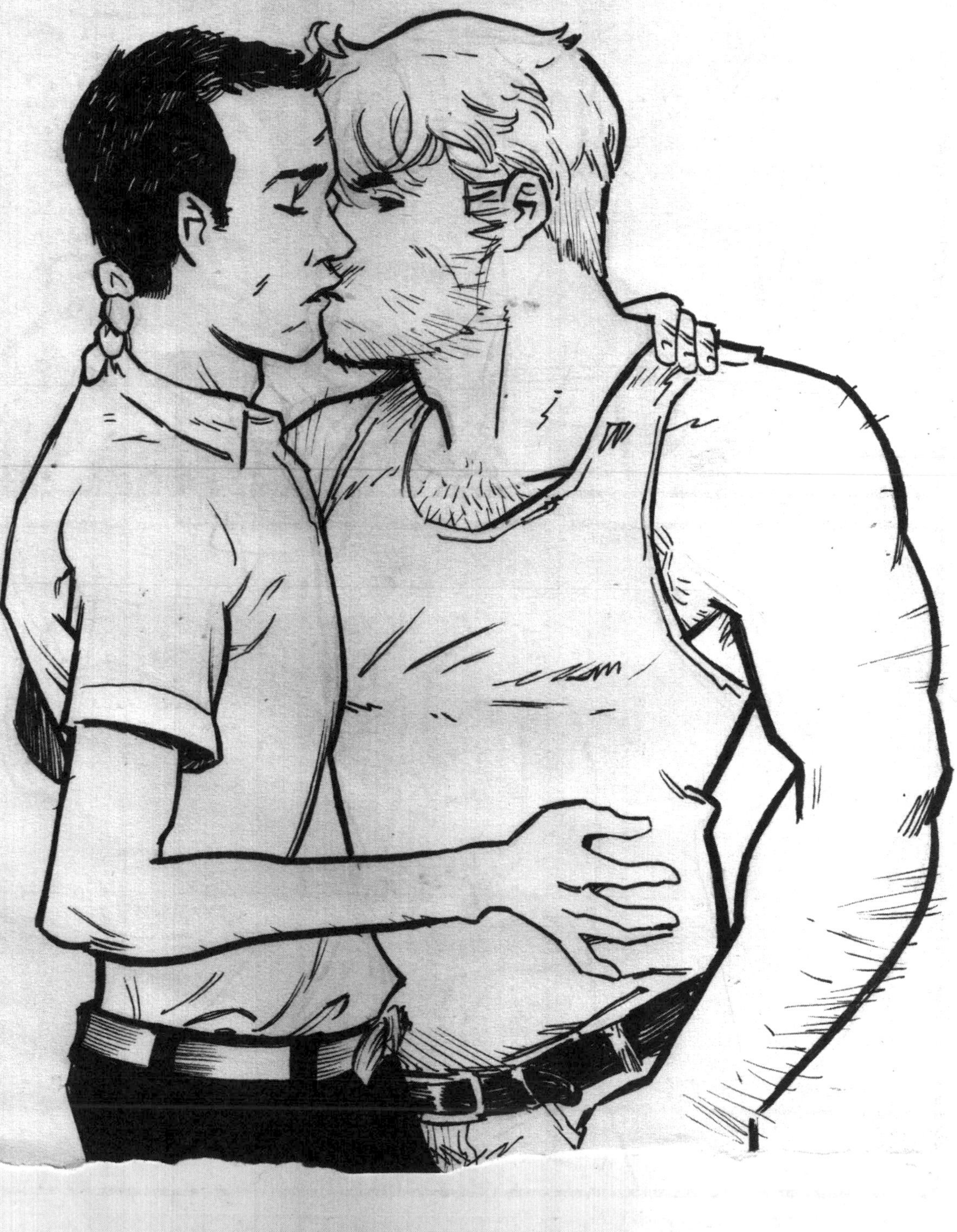

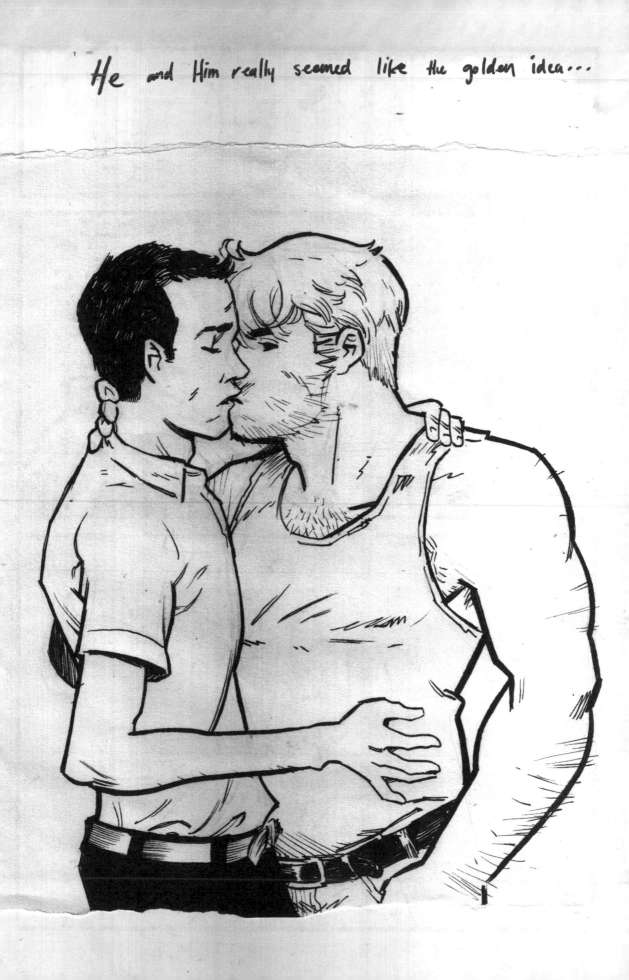

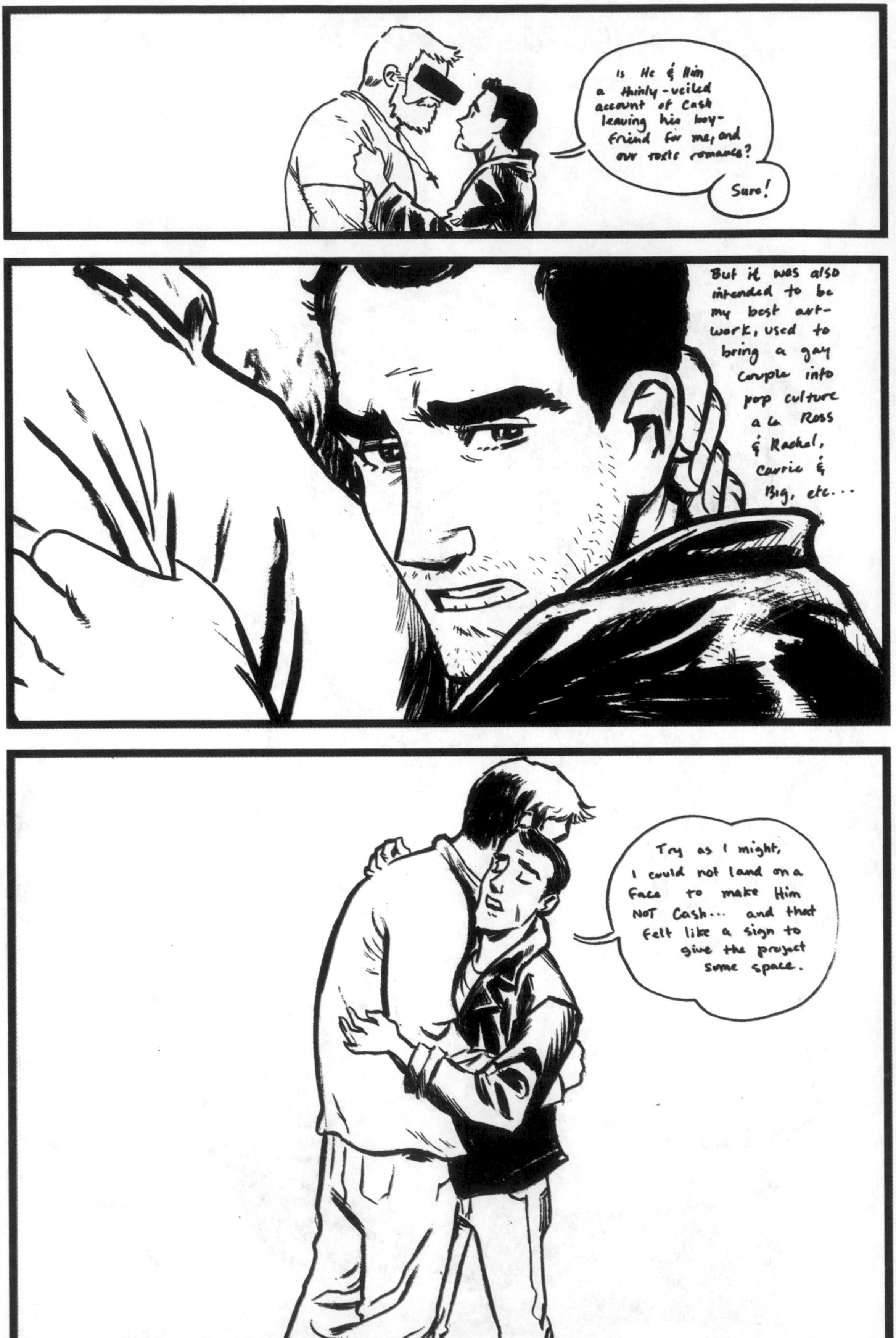
Is He & Him a thinly-veiled account of Cash leaving his boy-friend for me, and our toxic romance?
Sure!
But it was also intended to be my best art-work, used to bring a gay couple into pop culture a la Ross & Rachel, Carrie & Big, etc...
Try as I might, I could not land on a face to make Him NOT Cash... and that felt like a sign to give the project some space.

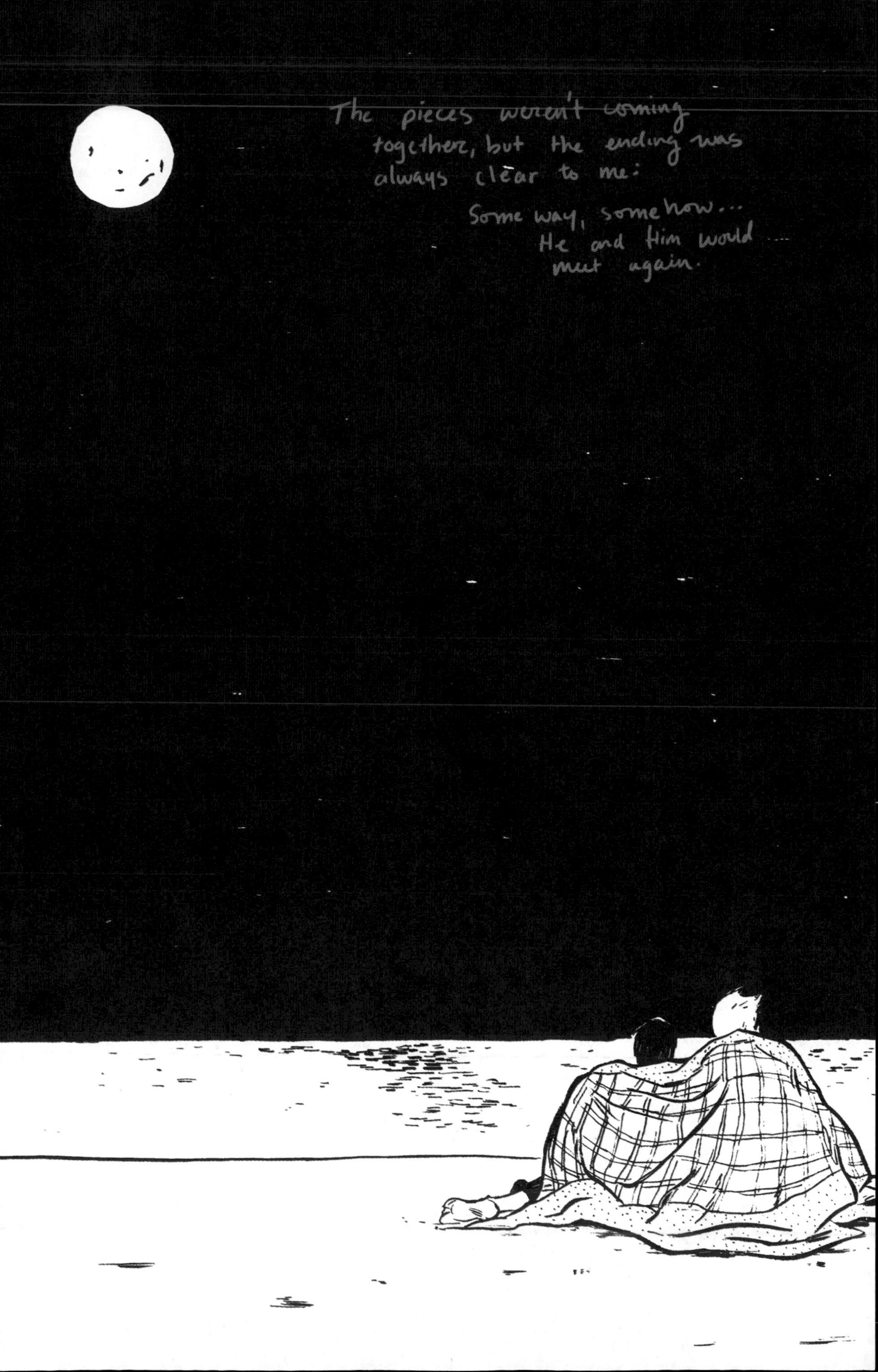
The pieces weren't coming together, but the ending was always clear to me:
Some way, somehow... He and Him would meet again.

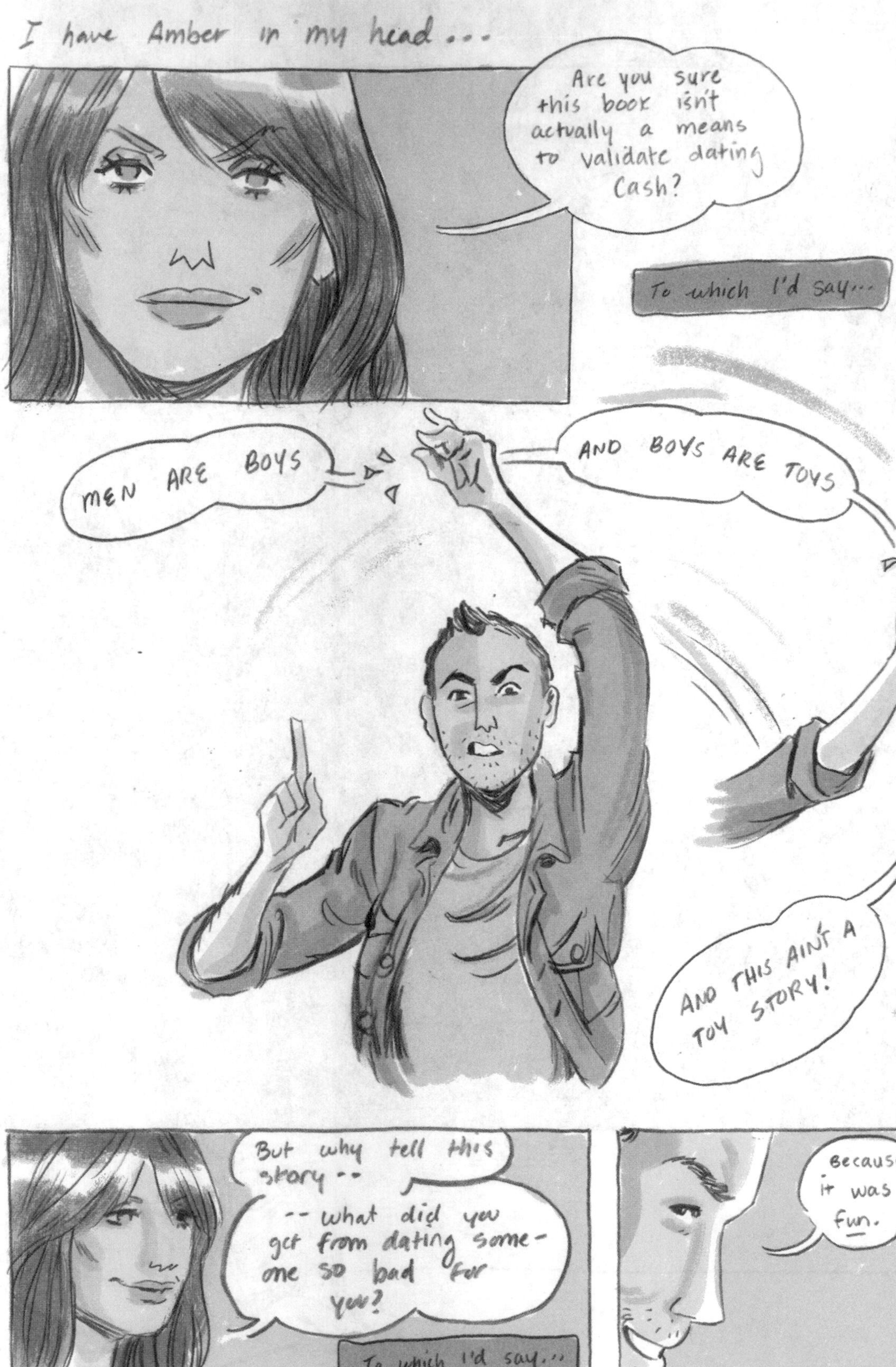
I have Amber in my head...
Are you sure this book isn't actually a means to validate dating Cash?
To which I'd say...
MEN ARE BOYS
AND BOYS ARE TOYS
AND THIS AIN'T A TOY STORY!
But why tell this story --
-- what did you get from dating some-one so bad for you?
To which I'd say...
Because it was fun.
(No, predictive friending is not fun.)

I have a story that
gets worked on in a
tiny note pad, about
one of the central forces
used in my first book,
Not My Bag.

named
after a
Rilo
kiley song

the book- "That's How I
choose to Remember It" is
a good exercise for me
to reconcile that
relationship . . .

But is it a
book???

There are over 3500 students at my school, which sits a mere mile away from the Santa Monica beach.

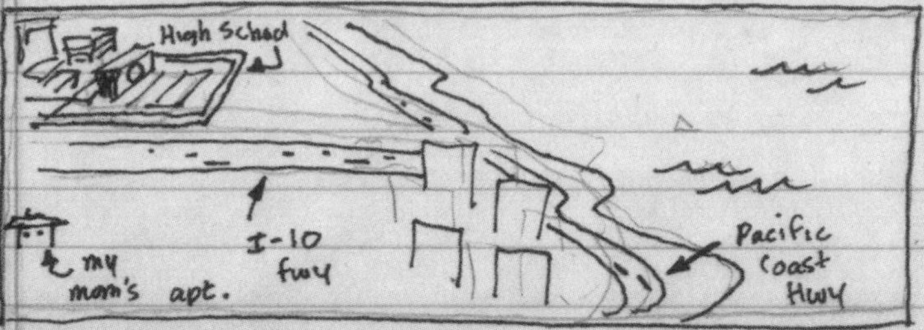

High School
I-10 fwy
my mom's apt.
Pacific Coast Hwy

Before lunchtime is over, an old bully approaches me for absolution, and I've fallen for my 4th period teacher.

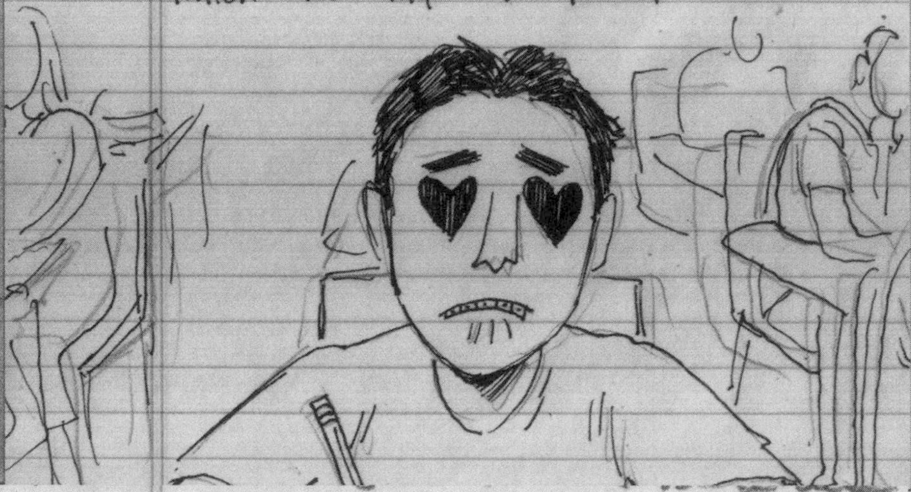

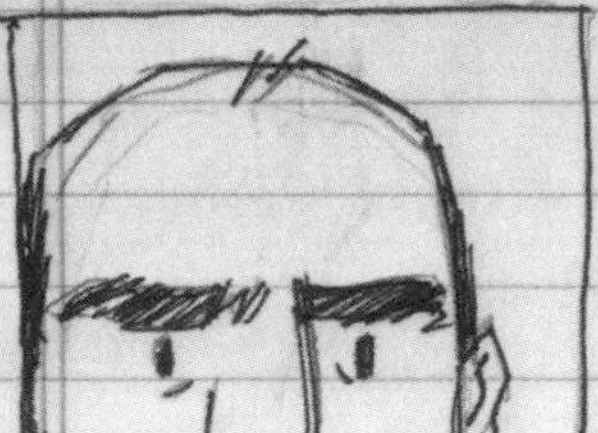

He makes a face when saying my name during roll call.

At a later point, he tells me it's because he assumed I was a girl.

That night, I jerk off to him before bed.

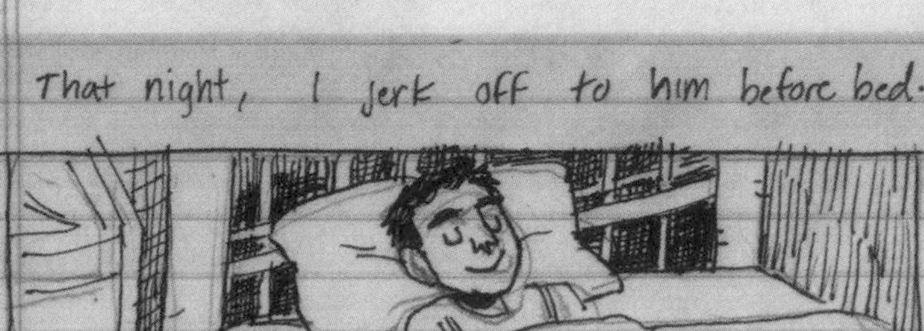

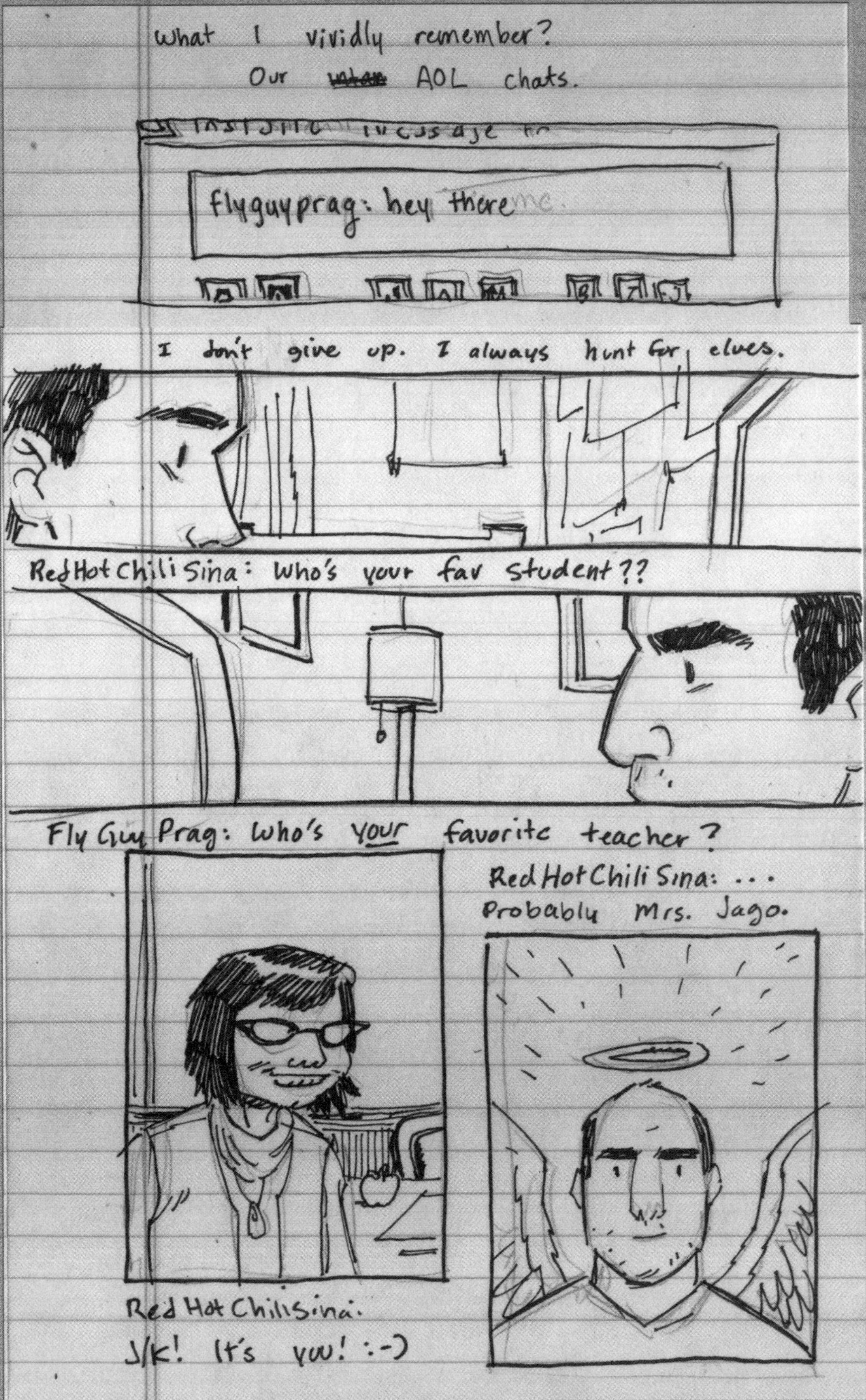
What I vividly remember?
Our AOL chats.
flyguyprag: hey there
I don't give up. I always hunt for clues.
RedHotChiliSina: Who's your fav student??
Fly Guy Prag: Who's YOUR favorite teacher?
RedHotChiliSina: ...
Probably Mrs. Jago.
Red Hot ChiliSina:
J/K! It's you! :-)

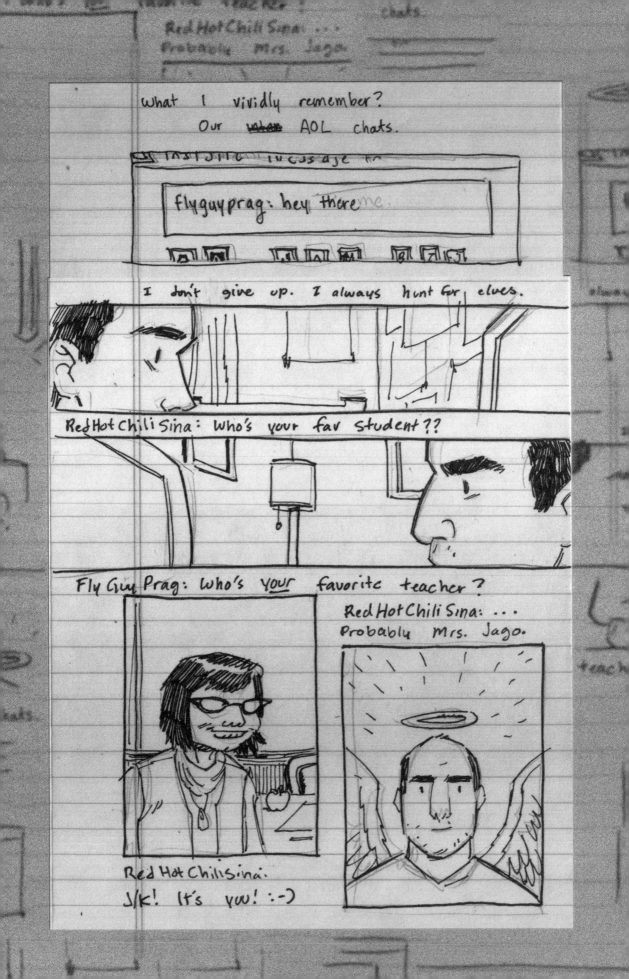

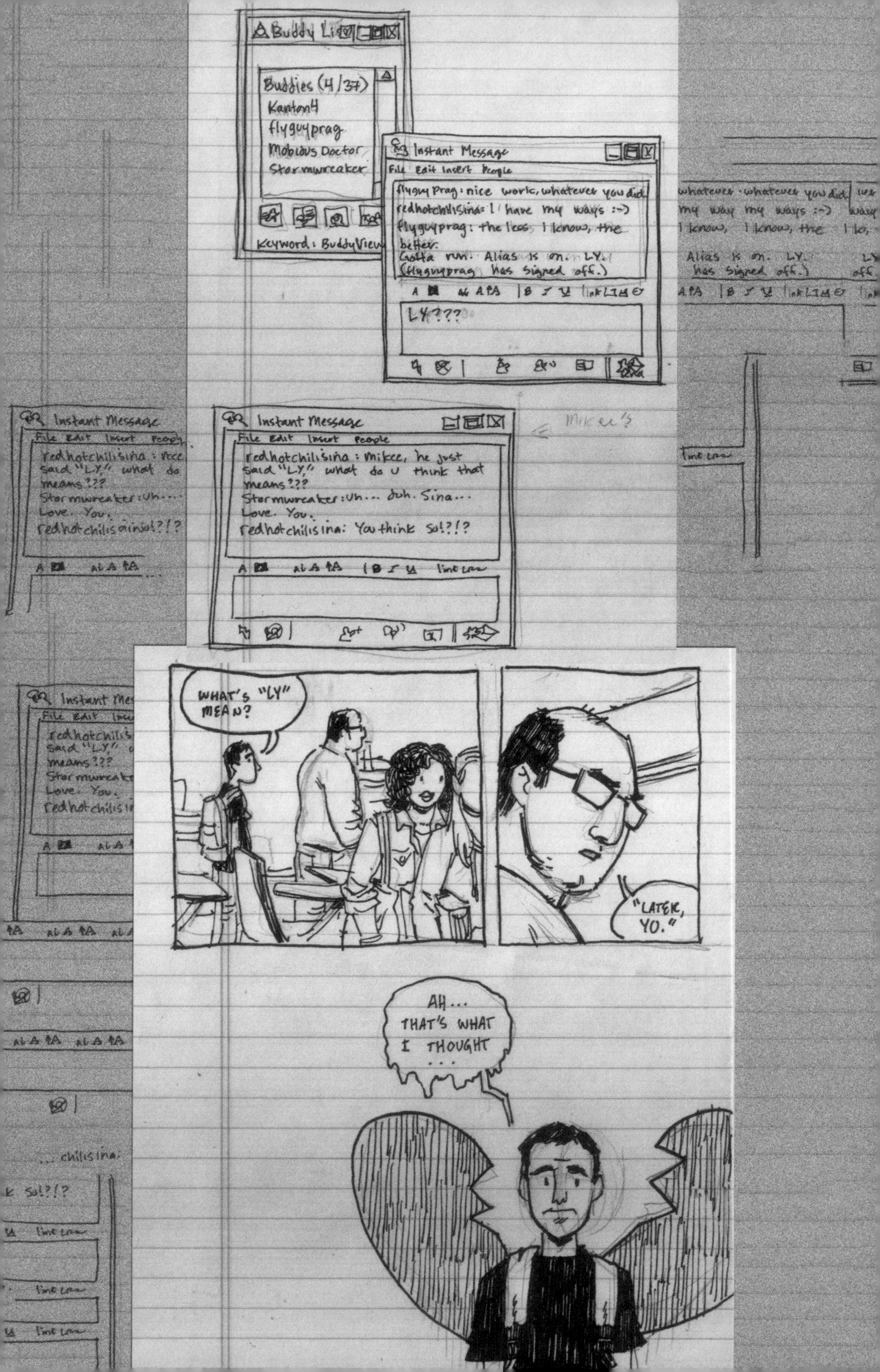
Buddy List
Buddies (4/37)
Kanton4
flyguyprag
Mobius Doctor
Stormwreaker
Keyword: BuddyView
Instant Message
File Edit Insert People
flyguyprag: nice work, whatever you did.
redhotchilisina: I have my ways :-)
flyguyprag: the less I know, the better.
Gotta run. Alias is on. LY.
(flyguyprag has signed off.)
LY???
Mikee's
Instant Message
File Edit Insert People
redhotchilisina: mikee, he just said "LY," what do u think that means???
Stormwreaker: Uh... duh. Sina... Love. You.
redhotchilisina: You think so!?!?
WHAT'S "LY" MEAN?
"LATER, YO."
AH... THAT'S WHAT I THOUGHT...

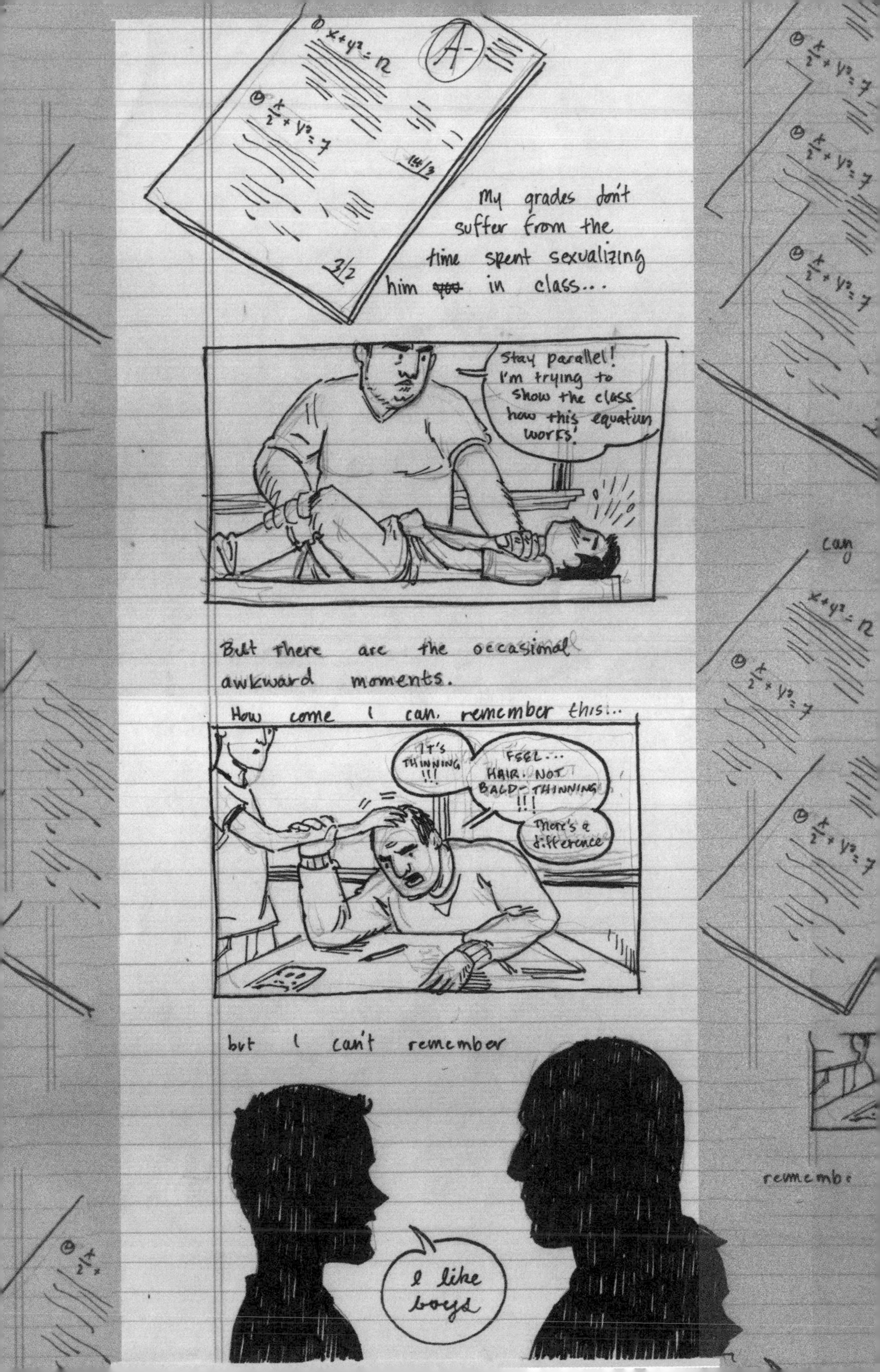
A-
x+y² = 12
x/2 + y² = 7
14/3
3/2
My grades don't suffer from the time spent sexualizing him ~~you~~ in class...
Stay parallel! I'm trying to show the class how this equation works!
But there are the occasional awkward moments.
How come I can remember this...
IT'S THINNING!!!
FEEL... HAIR. NOT BALD- THINNING!!!
There's a difference
but I can't remember
I like boys

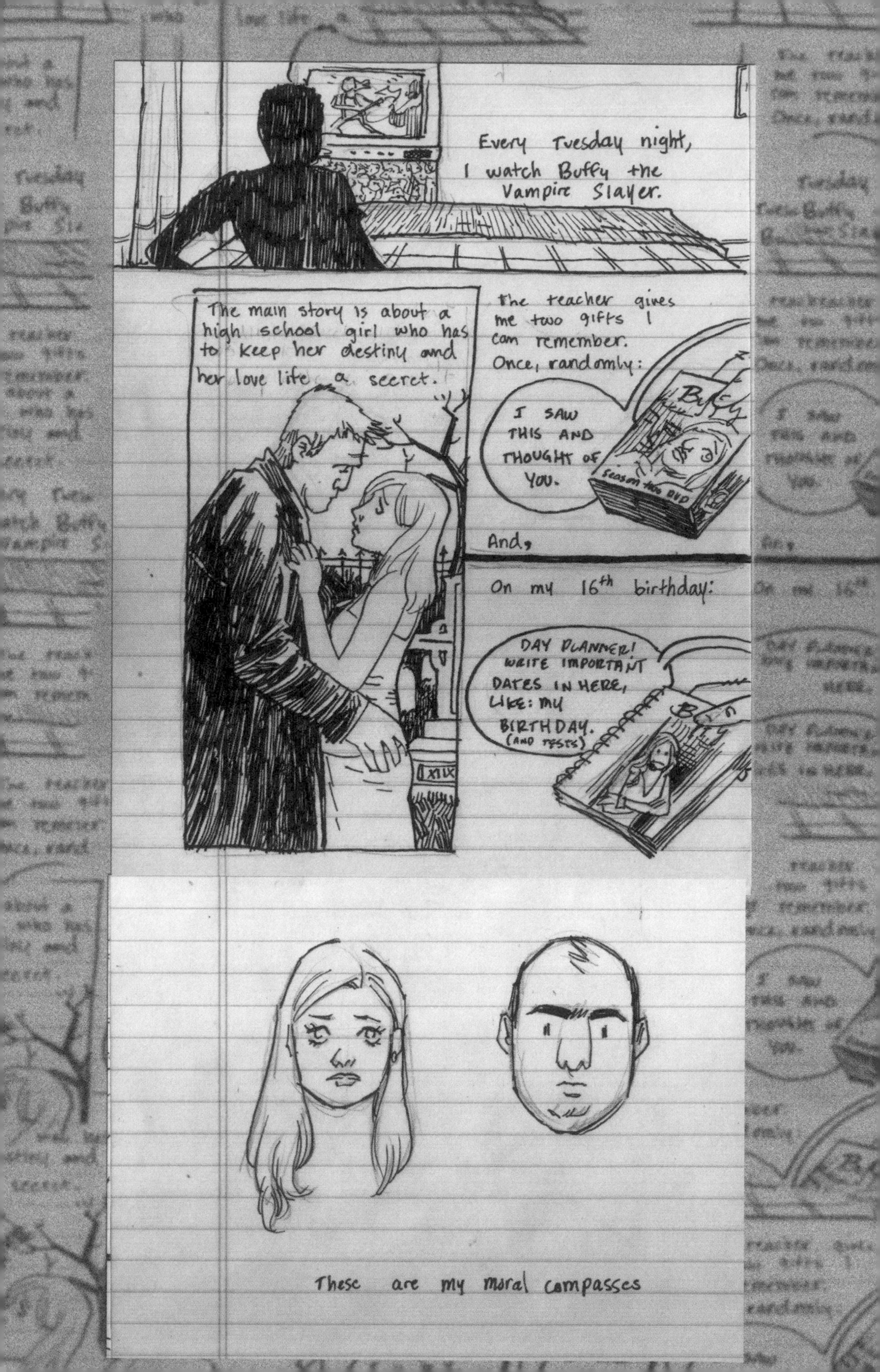
Every Tuesday night, I watch Buffy the Vampire Slayer.
The main story is about a high school girl who has to keep her destiny and her love life a secret.
The teacher gives me two gifts I can remember. Once, randomly:
I SAW THIS AND THOUGHT OF YOU.
Season two DVD
And,
On my 16th birthday:
DAY PLANNER! WRITE IMPORTANT DATES IN HERE, LIKE: MY BIRTHDAY. (AND TESTS)
These are my moral compasses

happen" Euthing I wantecthing I
hoccn for mysen for

Euryth
happeo

I h
at m
comlc

this page should happen later

Everything I wanted in life I made
happen for myself.

I have an internship
at my favorite
comic book publisher.

I work at my
favorite comic
shop...

I feel "cool,"
accepted, and I
make money enough
to dress how I
please.

"cool,
and I
ey enough
how I

I cannot will a
teacher to love me.

I
at m
coml

nship

blcher.

I have an interno
at my favorite
comic book publict.

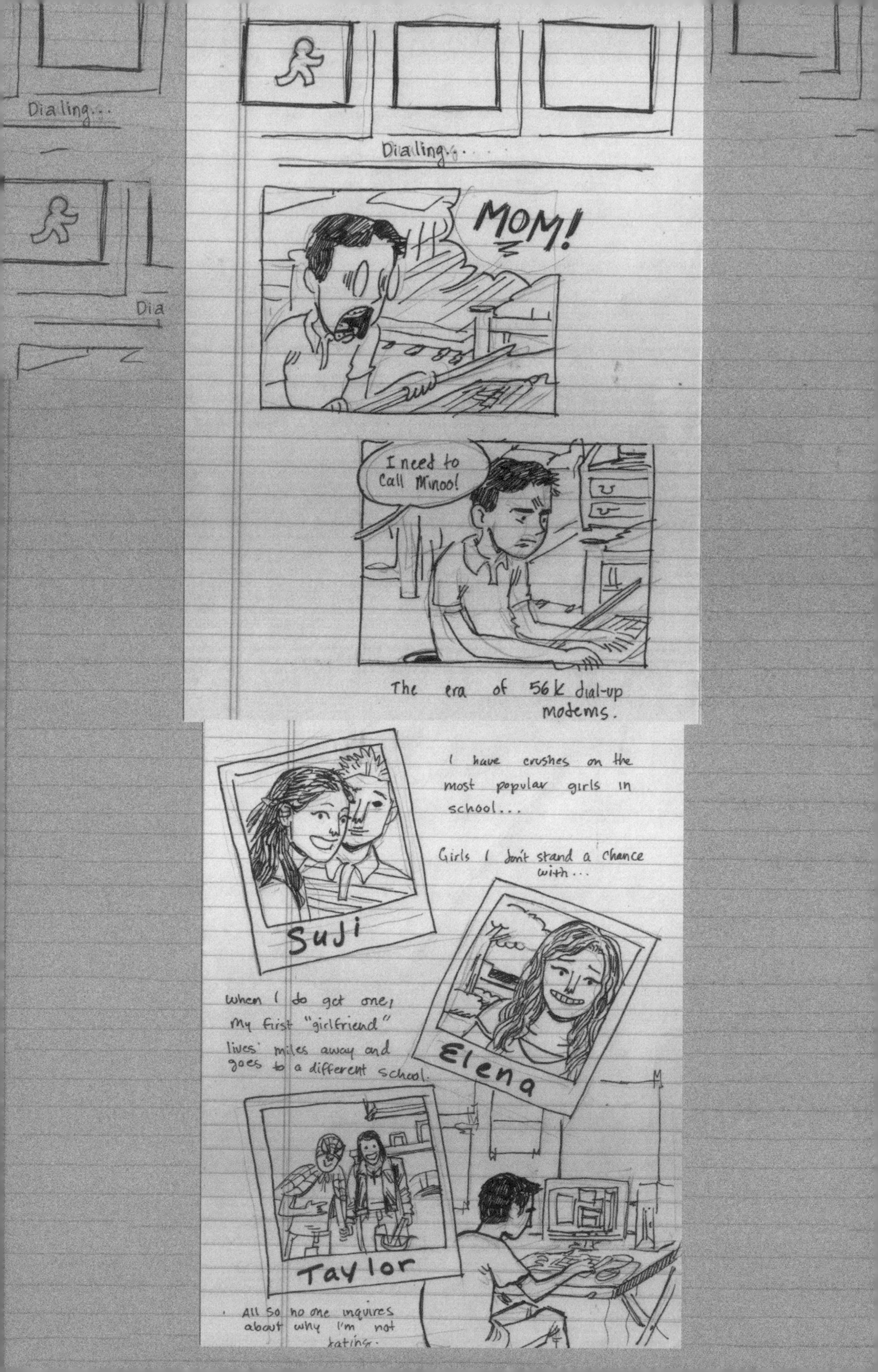
Dialing...
Dialing...
Dia
MOM!
I need to call Minoo!
The era of 56k dial-up modems.
I have crushes on the most popular girls in school...
Girls I don't stand a chance with...
Suji
Elena
When I do get one, my first "girlfriend" lives miles away and goes to a different school.
Taylor
All so no one inquires about why I'm not dating.

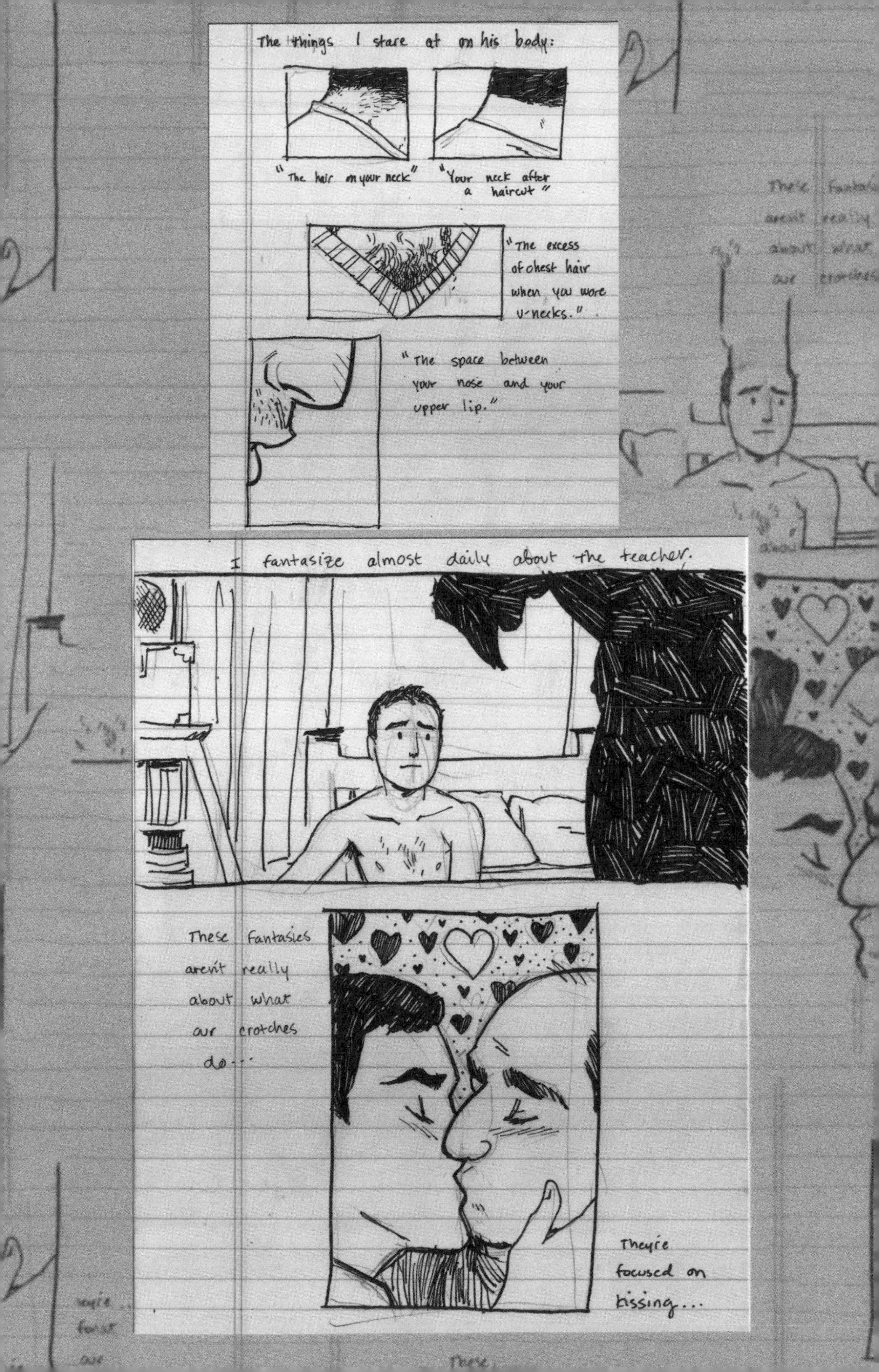

The things I stare at on his body:
"The hair on your neck"
"Your neck after a haircut"
"The excess of chest hair when you wore v-necks."
"The space between your nose and your upper lip."
I fantasize almost daily about the teacher.
These fantasies aren't really about what our crotches do...
They're focused on kissing...

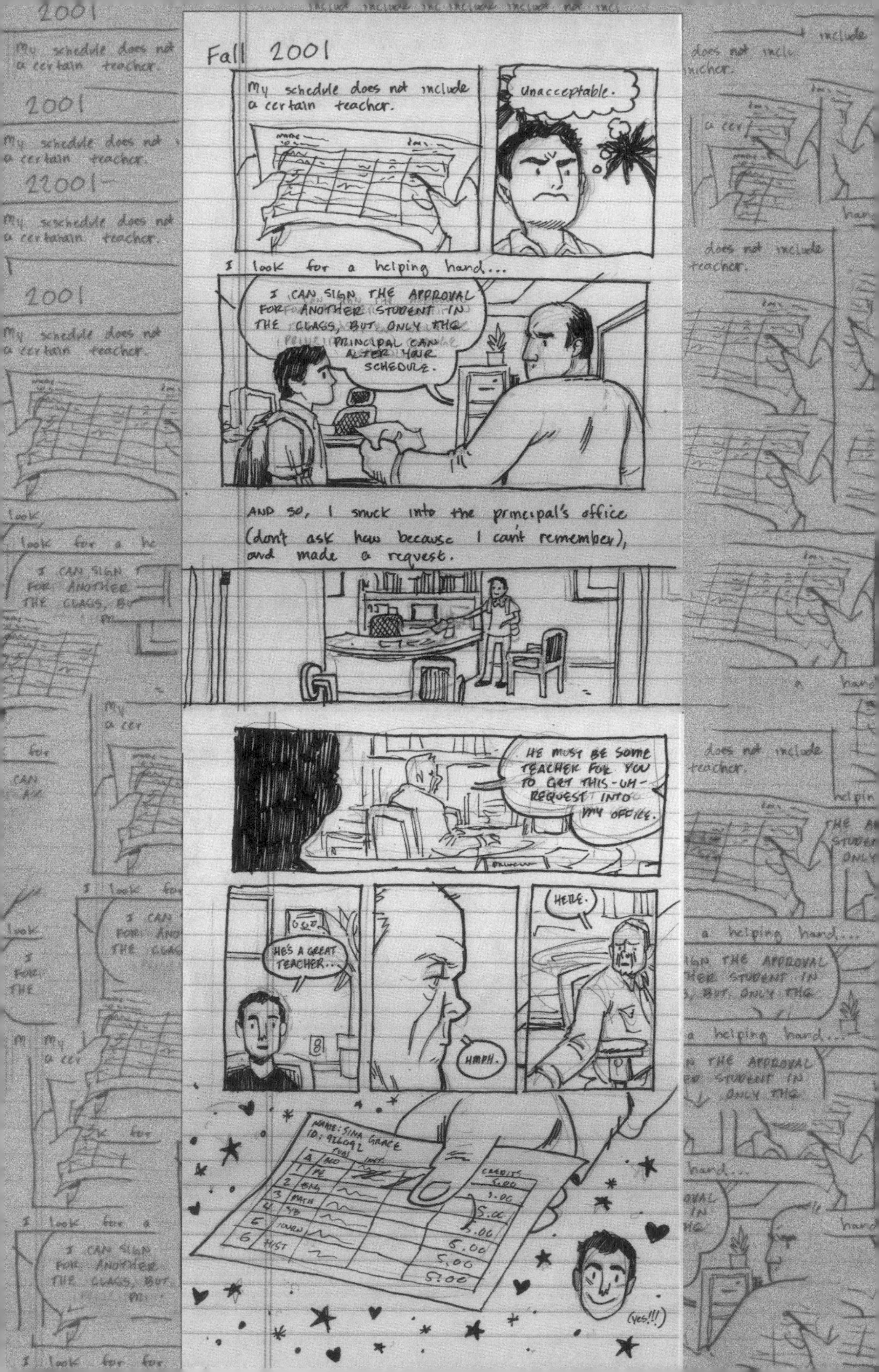
Fall 2001
My schedule does not include a certain teacher.
Unacceptable.
I look for a helping hand...
I CAN SIGN THE APPROVAL FOR ANOTHER STUDENT IN THE CLASS, BUT ONLY THE PRINCIPAL CAN ALTER YOUR SCHEDULE.
AND SO, I snuck into the principal's office (don't ask how because I can't remember), and made a request.
HE MUST BE SOME TEACHER FOR YOU TO GET THIS-UH-REQUEST INTO MY OFFICE.
HE'S A GREAT TEACHER...
HMPH.
HERE.
NAME: SINA GRACE
CREDITS
(yes!!!)

The teacher is 28.

I am 14.

I stay a virgin.

I get good grades.

I don't do drugs.

I do these things because
I think that's how he wants
me to be.

C+

MAUDLIN
AF!!!
and no ending...
he basically stopped
talking to me when
I called him
out on his
behavior...

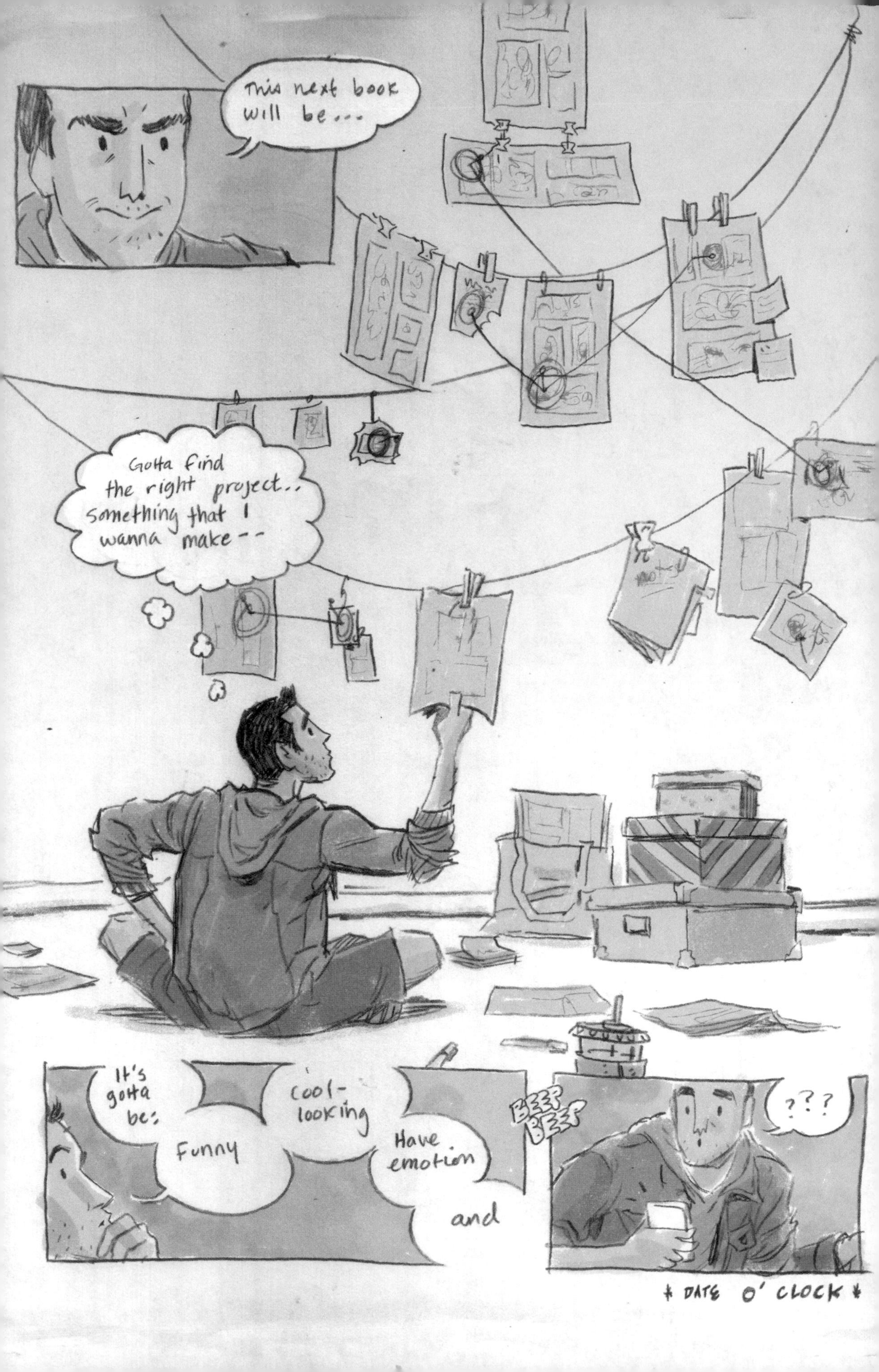
This next book will be...
Gotta find the right project.. something that I wanna make--
It's gotta be:
Funny
cool-looking
Have emotion
and
BEEP BEEP
???
* DATE O' CLOCK *

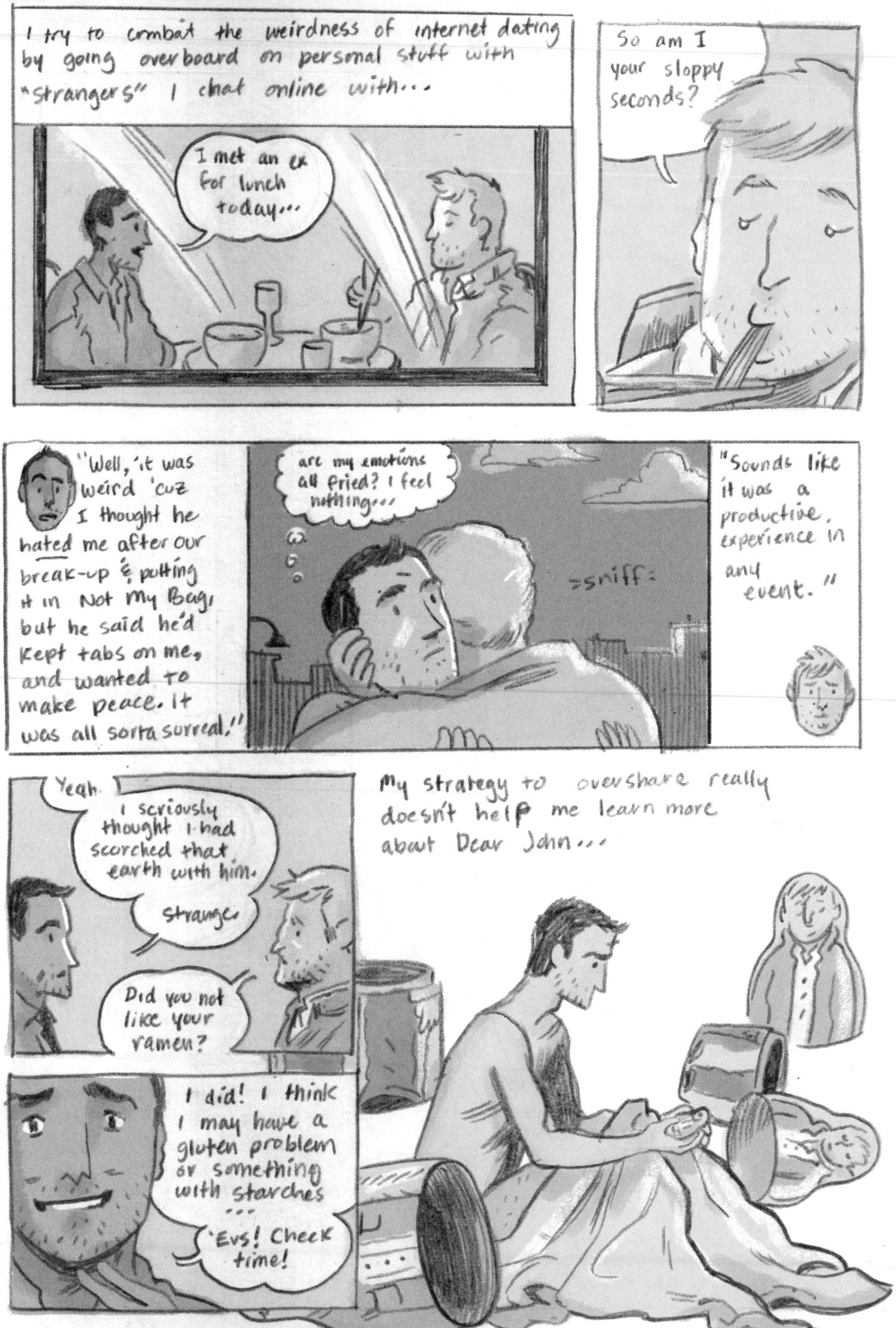

I try to combat the weirdness of internet dating by going overboard on personal stuff with "strangers" I chat online with...
I met an ex for lunch today...
So am I your sloppy seconds?
"Well, it was weird 'cuz I thought he hated me after our break-up & putting it in Not My Bag, but he said he'd kept tabs on me, and wanted to make peace. It was all sorta surreal."
are my emotions all fried? I feel nothing...
=sniff=
"Sounds like it was a productive experience in any event."
Yeah.
I seriously thought I had scorched that earth with him.
Strange.
Did you not like your ramen?
I did! I think I may have a gluten problem or something with starches...
'Evs! Check time!
My strategy to overshare really doesn't help me learn more about Dear John...

things I can't say three dates in...

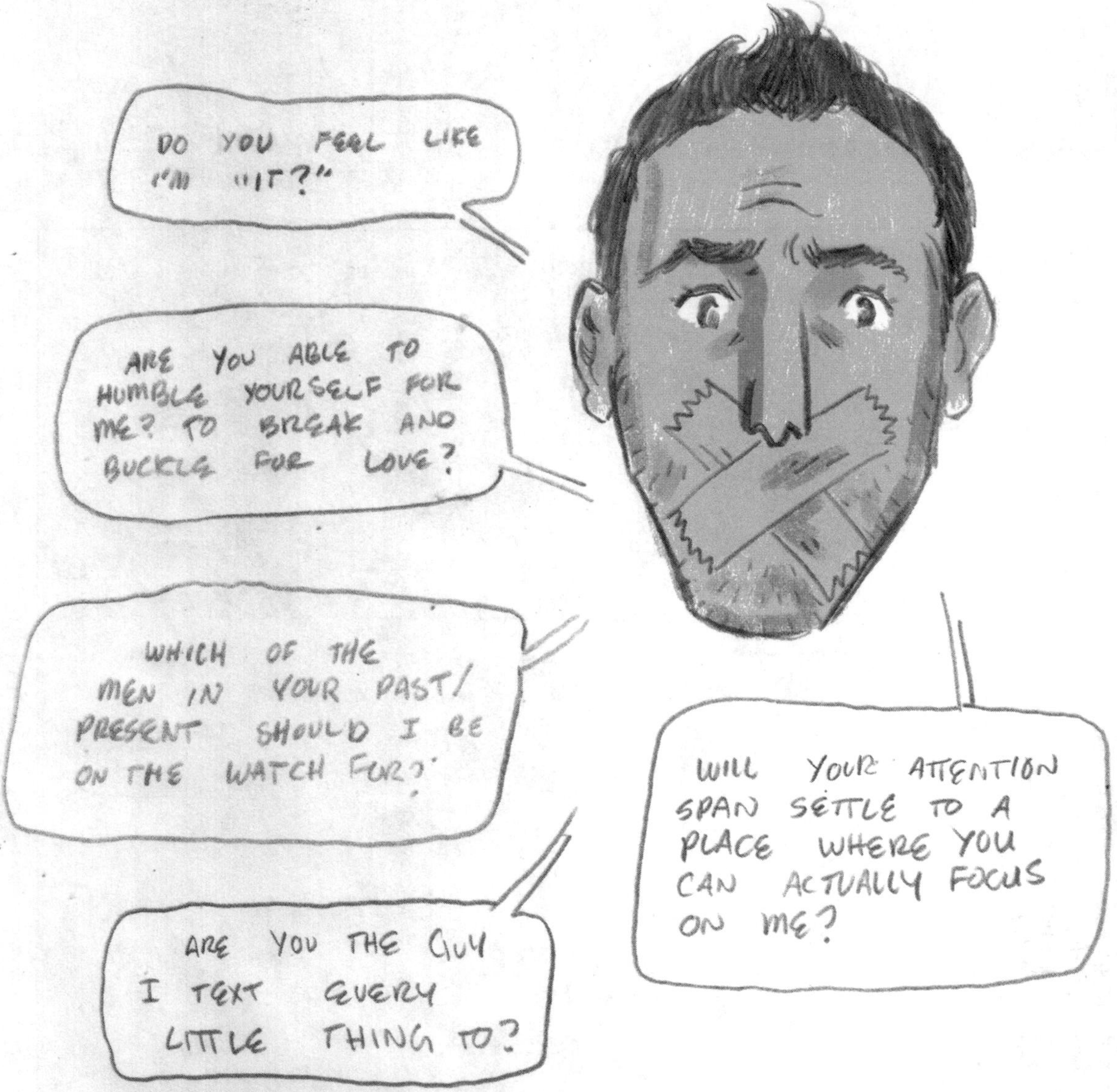
DO YOU FEEL LIKE I'M "IT?"
ARE YOU ABLE TO HUMBLE YOURSELF FOR ME? TO BREAK AND BUCKLE FOR LOVE?
WHICH OF THE MEN IN YOUR PAST/PRESENT SHOULD I BE ON THE WATCH FOR?
ARE YOU THE GUY I TEXT EVERY LITTLE THING TO?
WILL YOUR ATTENTION SPAN SETTLE TO A PLACE WHERE YOU CAN ACTUALLY FOCUS ON ME?

4.

1.

四

四

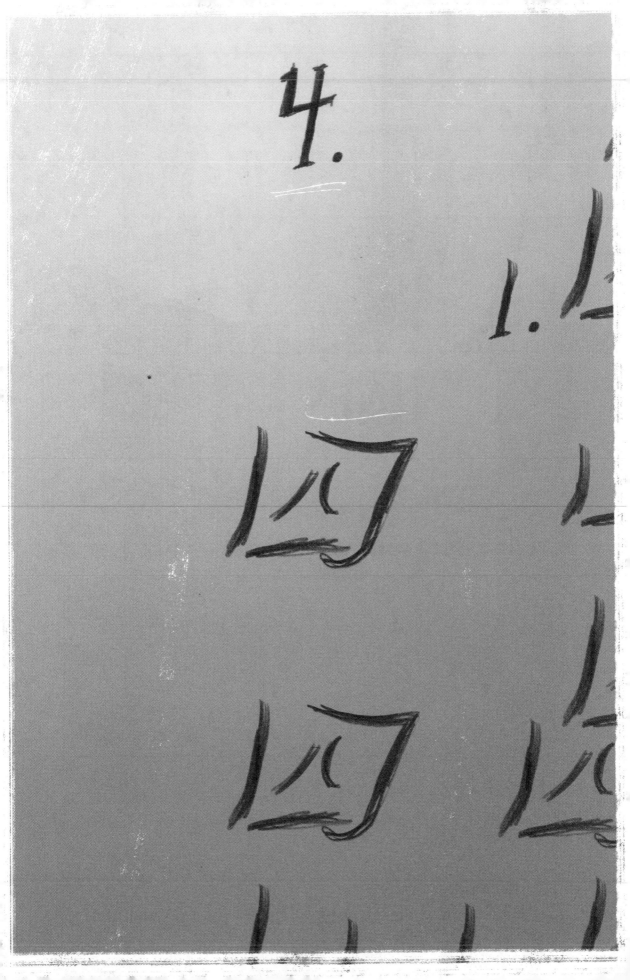

· a memory (the time I cut myself...)

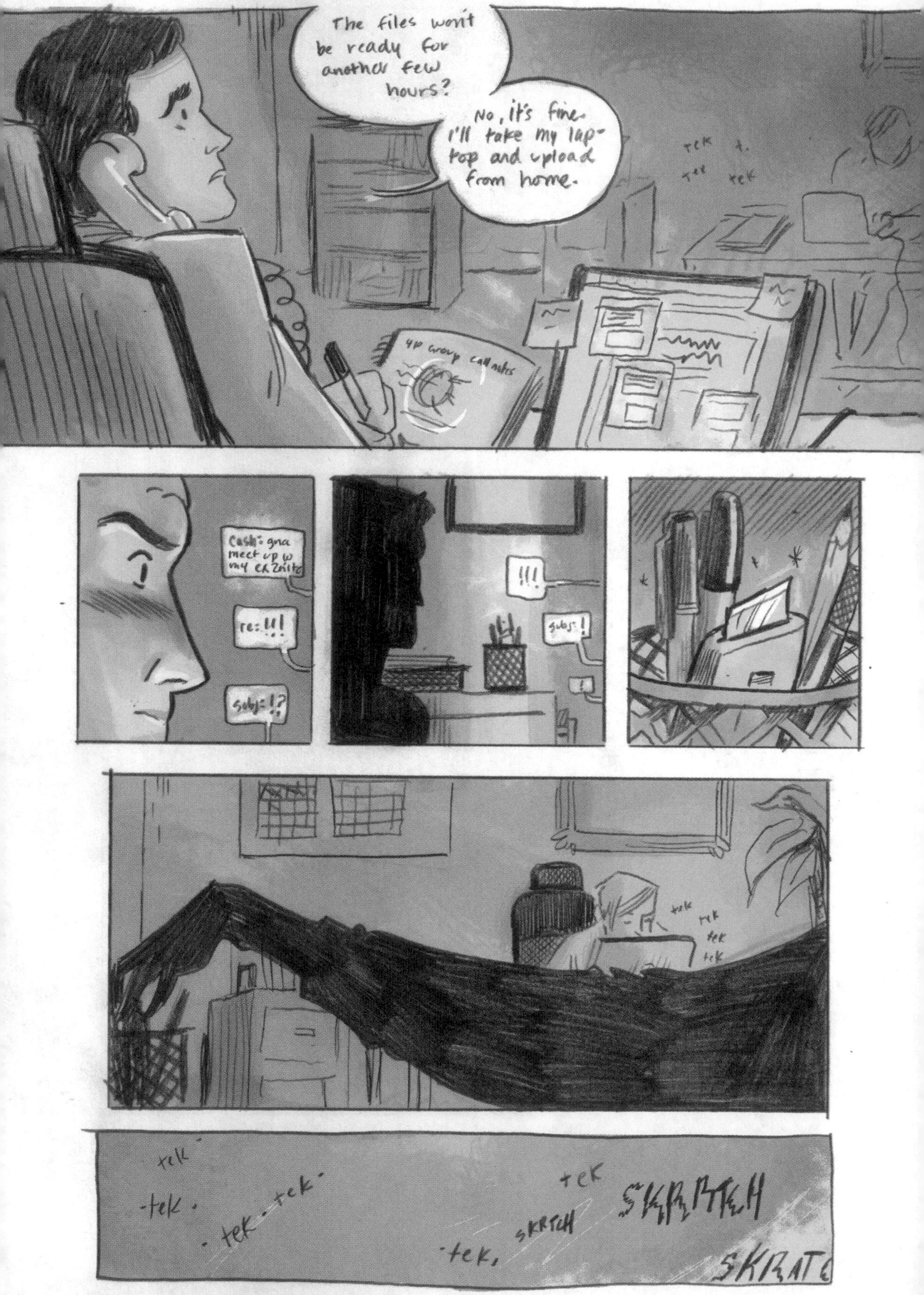

The files won't be ready for another few hours?
No, it's fine. I'll take my laptop and upload from home.
tek t. tek tek
Cash: gna meet up w my ex2nite
re: !!!
subj: !?
!!!
subj: !
tek tek tek tek
tek
-tek.
tek. tek
tek
-tek, SKRTCH
SKRTCH
SKRATC

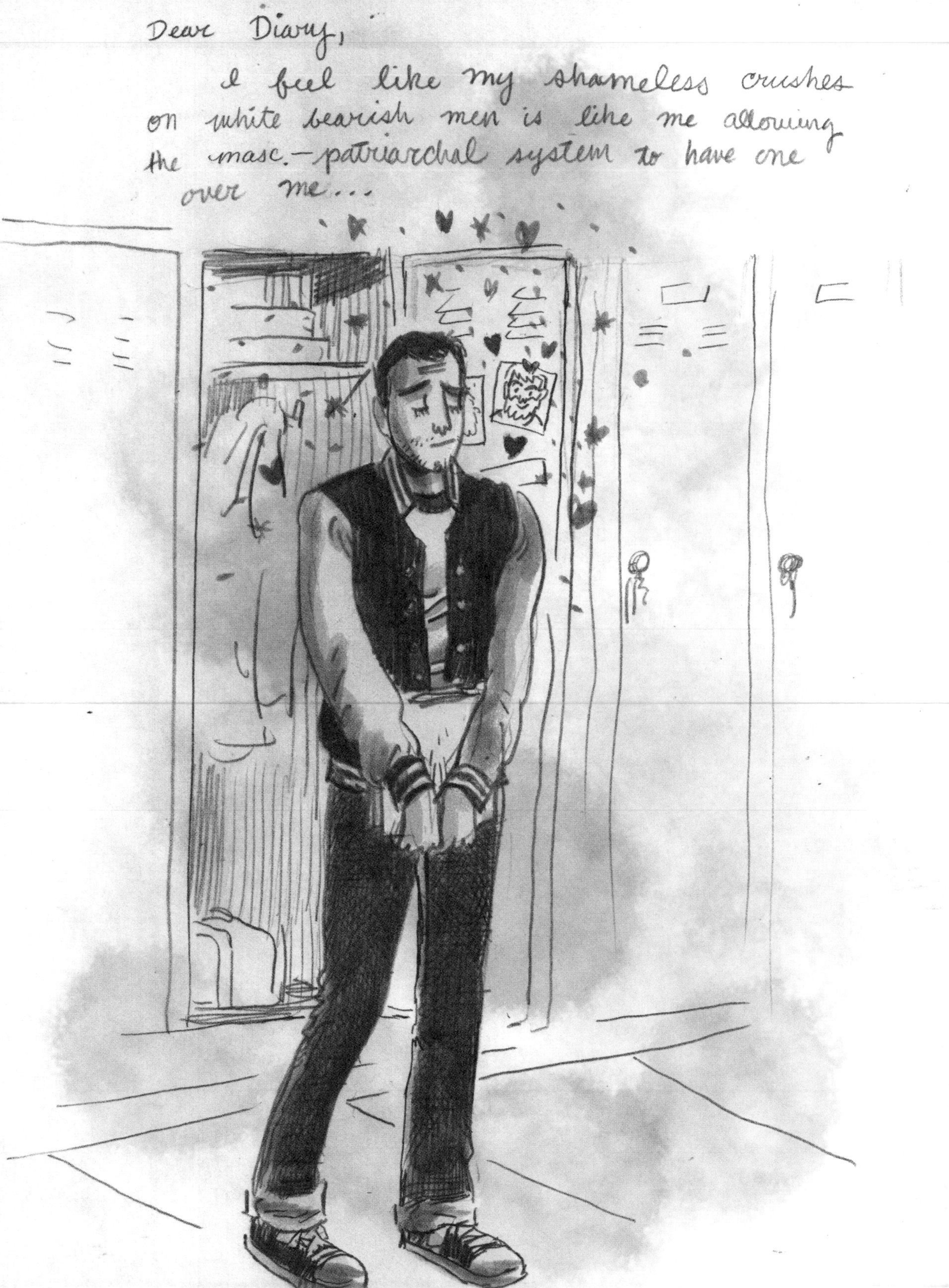
Dear Diary,
I feel like my shameless crushes on white bearish men is like me allowing the masc.-patriarchal system to have one over me...

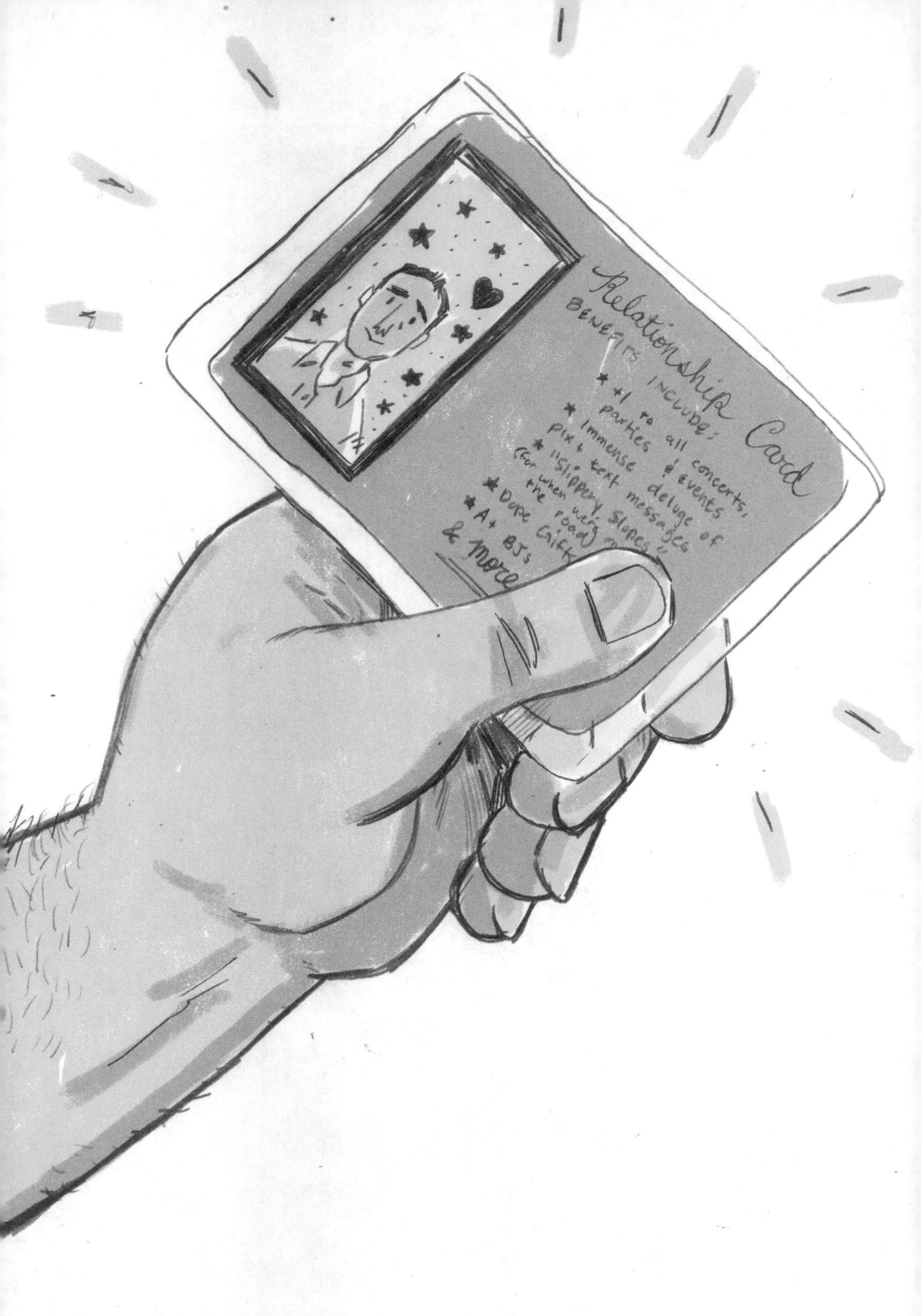
Relationship Card
BENEFITS INCLUDE:
* +1 to all concerts, parties & events
* Immense deluge of pix + text messages
* "Slippery slopes"
* Dope
* A+ BJs
& more

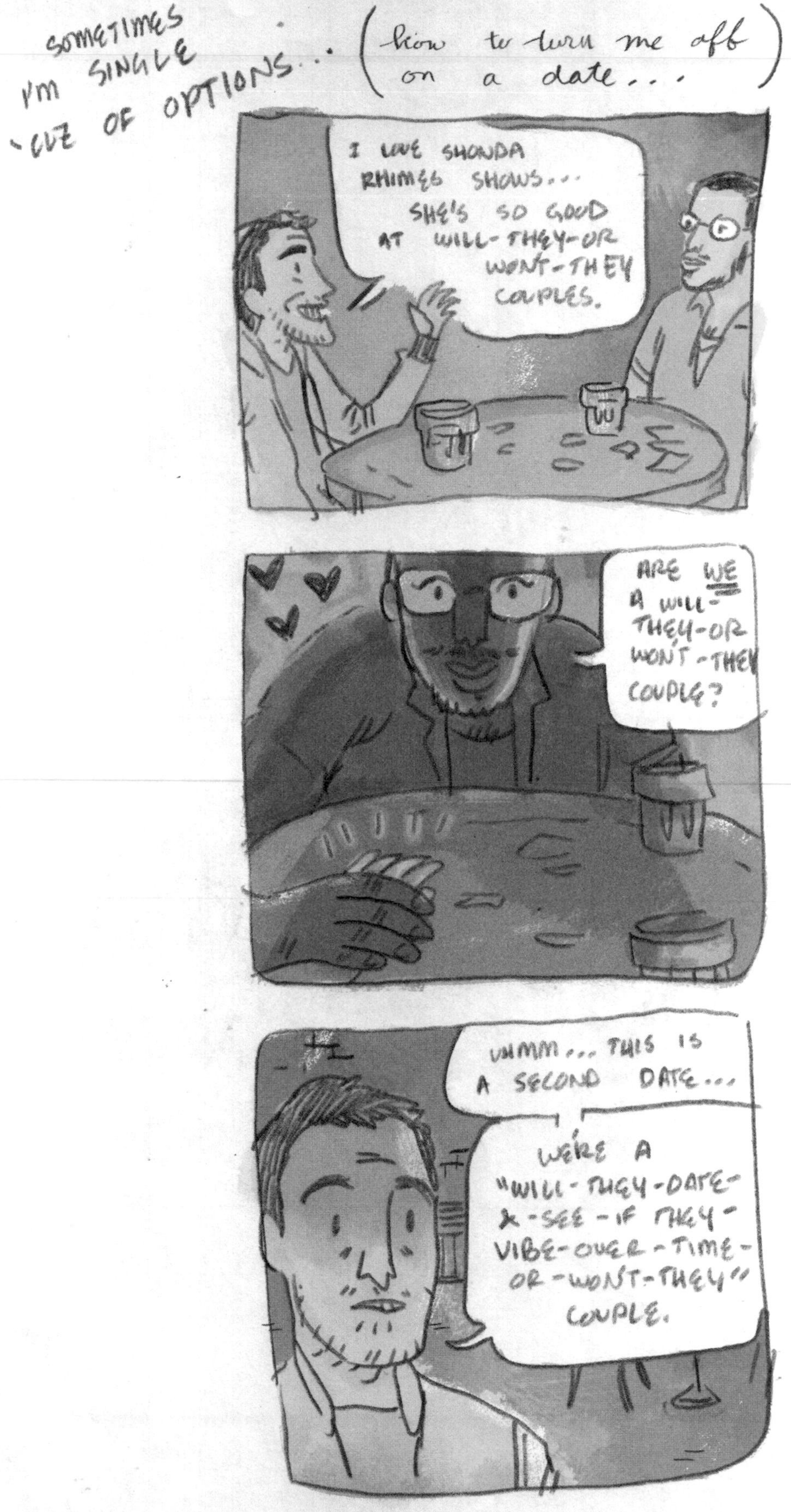
SOMETIMES I'M SINGLE 'CUZ OF OPTIONS...
(how to turn me off on a date...)
I LOVE SHONDA RHIMES SHOWS... SHE'S SO GOOD AT WILL-THEY-OR WON'T-THEY COUPLES.
ARE WE A WILL-THEY-OR WON'T-THEY COUPLE?
UMMM... THIS IS A SECOND DATE...
WE'RE A "WILL-THEY-DATE-&-SEE-IF THEY-VIBE-OVER-TIME-OR-WON'T-THEY" COUPLE.

BUT ALSO...

WHY I'M REALLY SINGLE:

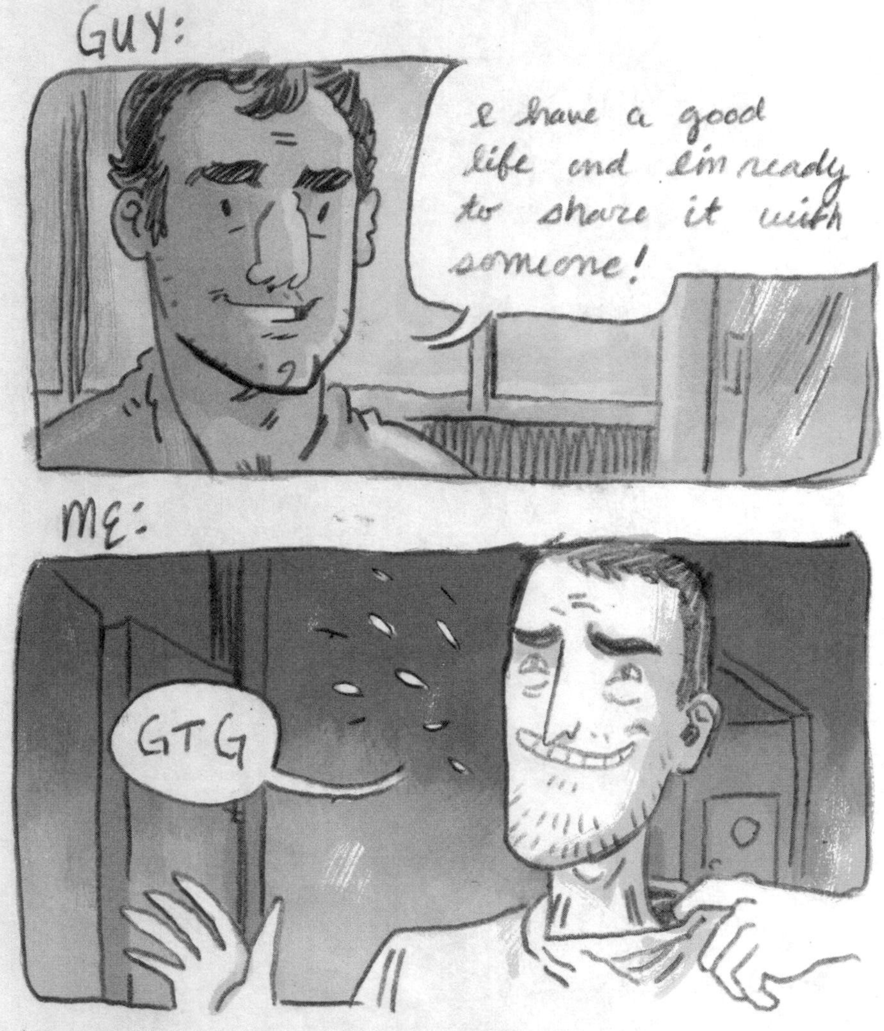
GUY:
I have a good life and im ready to share it with someone!
ME:
GTG

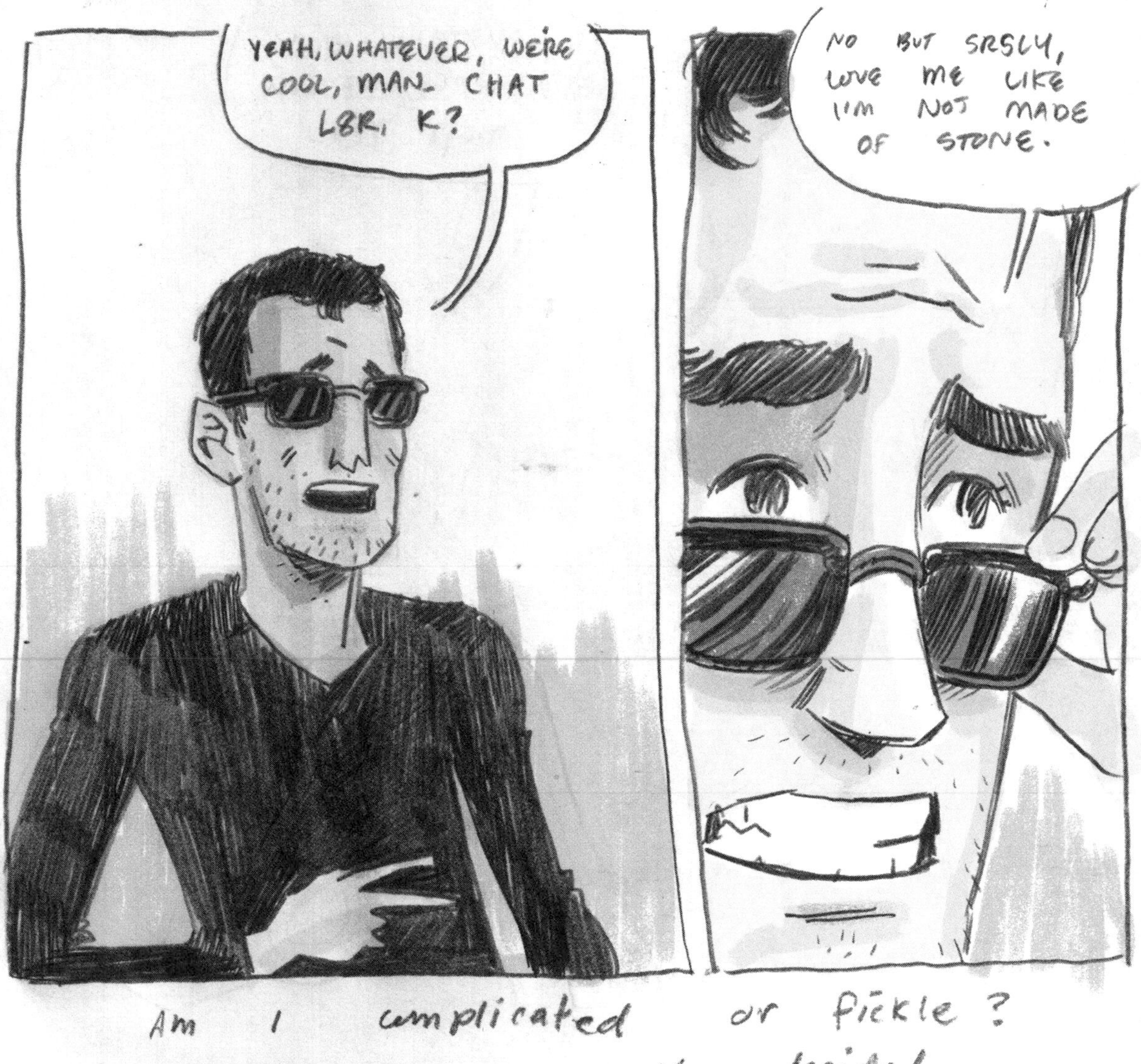
YEAH, WHATEVER, WE'RE COOL, MAN. CHAT L8R, K?
NO BUT SRSLY, LOVE ME LIKE I'M NOT MADE OF STONE.

Am I complicated or fickle? You decide!

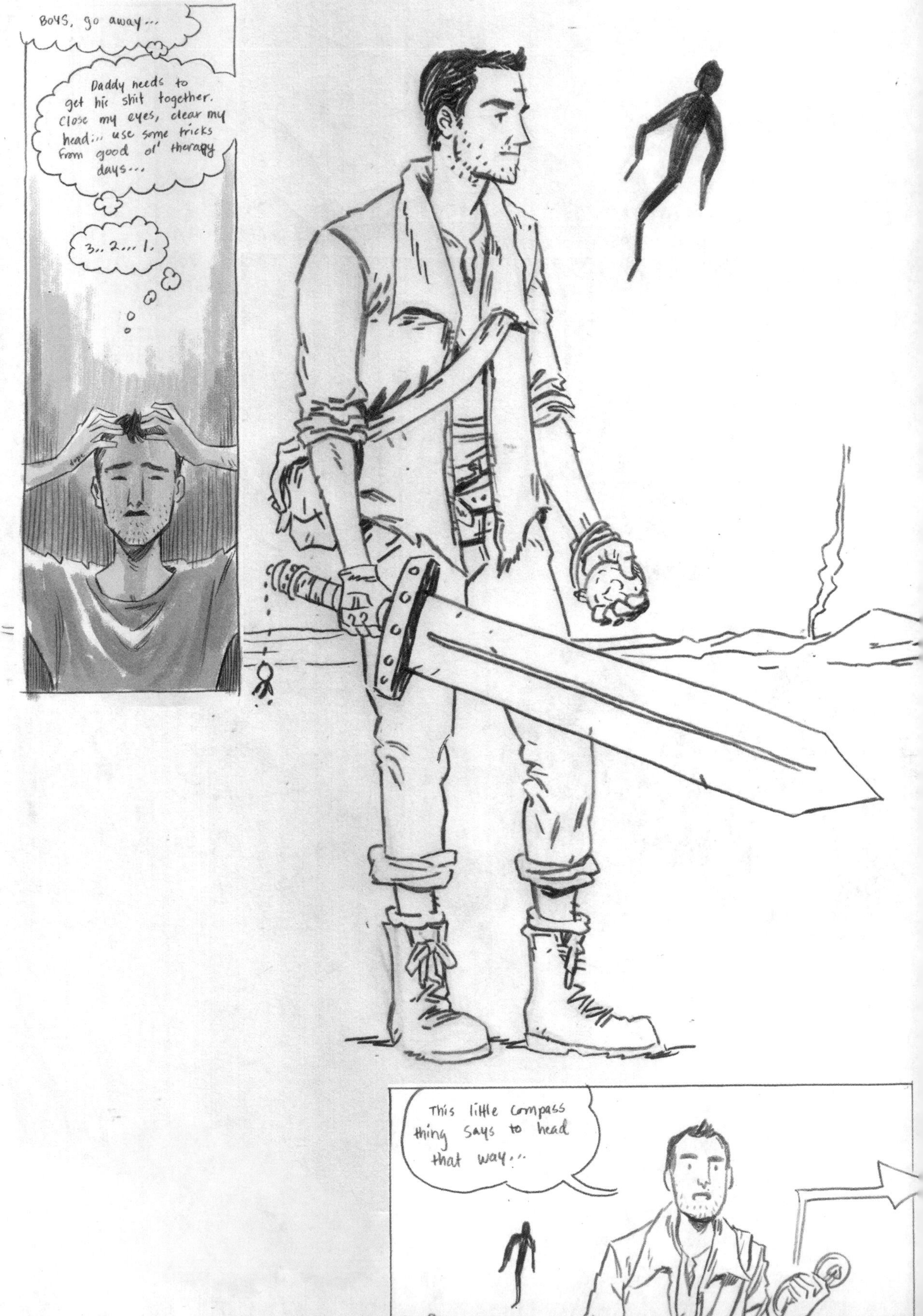
Boys, go away...
Daddy needs to get his shit together. Close my eyes, clear my head... use some tricks from good ol' therapy days...
3.. 2... 1.
This little compass thing says to head that way...

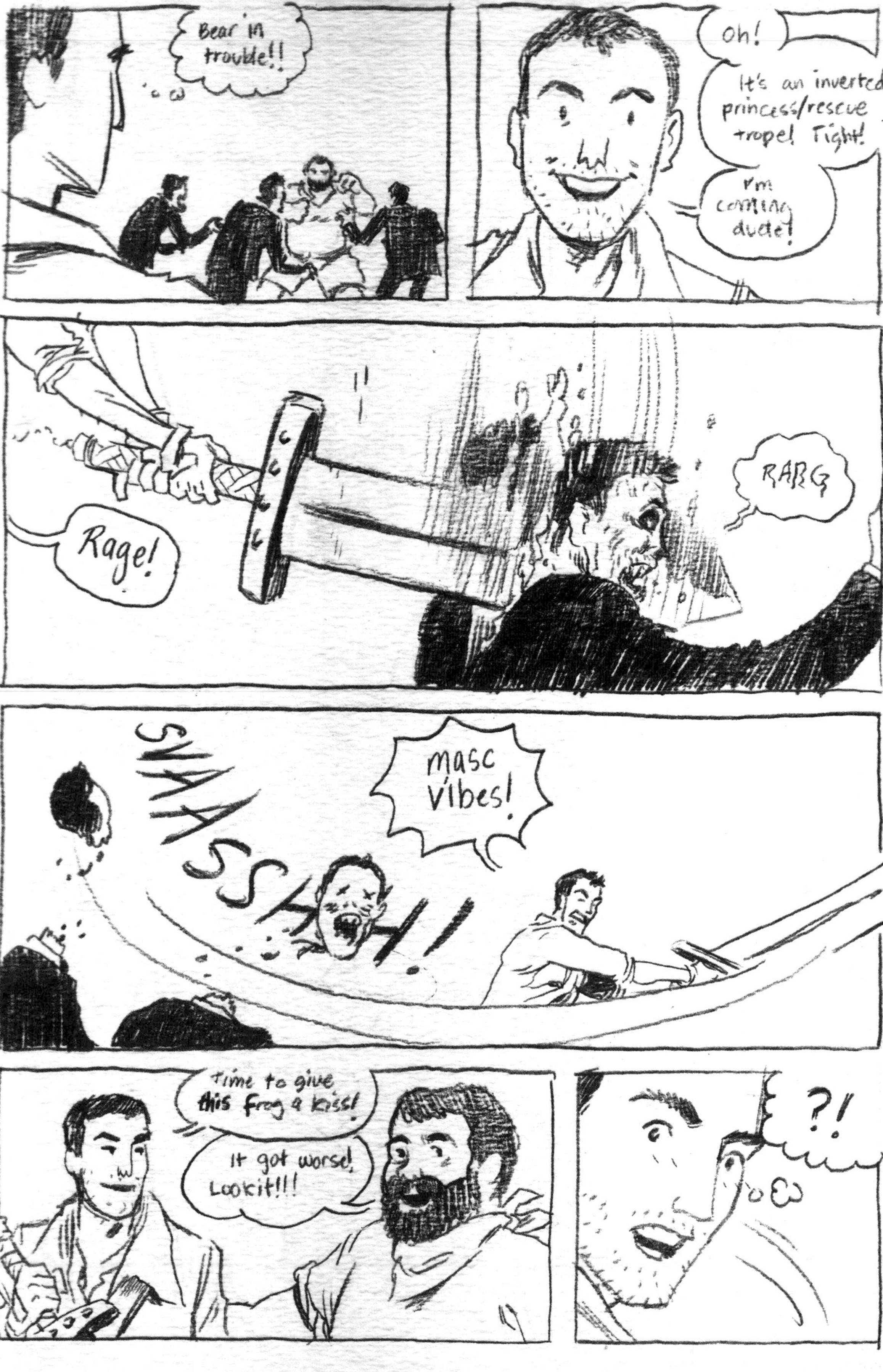

Bear in trouble!!
Oh!
It's an inverted princess/rescue trope! Tight!
I'm coming dude!
Rage!
RABG
masc vibes!
SHAAASSHH!!
Time to give this frog a kiss!
It got worse! Lookit!!!
?!

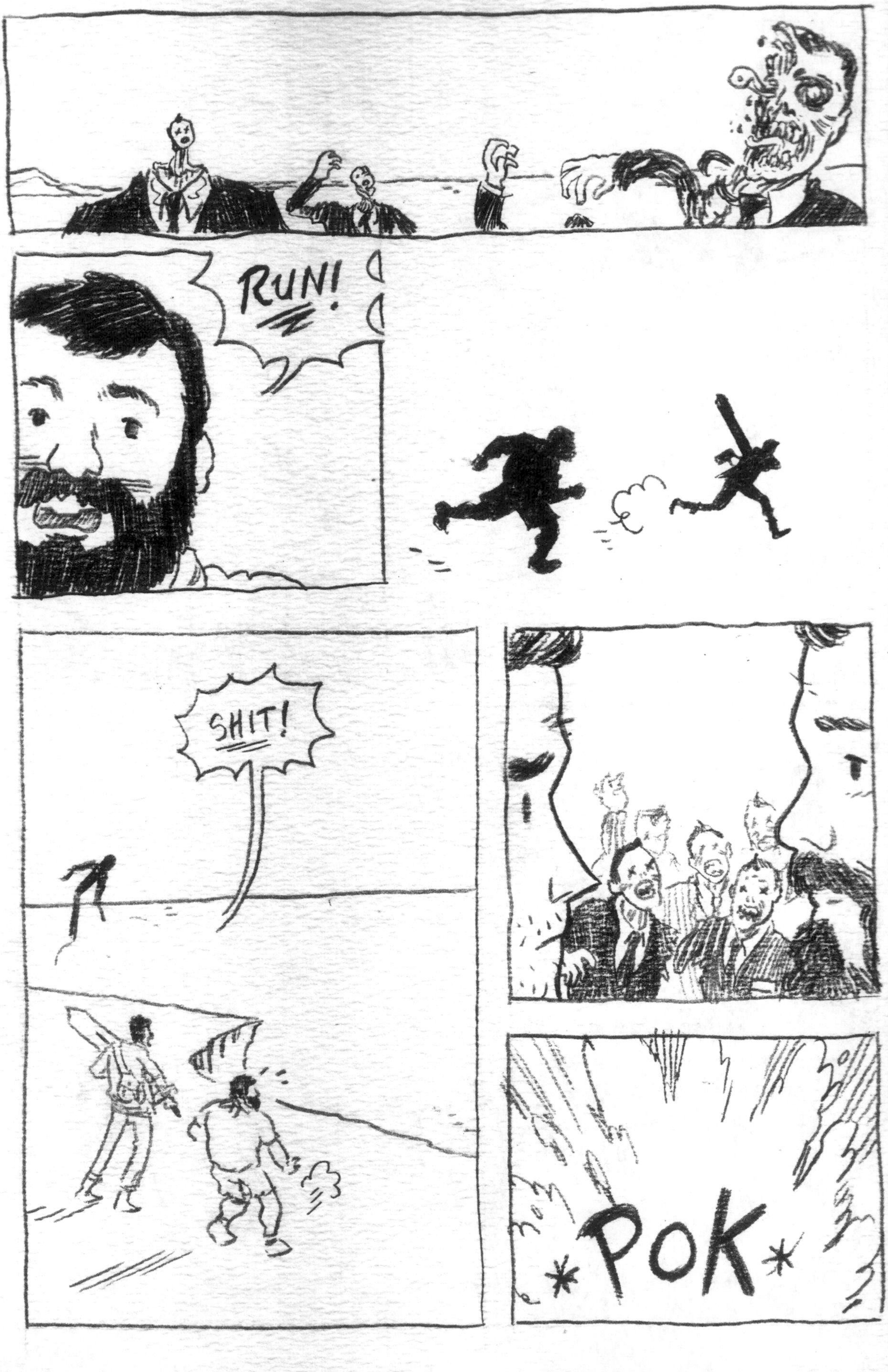
RUN!
SHIT!
POK

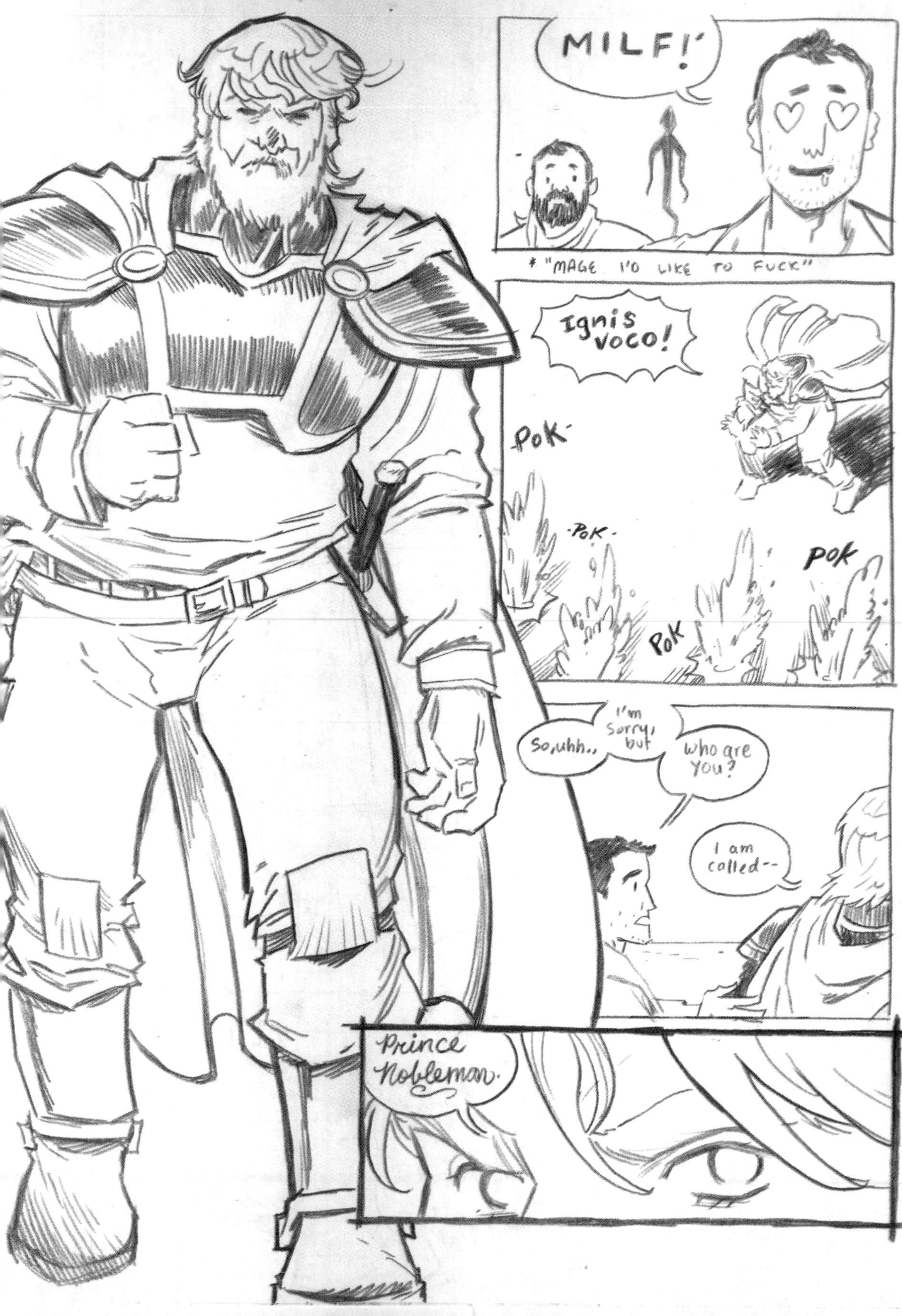
MILF!*
* "MAGE I'D LIKE TO FUCK"
Ignis voco!
POK
POK
POK
POK
So, uhh..
I'm sorry, but
who are you?
I am called--
Prince Nobleman.

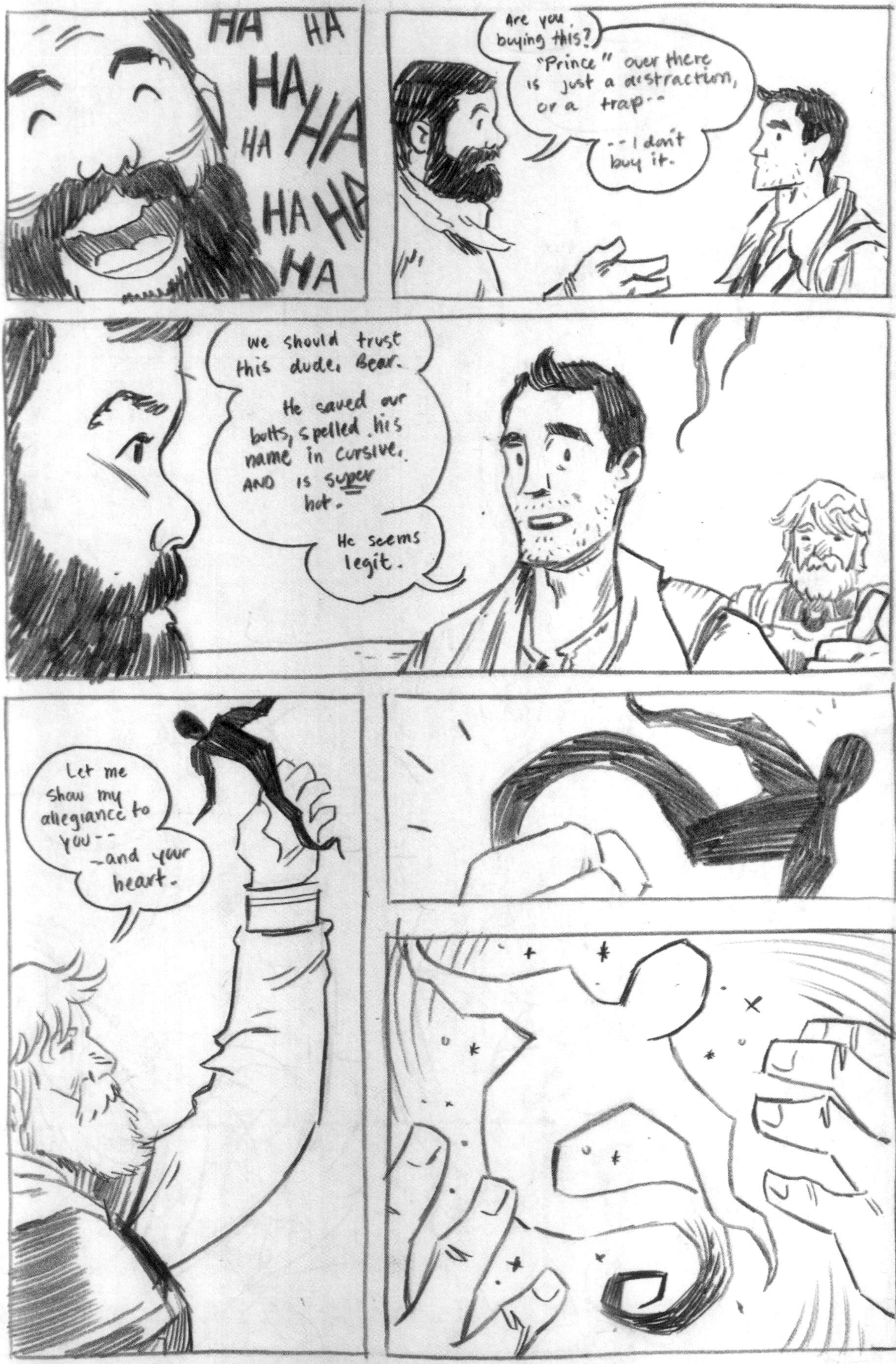
HA HA HA HA HA HA HA HA HA
Are you buying this?
"Prince" over there is just a distraction, or a trap--
--I don't buy it.
We should trust this dude, Bear.
He saved our butts, spelled his name in cursive, AND is super hot.
He seems legit.
Let me show my allegiance to you--
--and your heart.

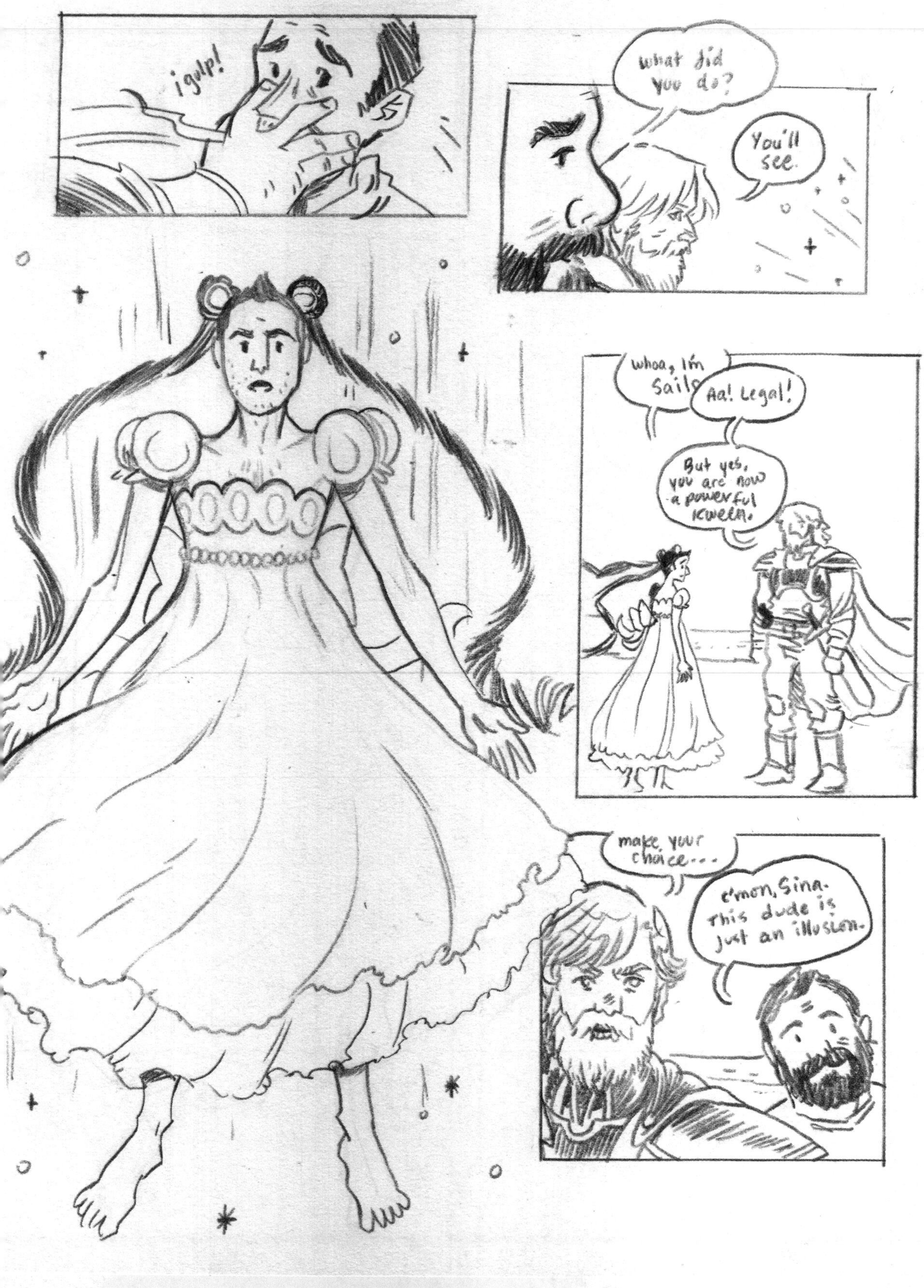
¡gulp!
what did you do?
You'll see.
whoa, I'm Sailo
Aa! Legal!
But yes, you are now a powerful kween.
make your choice...
c'mon, Sina. This dude is just an illusion.

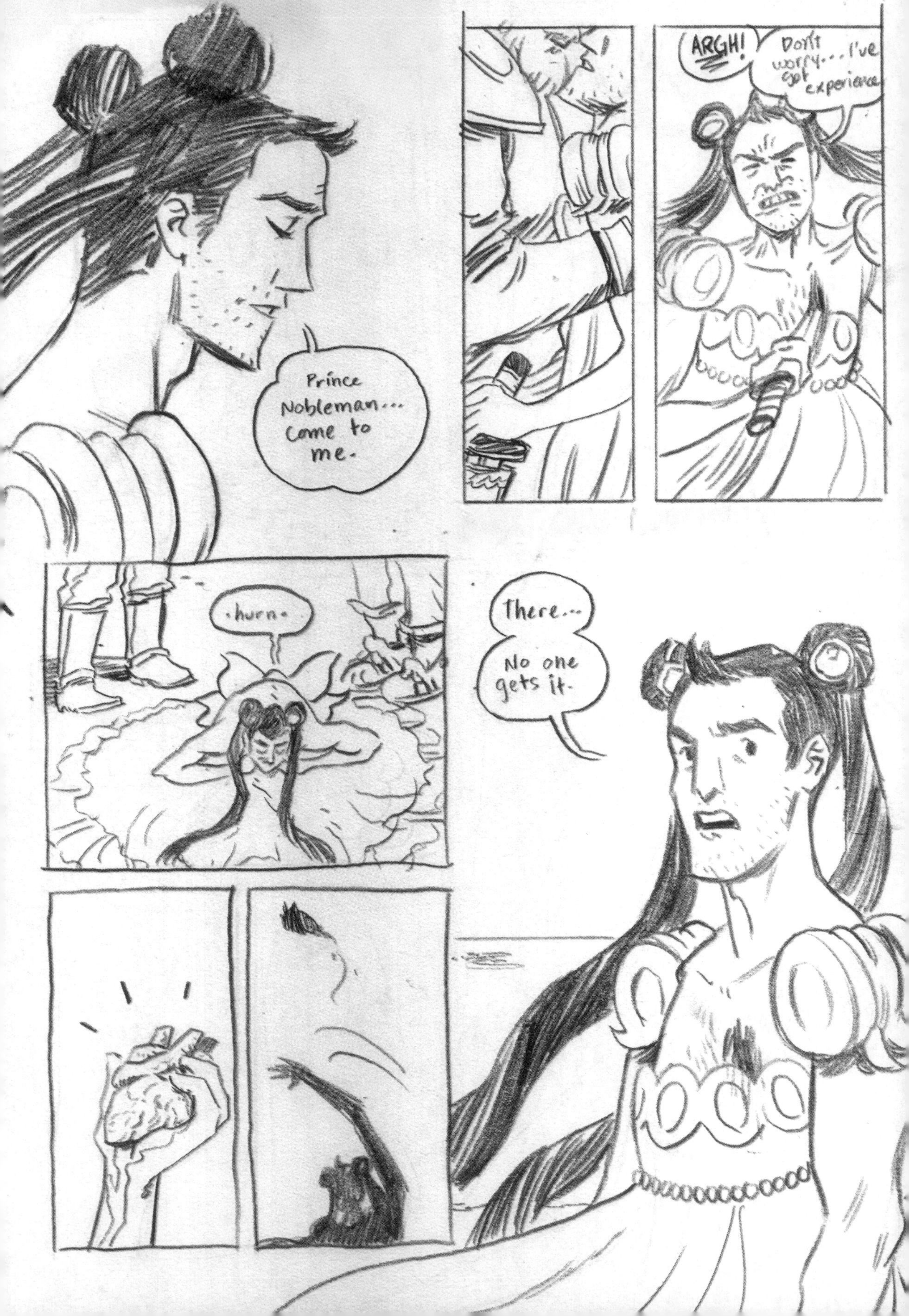
Prince Nobleman... come to me.
ARGH!
Don't worry... I've got experience
·hurn·
There...
No one gets it.

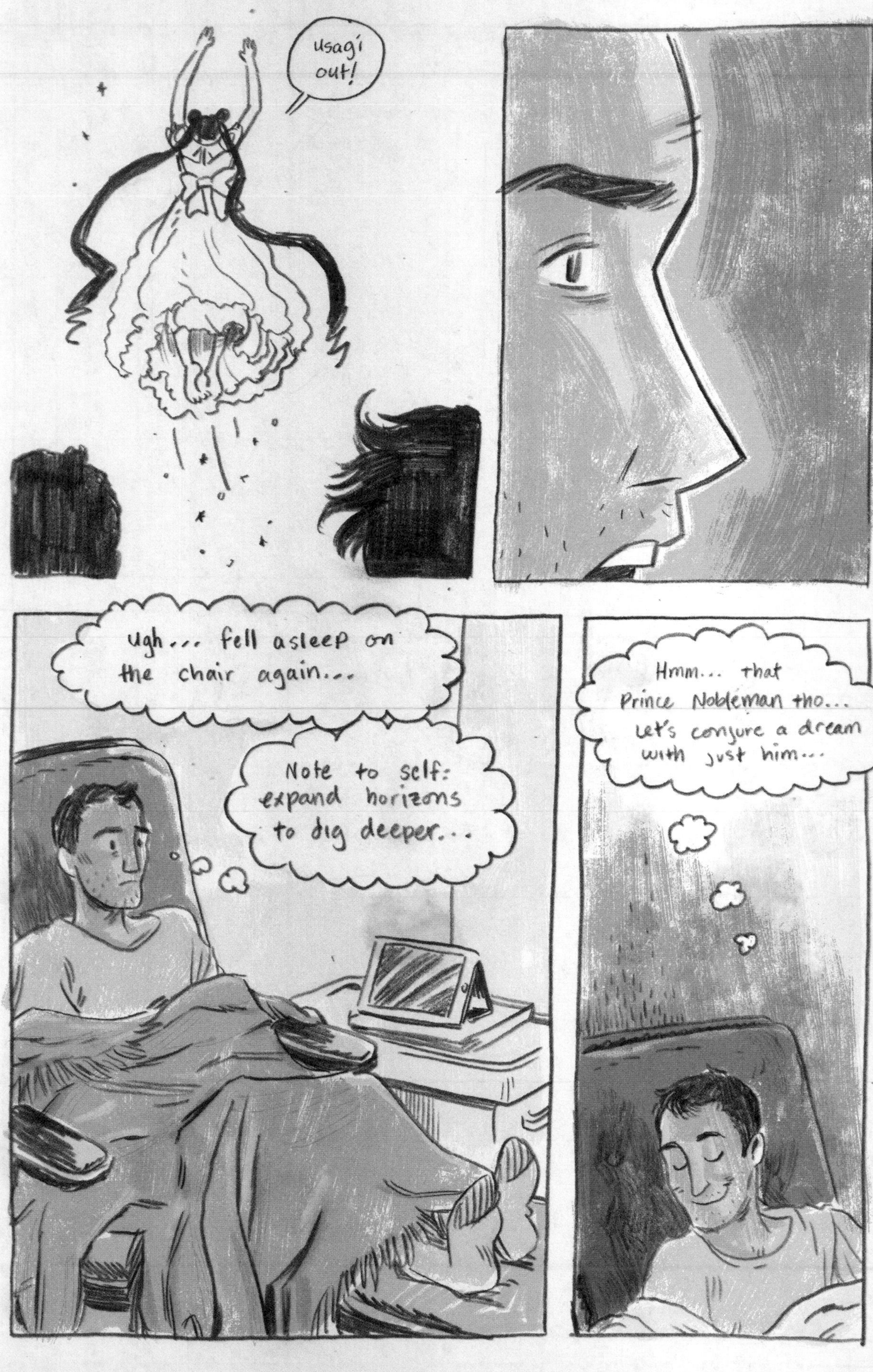
usagi out!
ugh... fell asleep on the chair again...
Note to self: expand horizons to dig deeper...
Hmm... that Prince Nobleman tho... Let's conjure a dream with just him...

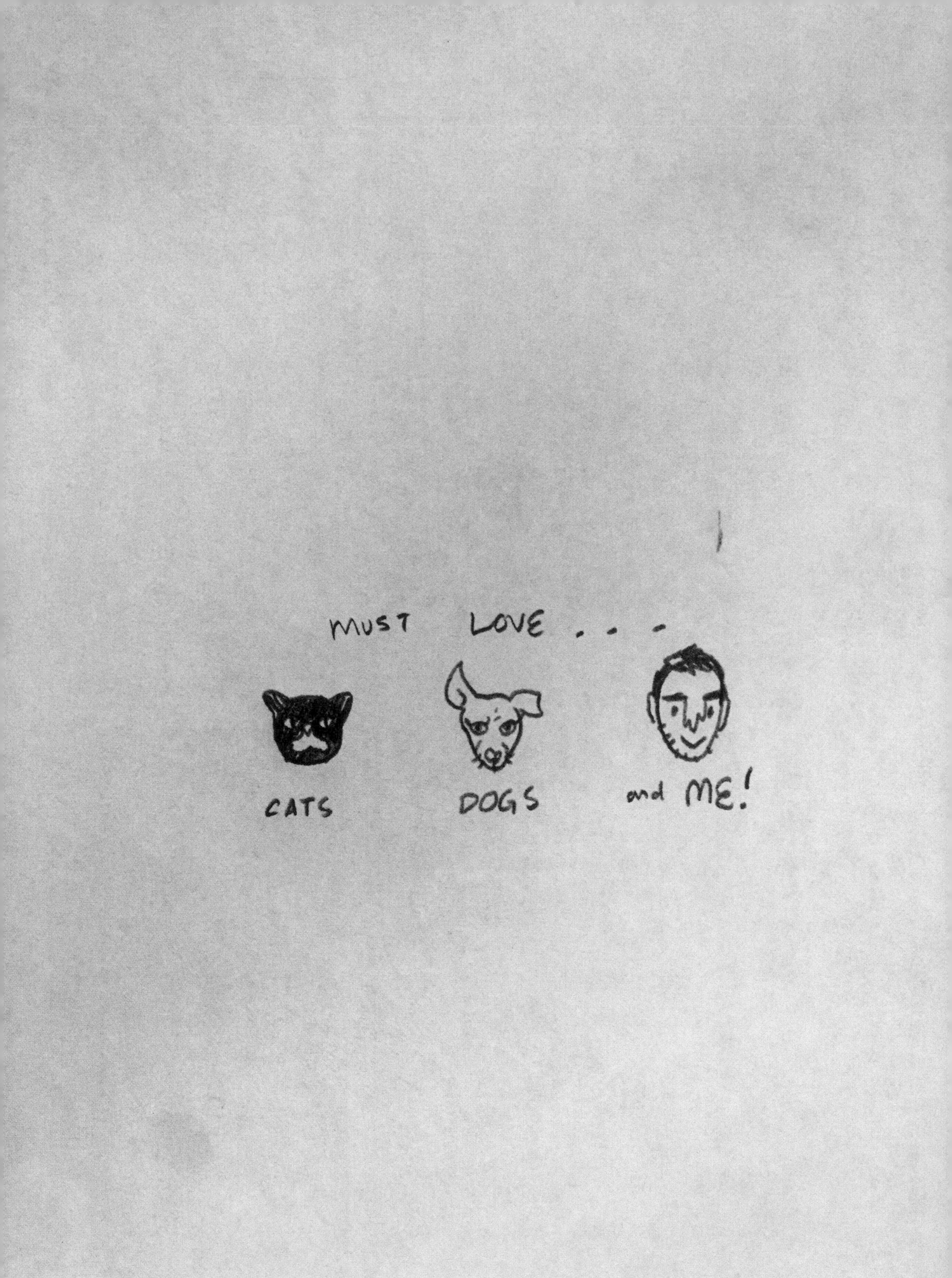
MUST LOVE . . .
CATS
DOGS
and ME!

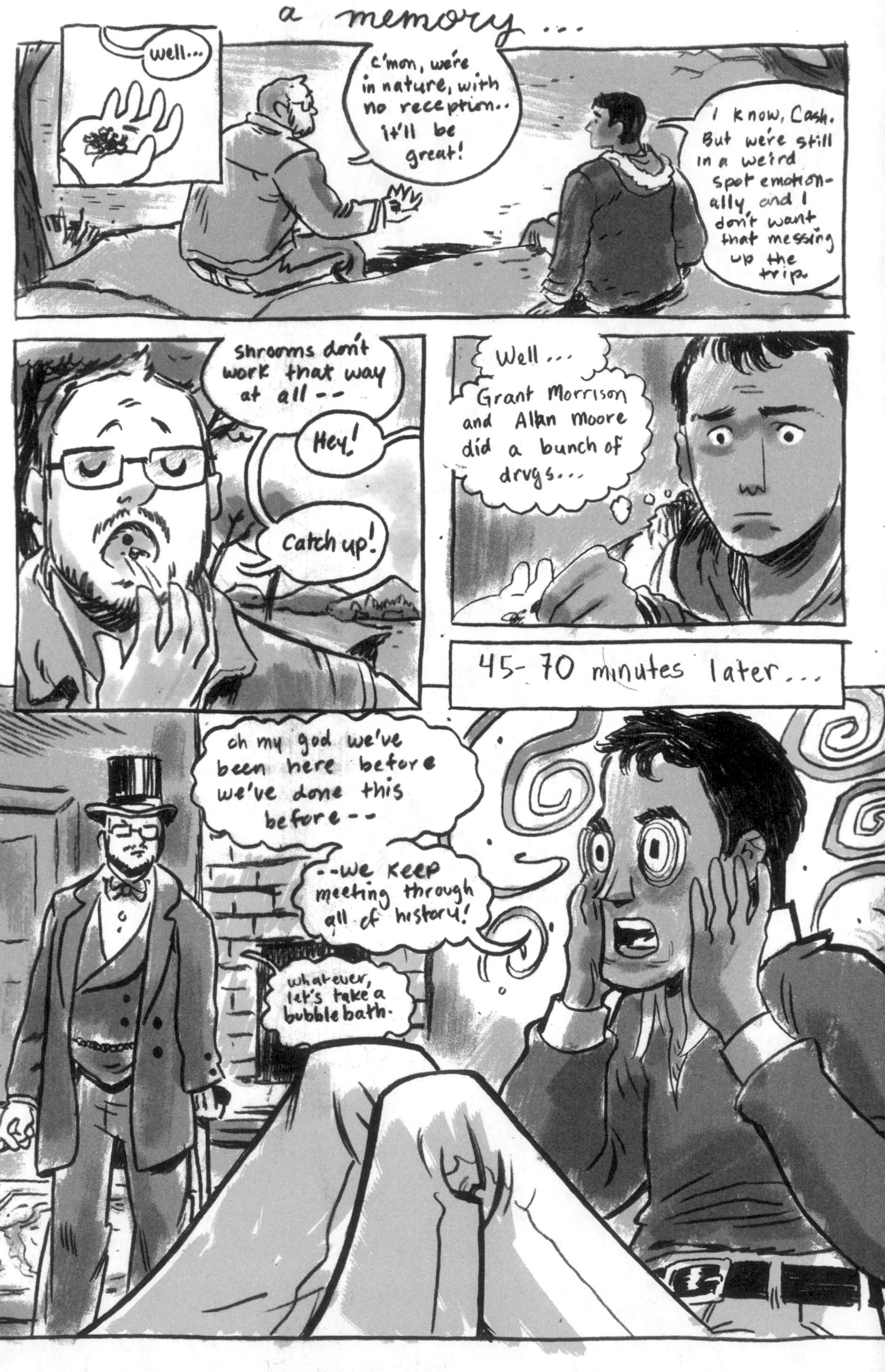
a memory...
well...
c'mon, we're in nature, with no reception.. it'll be great!
I know, Cash. But we're still in a weird spot emotionally and I don't want that messing up the trip.
shrooms don't work that way at all --
Hey!
Catch up!
Well... Grant Morrison and Allan Moore did a bunch of drugs...
45-70 minutes later...
oh my god we've been here before we've done this before --
--we keep meeting through all of history!
whatever, let's take a bubble bath.

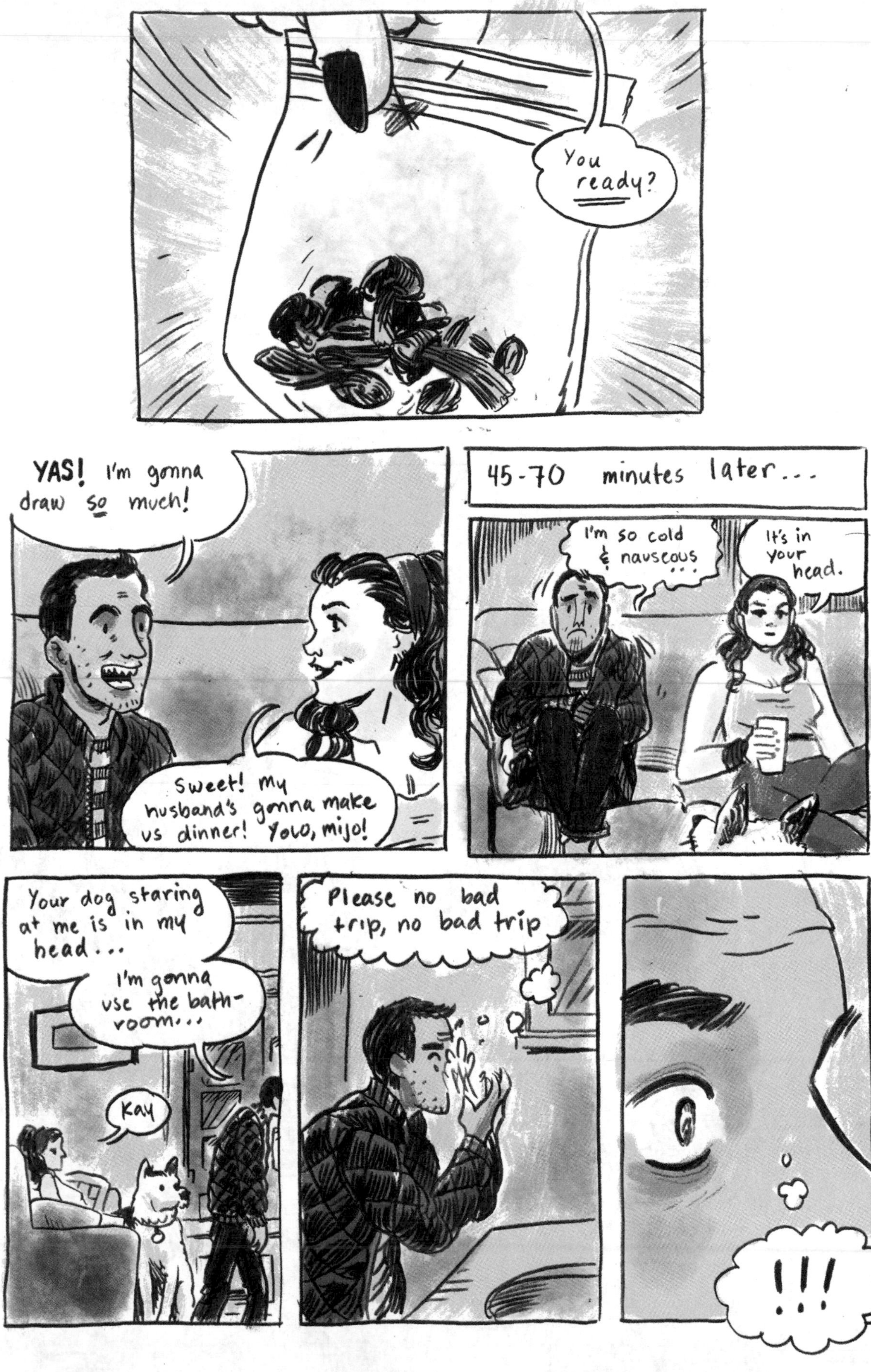

You ready?
YAS! I'm gonna draw so much!
Sweet! my husband's gonna make us dinner! Yolo, mijo!
45-70 minutes later...
I'm so cold & nauseous...
It's in your head.
Your dog staring at me is in my head...
I'm gonna use the bathroom...
Kay
Please no bad trip, no bad trip
!!!

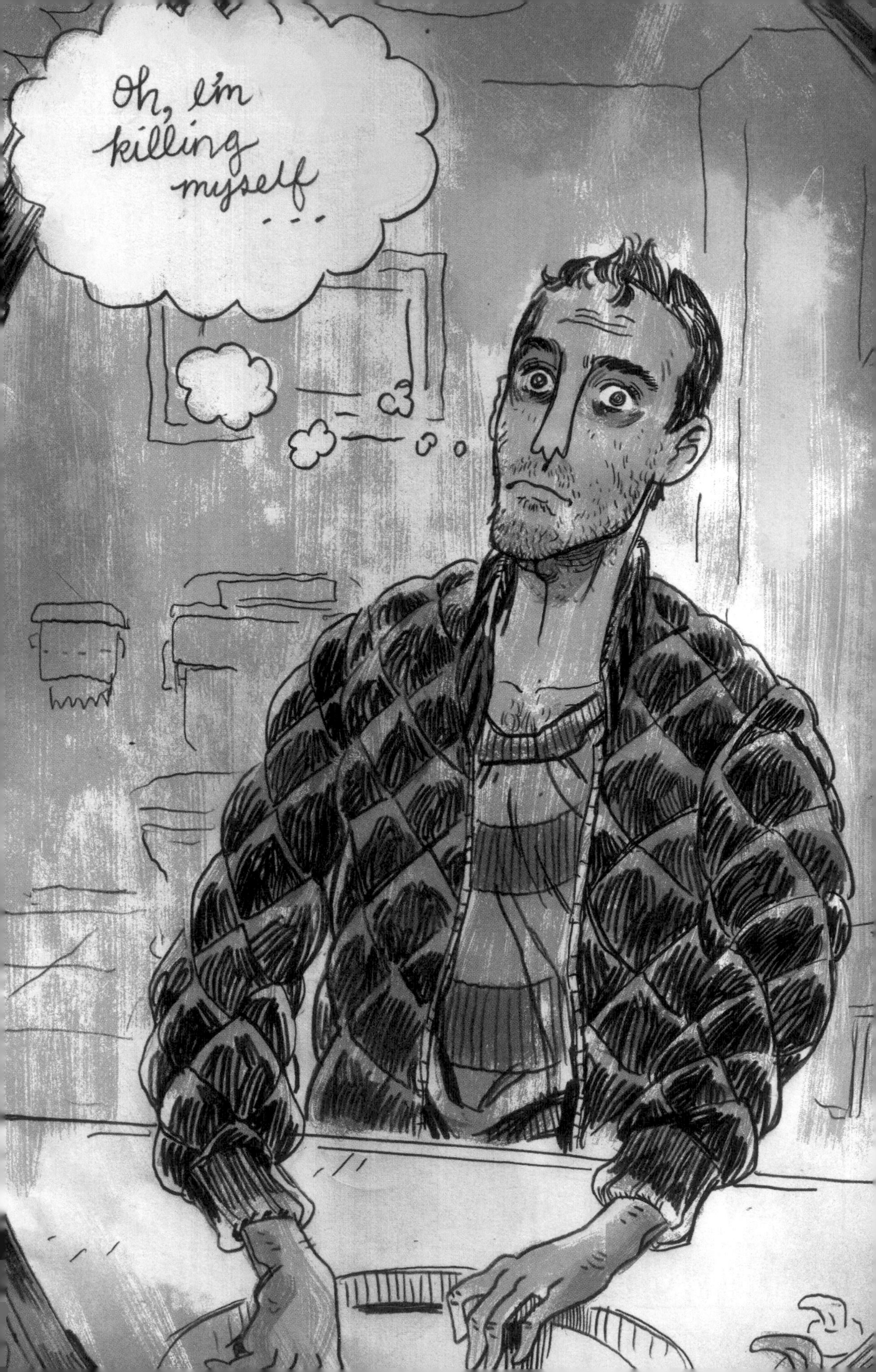
Oh, I'm killing myself . . .

my cheeks won't unsink

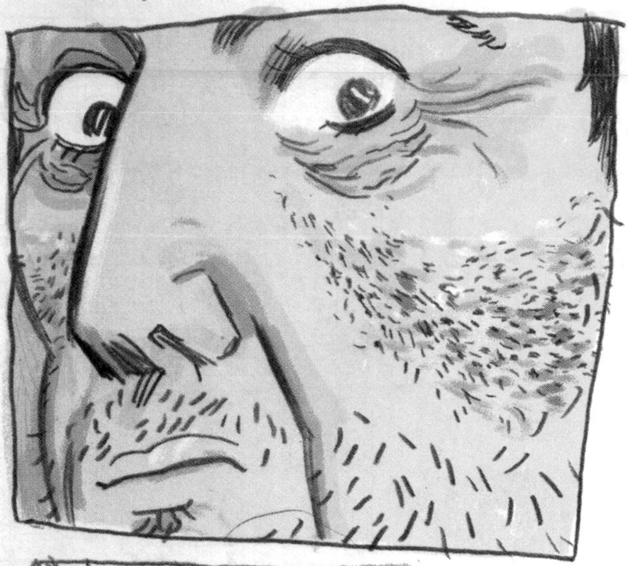

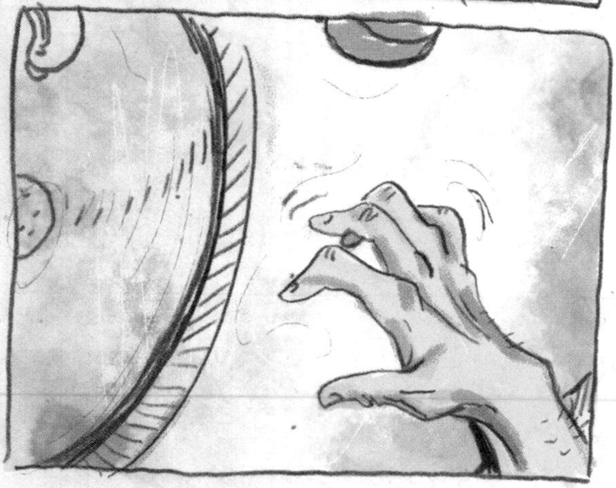

when did all my tendons start to be so... exposed?

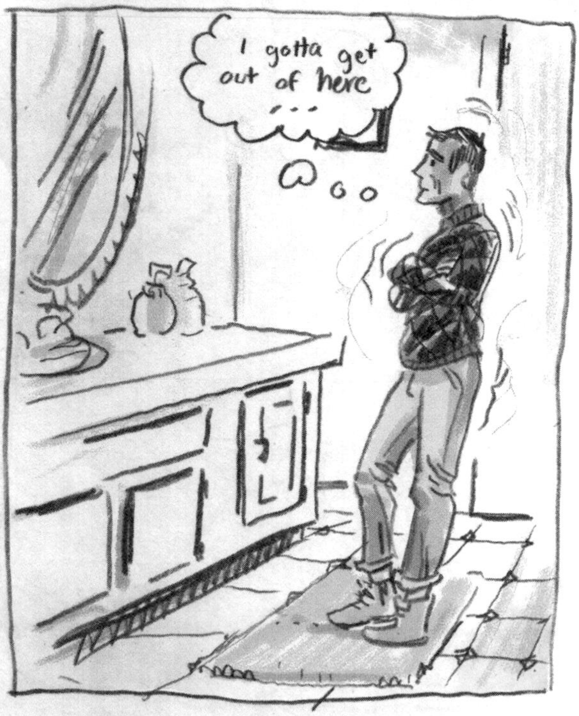
I gotta get out of here
...

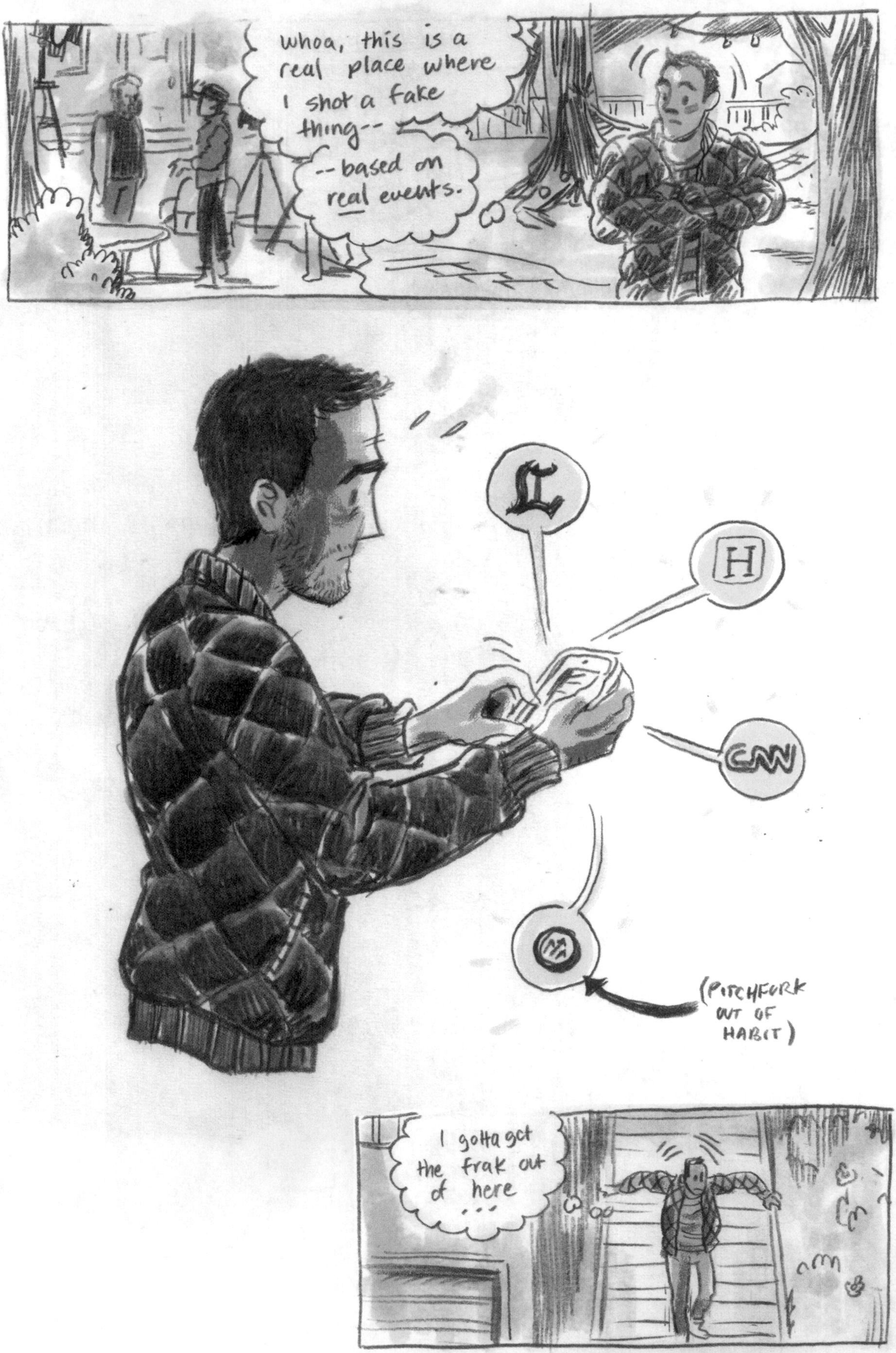
whoa, this is a real place where I shot a fake thing--
--based on real events.
(PITCHFORK OUT OF HABIT)
I gotta get the frak out of here ...

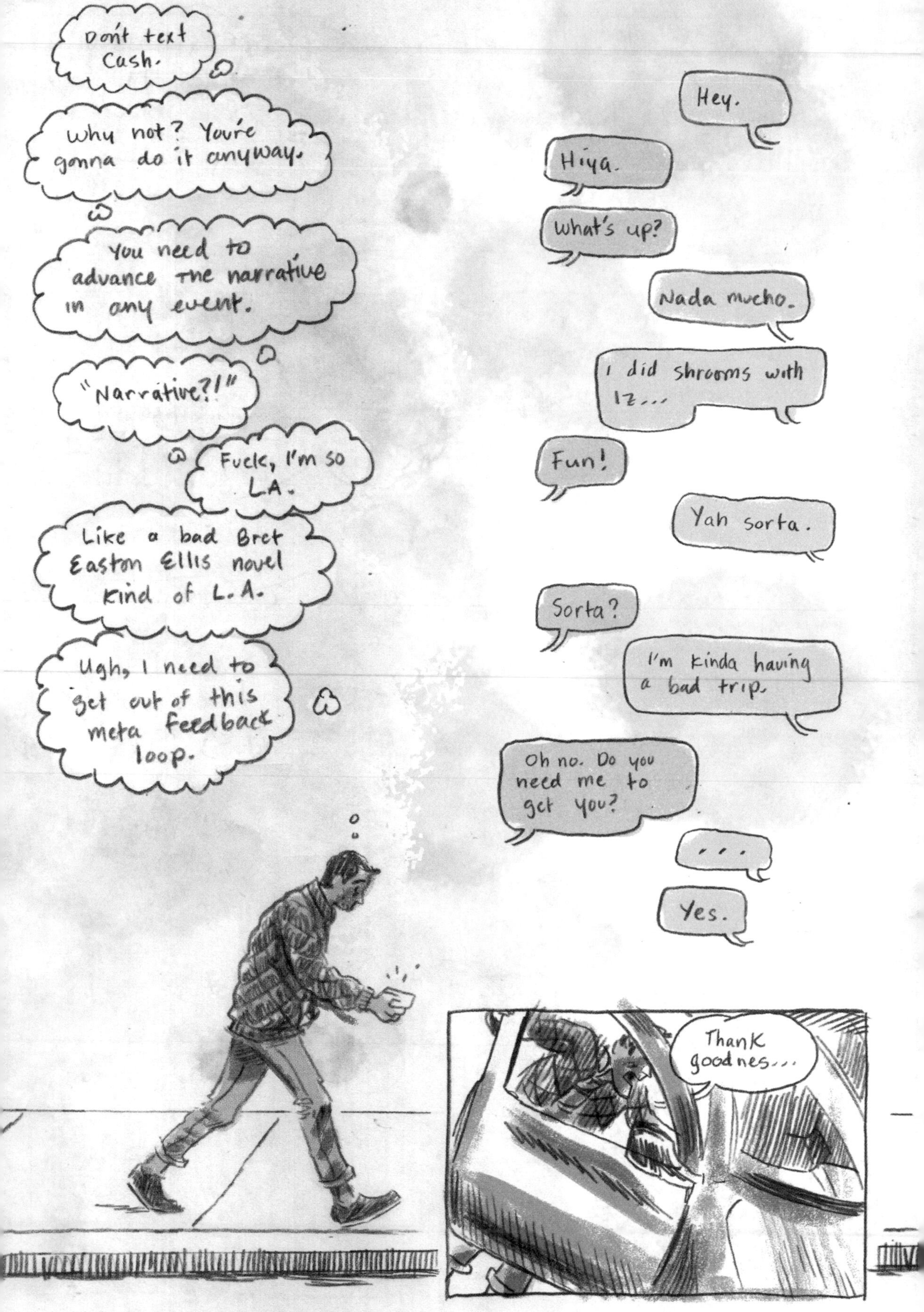
Don't text Cash.
Why not? You're gonna do it anyway.
You need to advance the narrative in any event.
"Narrative?!"
Fuck, I'm so L.A.
Like a bad Bret Easton Ellis novel kind of L.A.
Ugh, I need to get out of this meta feedback loop.
Hey.
Hiya.
What's up?
Nada mucho.
I did shrooms with Iz...
Fun!
Yah sorta.
Sorta?
I'm kinda having a bad trip.
Oh no. Do you need me to get you?
...
Yes.
Thank goodnes...

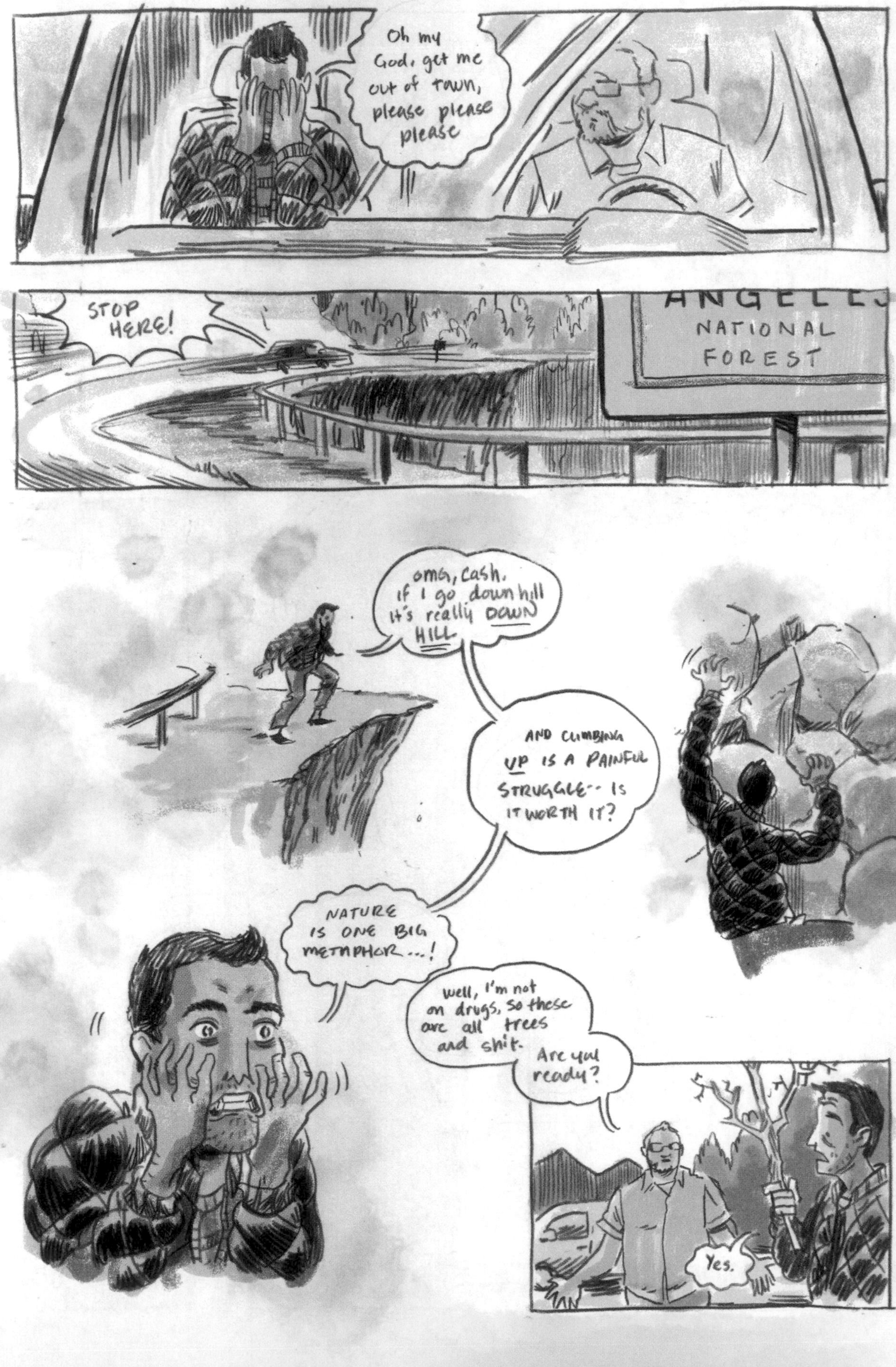
Oh my God, get me out of town, please please please
STOP HERE!
ANGELES
NATIONAL FOREST
omg, cash. If I go down hill it's really DOWN HILL
AND CLIMBING UP IS A PAINFUL STRUGGLE-- IS IT WORTH IT?
NATURE IS ONE BIG METAPHOR...!
well, I'm not on drugs, so these are all trees and shit.
Are you ready?
Yes.

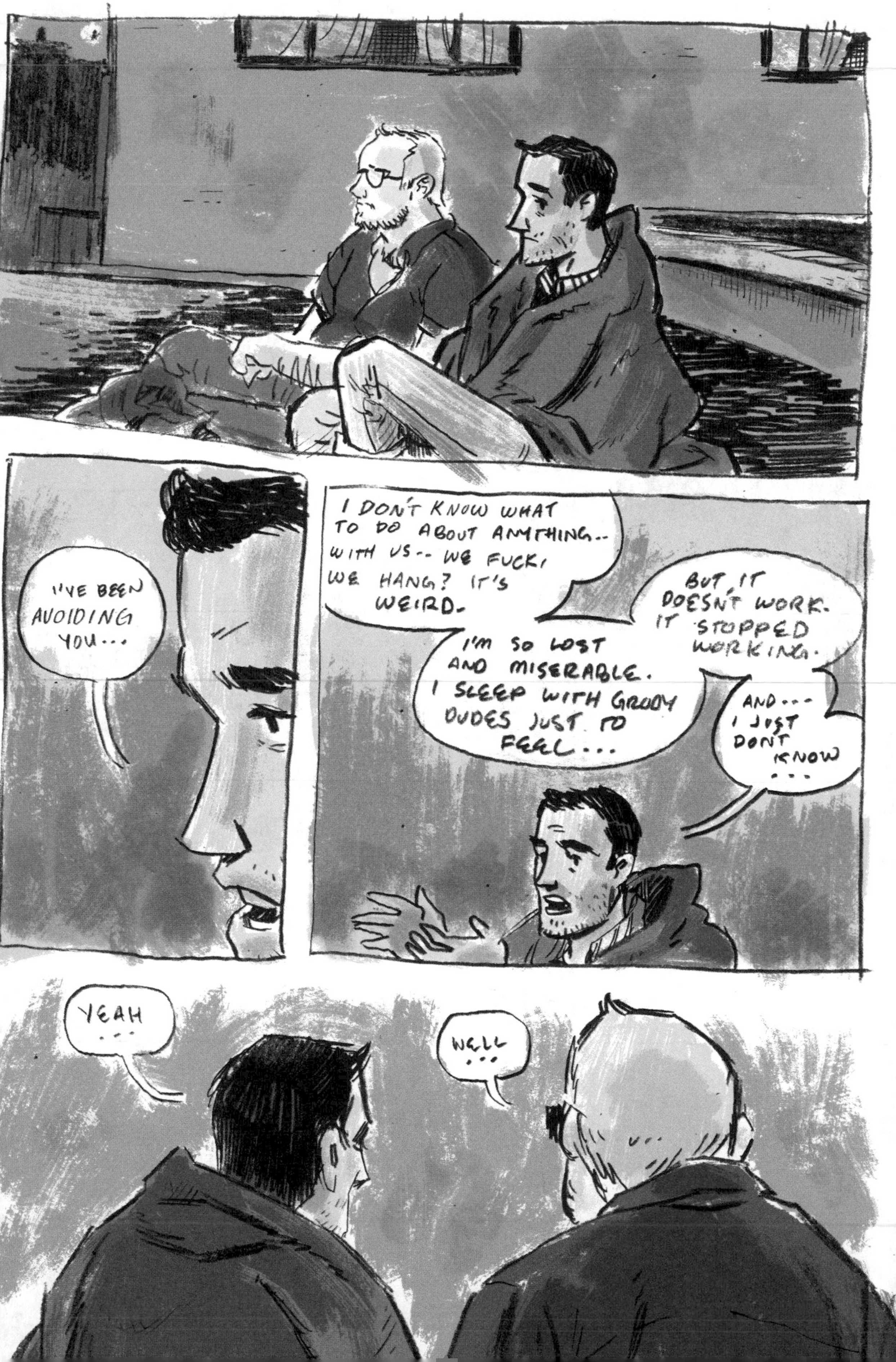
I'VE BEEN AVOIDING YOU...
I DON'T KNOW WHAT TO DO ABOUT ANYTHING.. WITH US.. WE FUCK, WE HANG? IT'S WEIRD.
BUT IT DOESN'T WORK. IT STOPPED WORKING.
I'M SO LOST AND MISERABLE. I SLEEP WITH GROSS DUDES JUST TO FEEL...
AND... I JUST DONT KNOW...
YEAH...
WELL...

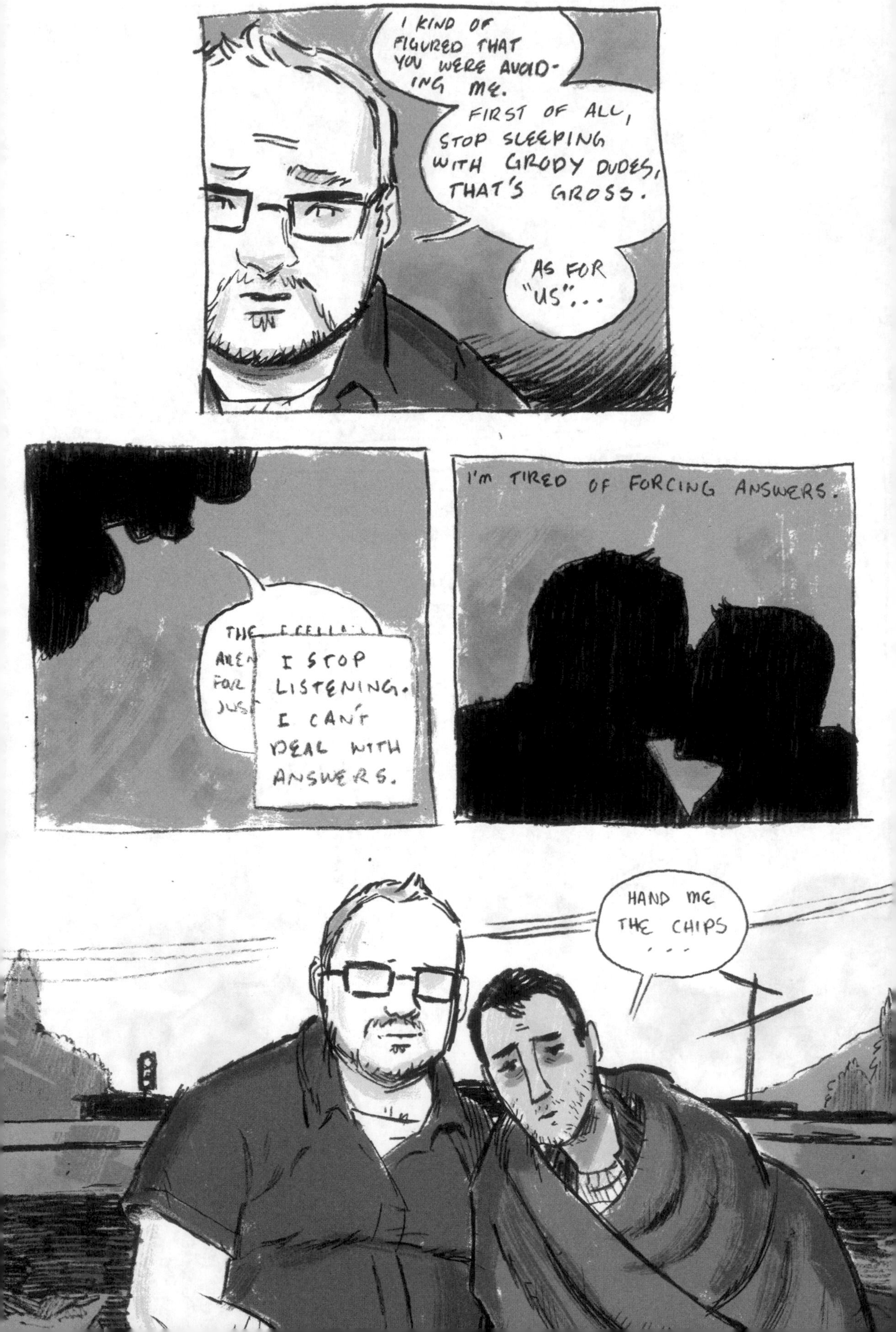
I KIND OF FIGURED THAT YOU WERE AVOIDING ME.
FIRST OF ALL, STOP SLEEPING WITH GRODY DUDES, THAT'S GROSS.
AS FOR "US"...
I STOP LISTENING. I CAN'T DEAL WITH ANSWERS.
I'M TIRED OF FORCING ANSWERS.
HAND ME THE CHIPS ...

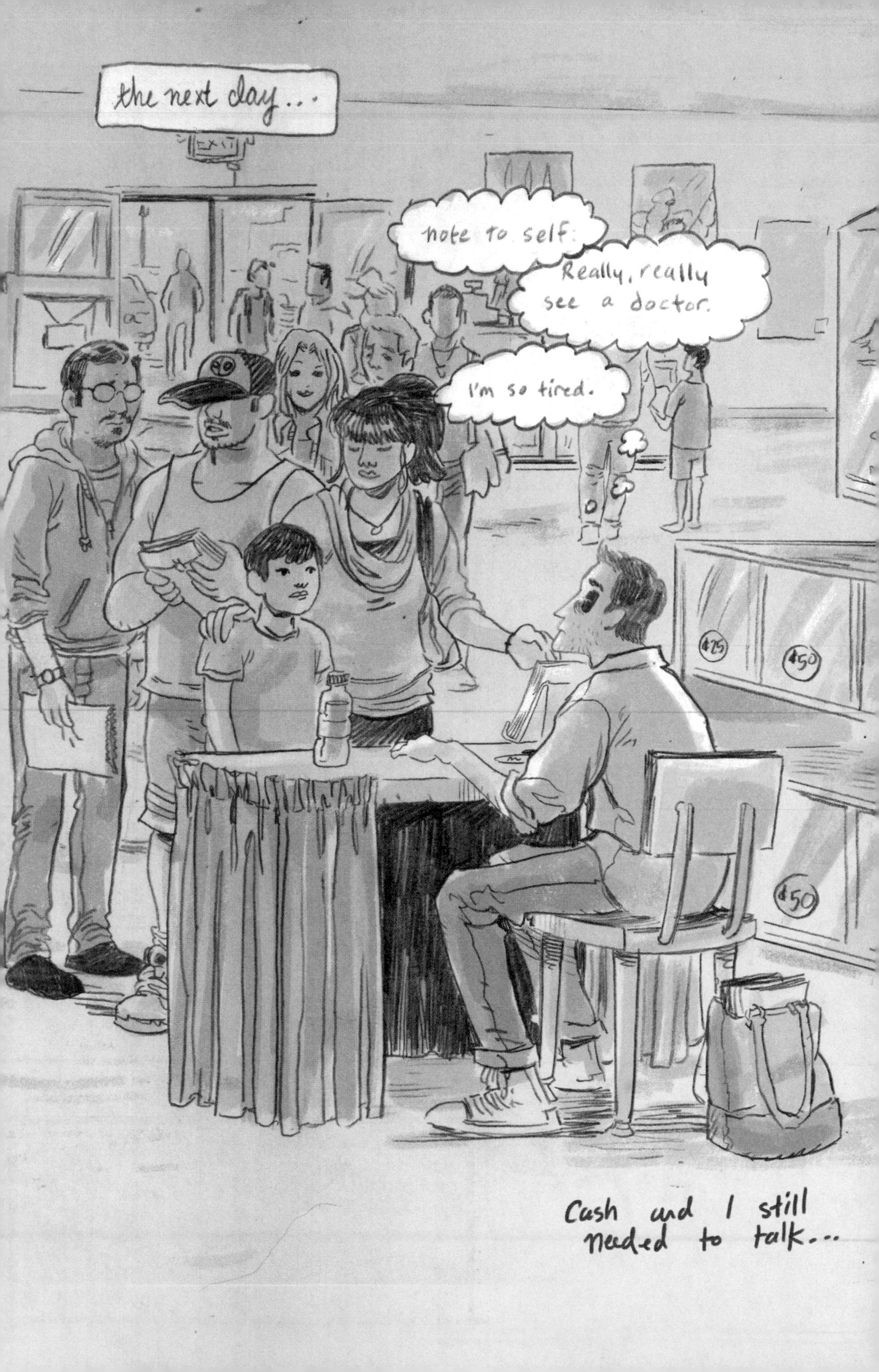
the next day...
note to self:
Really, really see a doctor.
I'm so tired.
$25
$50
$50
Cash and I still needed to talk...

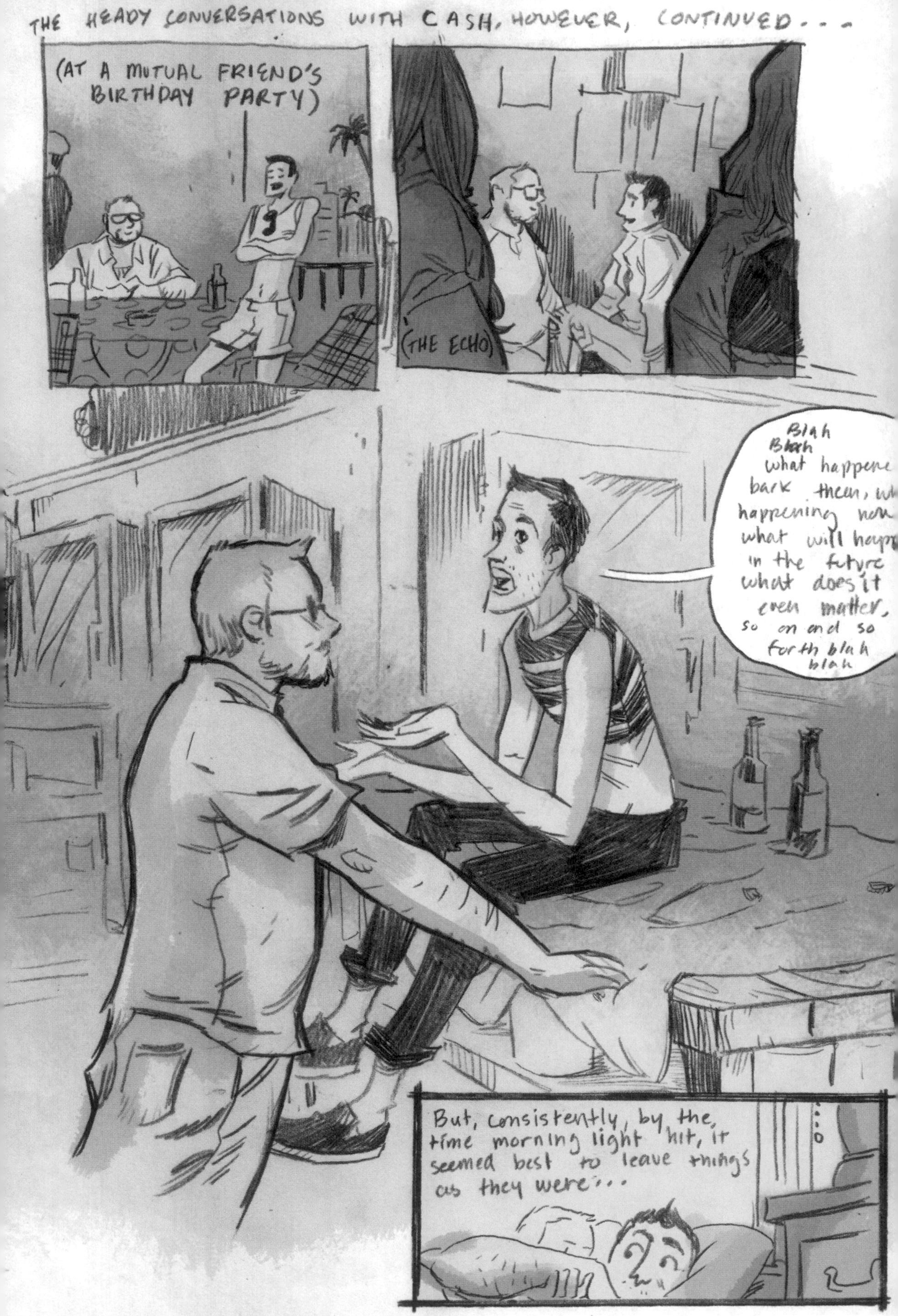
THE HEADY CONVERSATIONS WITH CASH, HOWEVER, CONTINUED...
(AT A MUTUAL FRIEND'S BIRTHDAY PARTY)
(THE ECHO)
Blah Blah what happene bark then, w happening now what will happ in the future what does it even matter, so on and so forth blah blah
But, consistently, by the time morning light hit, it seemed best to leave things as they were...

a memory
(hanging with a friend who "made it.")

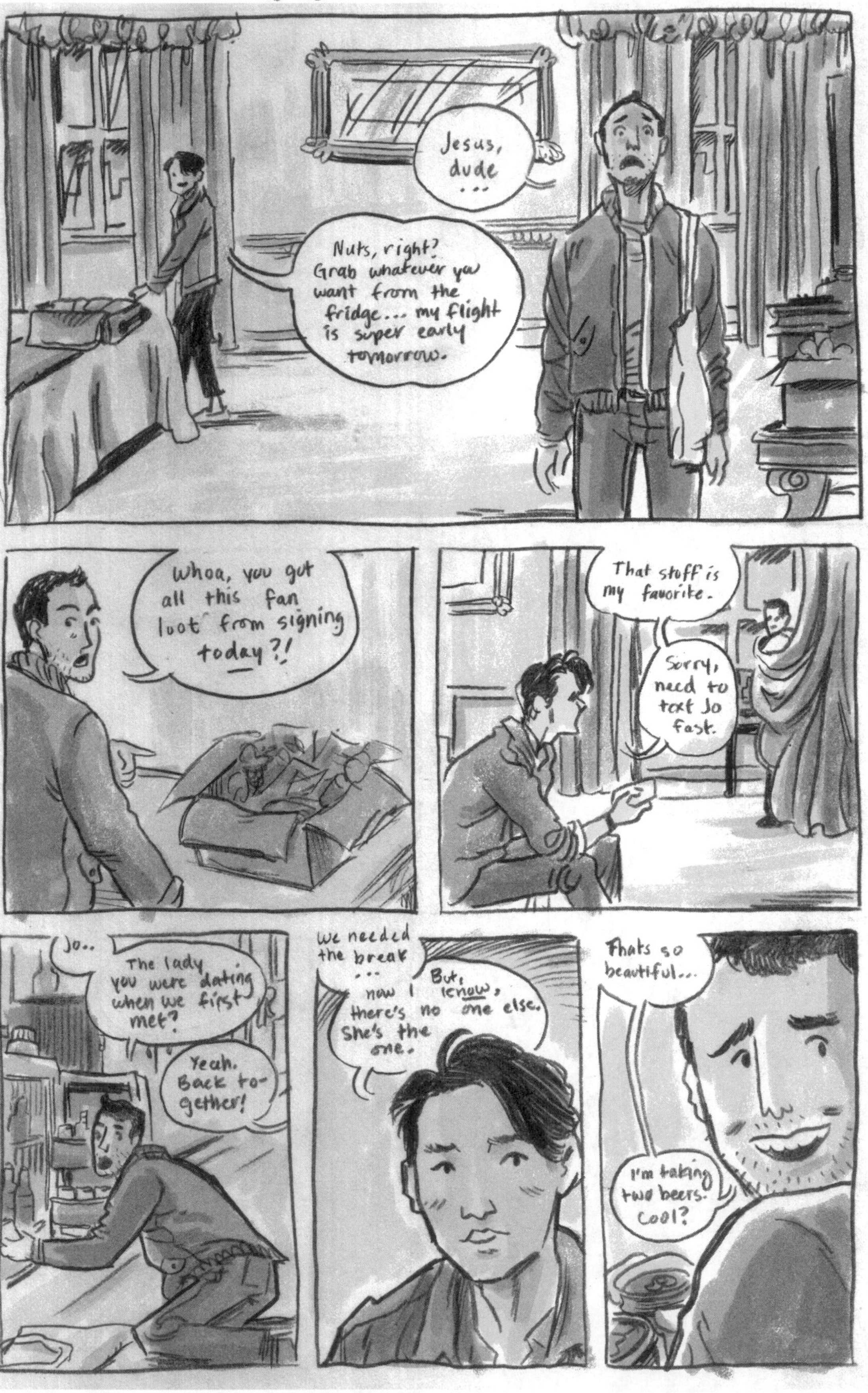

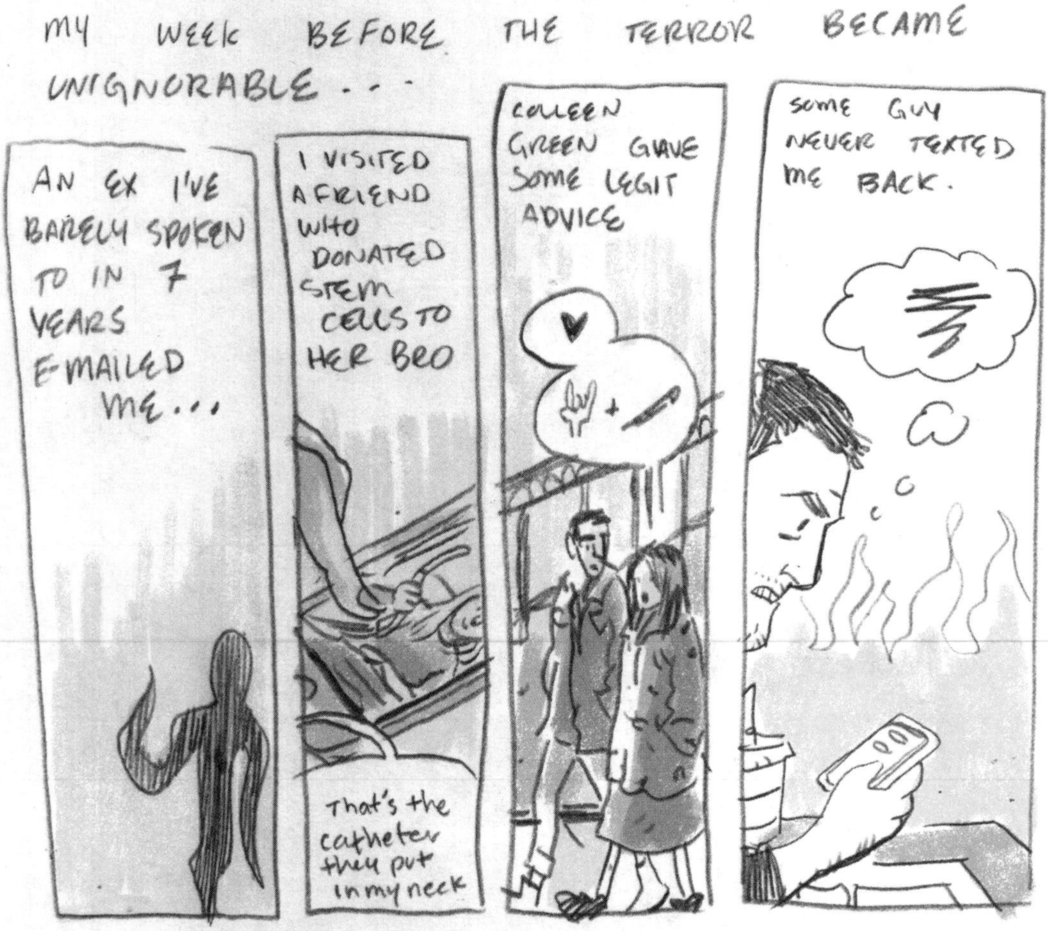
MY WEEK BEFORE THE TERROR BECAME UNIGNORABLE...
AN EX I'VE BARELY SPOKEN TO IN 7 YEARS E-MAILED ME...
I VISITED A FRIEND WHO DONATED STEM CELLS TO HER BRO
That's the catheter they put in my neck
COLLEEN GREEN GAVE SOME LEGIT ADVICE
SOME GUY NEVER TEXTED ME BACK.

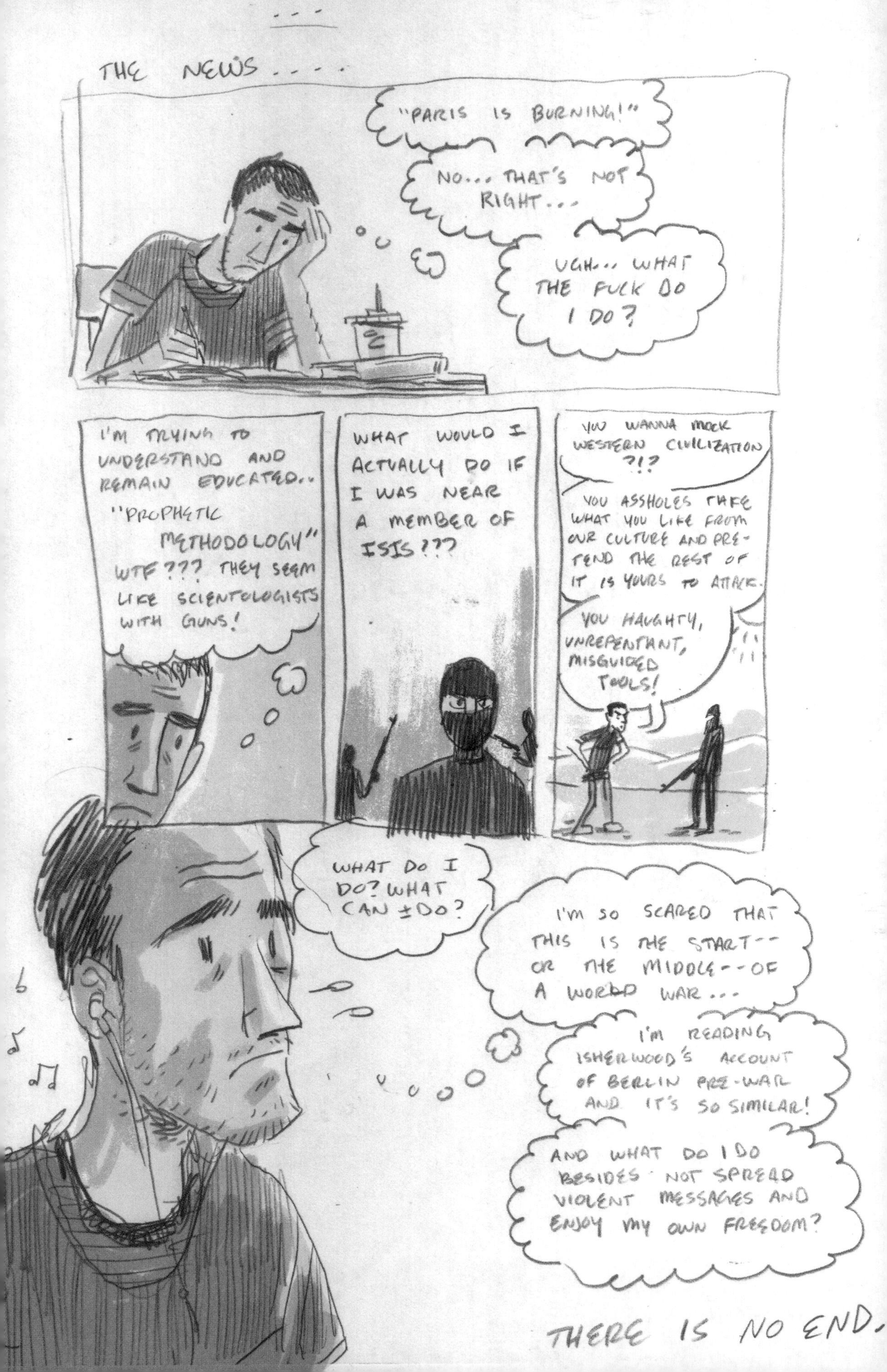
THE NEWS....
"PARIS IS BURNING!"
NO... THAT'S NOT RIGHT...
UGH... WHAT THE FUCK DO I DO?
I'M TRYING TO UNDERSTAND AND REMAIN EDUCATED.. "PROPHETIC METHODOLOGY" WTF??? THEY SEEM LIKE SCIENTOLOGISTS WITH GUNS!
WHAT WOULD I ACTUALLY DO IF I WAS NEAR A MEMBER OF ISIS???
YOU WANNA MOCK WESTERN CIVILIZATION?!?
YOU ASSHOLES TAKE WHAT YOU LIKE FROM OUR CULTURE AND PRETEND THE REST OF IT IS YOURS TO ATTACK.
YOU HAUGHTY, UNREPENTANT, MISGUIDED TOOLS!
WHAT DO I DO? WHAT CAN I DO?
I'M SO SCARED THAT THIS IS THE START-- OR THE MIDDLE--OF A WORLD WAR...
I'M READING ISHERWOOD'S ACCOUNT OF BERLIN PRE-WAR AND IT'S SO SIMILAR!
AND WHAT DO I DO BESIDES NOT SPREAD VIOLENT MESSAGES AND ENJOY MY OWN FREEDOM?
THERE IS NO END.

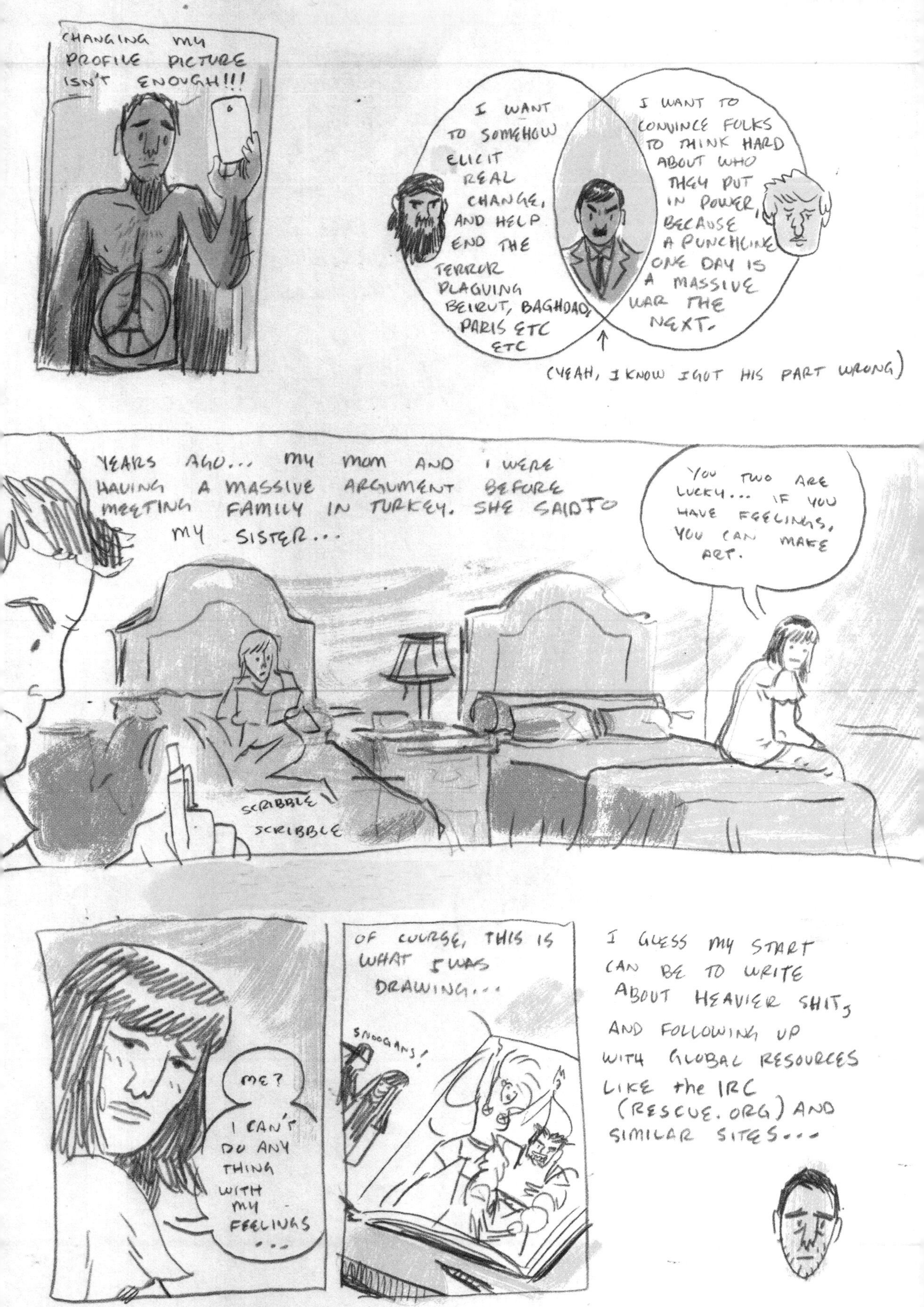
CHANGING MY PROFILE PICTURE ISN'T ENOUGH!!!
I WANT TO SOMEHOW ELICIT REAL CHANGE, AND HELP END THE TERROR PLAGUING BEIRUT, BAGHDAD, PARIS ETC ETC
I WANT TO CONVINCE FOLKS TO THINK HARD ABOUT WHO THEY PUT IN POWER, BECAUSE A PUNCHLINE ONE DAY IS A MASSIVE WAR THE NEXT.
(YEAH, I KNOW I GOT HIS PART WRONG)
YEARS AGO... MY MOM AND I WERE HAVING A MASSIVE ARGUMENT BEFORE MEETING FAMILY IN TURKEY. SHE SAID TO MY SISTER...
YOU TWO ARE LUCKY... IF YOU HAVE FEELINGS, YOU CAN MAKE ART.
SCRIBBLE
SCRIBBLE
ME?
I CAN'T DO ANY THING WITH MY FEELINGS...
OF COURSE, THIS IS WHAT I WAS DRAWING...
SNOOGANS!
I GUESS MY START CAN BE TO WRITE ABOUT HEAVIER SHIT, AND FOLLOWING UP WITH GLOBAL RESOURCES LIKE the IRC (RESCUE.ORG) AND SIMILAR SITES...

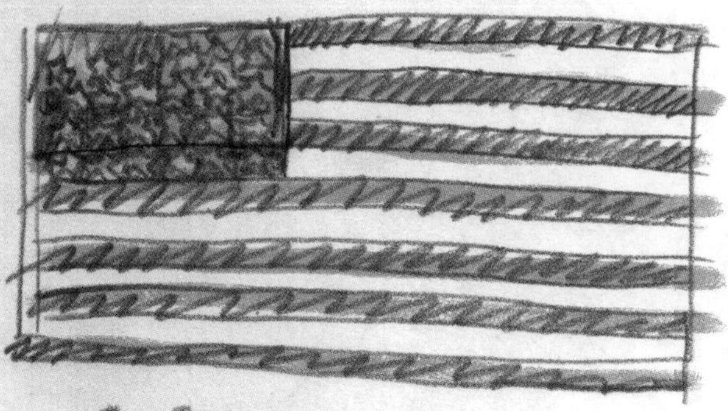

I FEEL PROTECTED
BY THIS FLAG

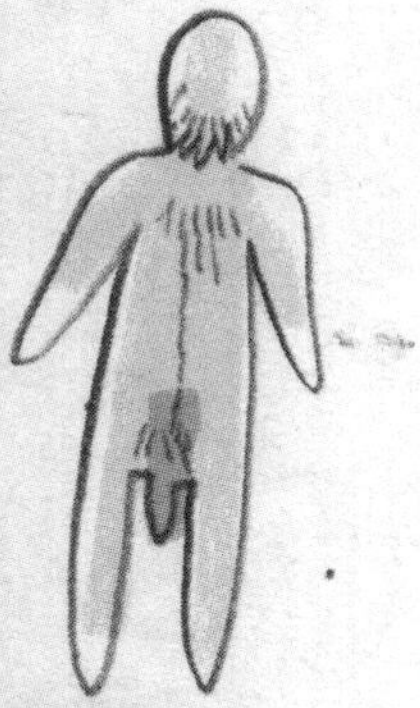

I FEEL PROTECTED
BY THIS MALE BODY.

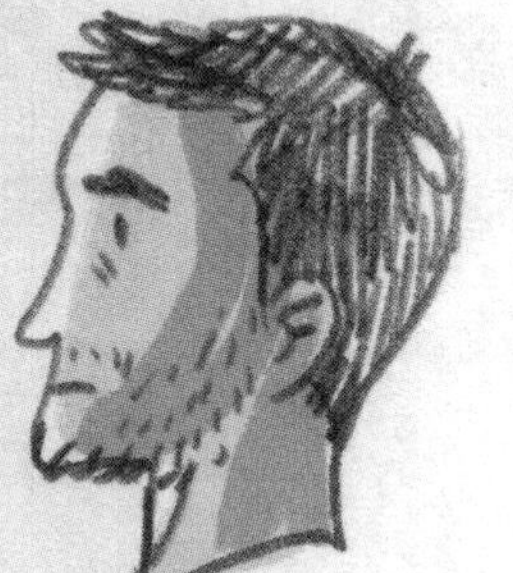

I FEEL PROTECTED
BY MY ETHNICALLY AMBIGUOUS
FLESHTONE.

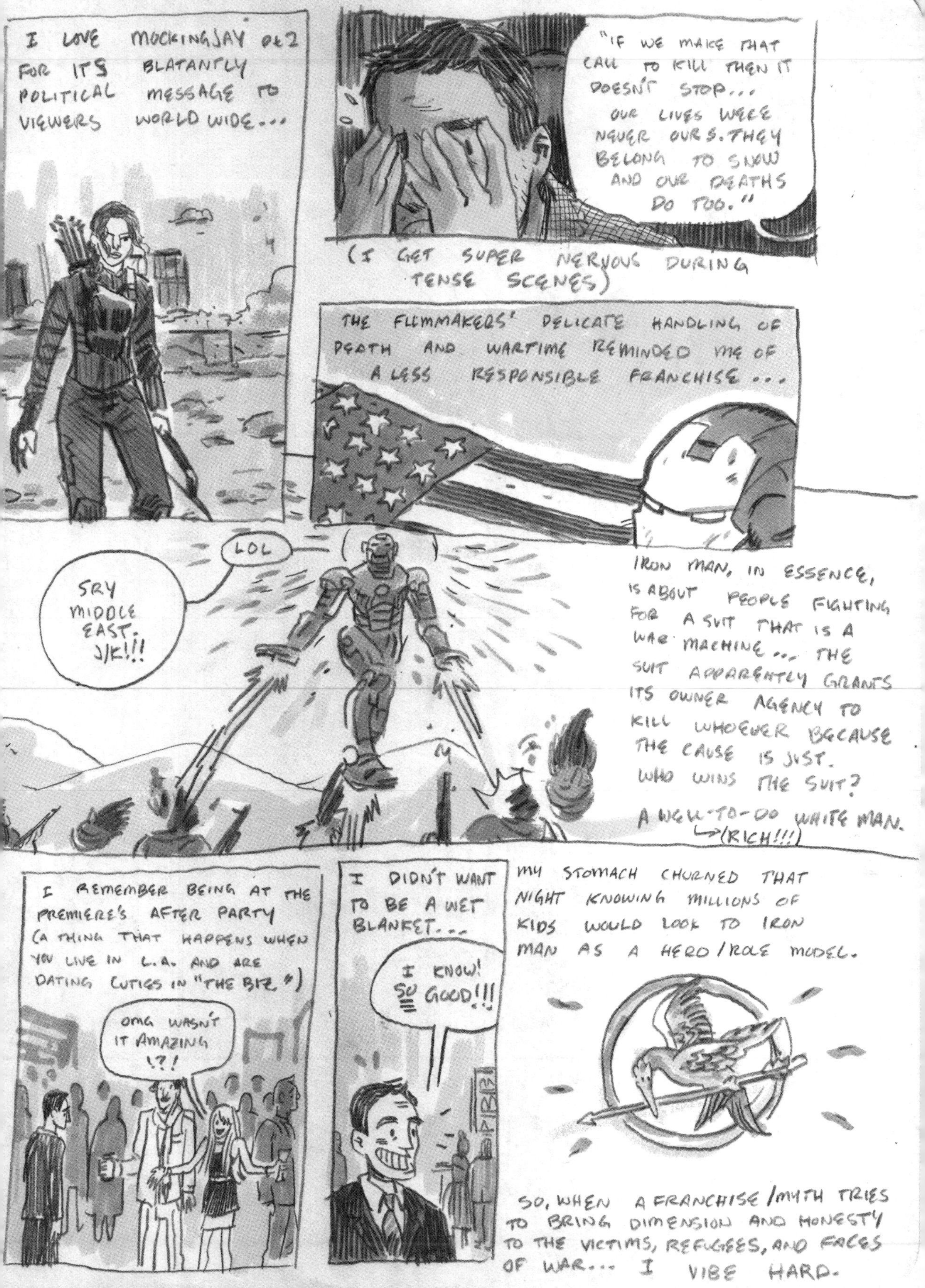
I LOVE MOCKINGJAY PT 2 FOR ITS BLATANTLY POLITICAL MESSAGE TO VIEWERS WORLD WIDE...
"IF WE MAKE THAT CALL TO KILL THEN IT DOESN'T STOP... OUR LIVES WERE NEVER OURS. THEY BELONG TO SNOW AND OUR DEATHS DO TOO."
(I GET SUPER NERVOUS DURING TENSE SCENES)
THE FILMMAKERS' DELICATE HANDLING OF DEATH AND WARTIME REMINDED ME OF A LESS RESPONSIBLE FRANCHISE...
LOL
SRY MIDDLE EAST. J/K!!!
IRON MAN, IN ESSENCE, IS ABOUT PEOPLE FIGHTING FOR A SUIT THAT IS A WAR MACHINE... THE SUIT APPARENTLY GRANTS ITS OWNER AGENCY TO KILL WHOEVER BECAUSE THE CAUSE IS JUST. WHO WINS THE SUIT? A WELL-TO-DO WHITE MAN.
(RICH!!!)
I REMEMBER BEING AT THE PREMIERE'S AFTER PARTY (A THING THAT HAPPENS WHEN YOU LIVE IN L.A. AND ARE DATING CUTIES IN "THE BIZ.")
OMG WASN'T IT AMAZING !?!
I DIDN'T WANT TO BE A WET BLANKET...
I KNOW! SO GOOD!!!
MY STOMACH CHURNED THAT NIGHT KNOWING MILLIONS OF KIDS WOULD LOOK TO IRON MAN AS A HERO/ROLE MODEL.
SO, WHEN A FRANCHISE/MYTH TRIES TO BRING DIMENSION AND HONESTY TO THE VICTIMS, REFUGEES, AND FACES OF WAR... I VIBE HARD.

"Waiting Room"

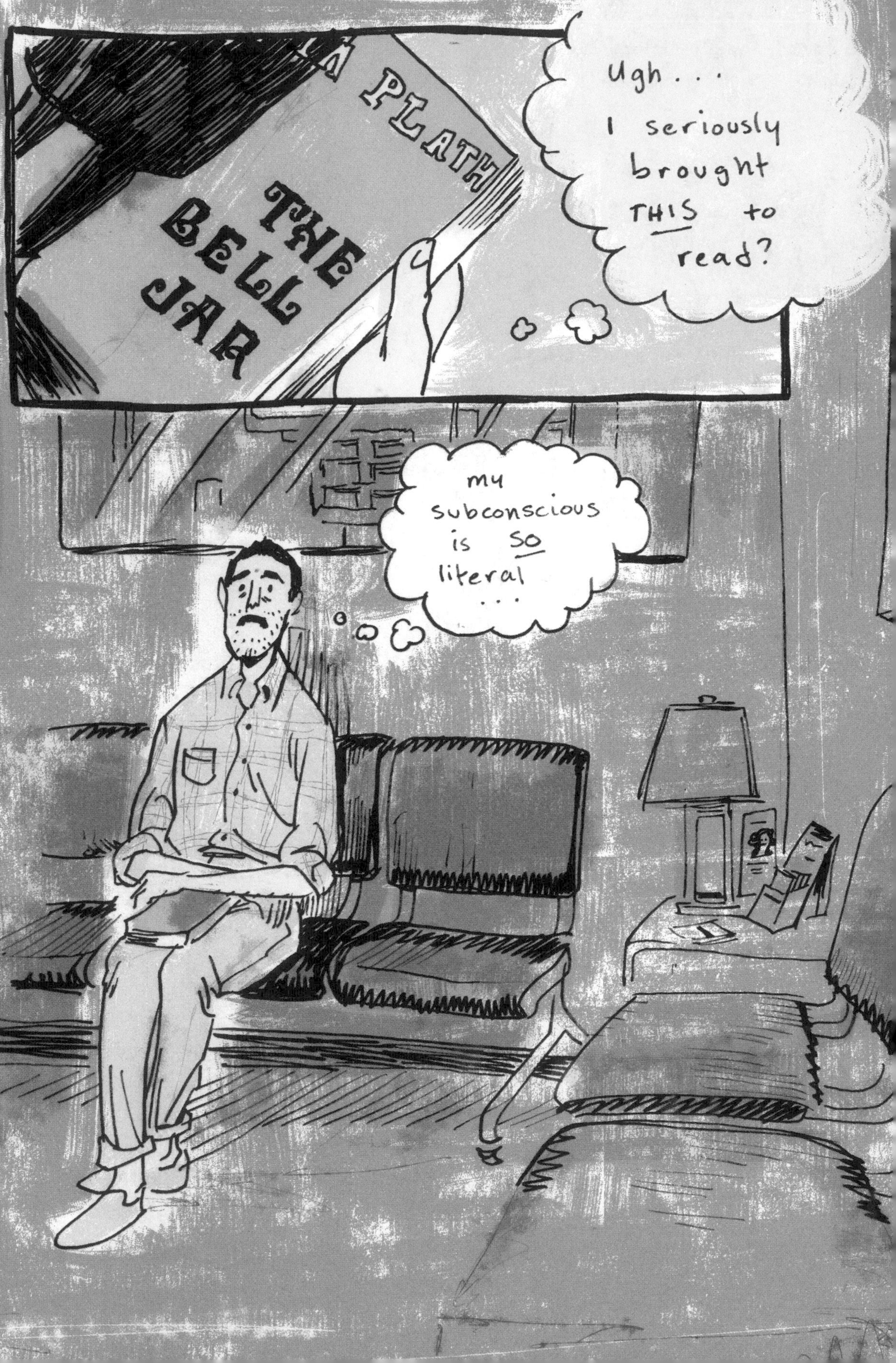

S. PLATH
THE BELL JAR
Ugh... I seriously brought THIS to read?
my subconscious is SO literal...

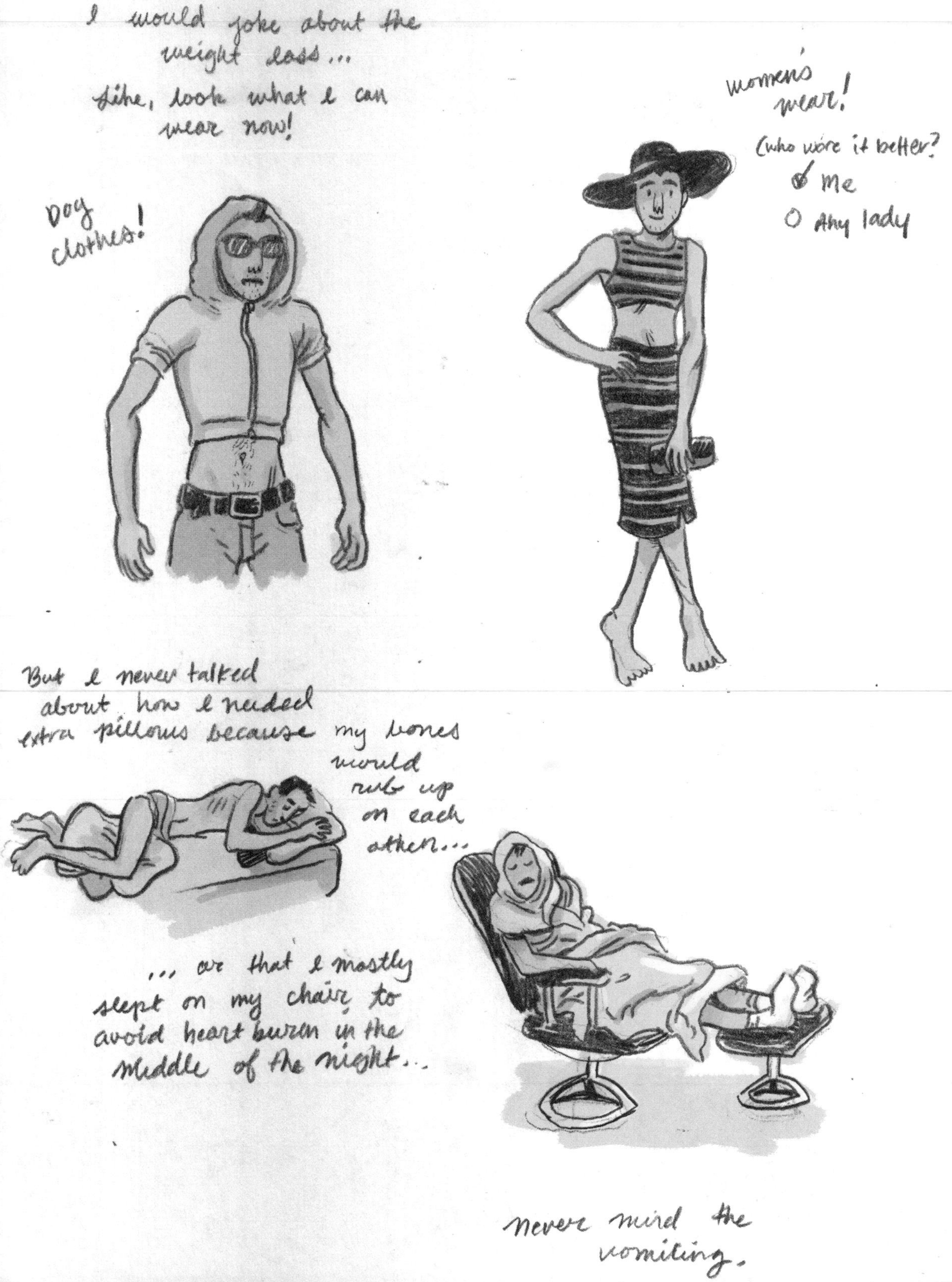
I would joke about the weight loss...
like, look what I can wear now!
Dog clothes!
women's wear!
(who wore it better?
✓ me
O any lady
But I never talked about how I needed extra pillows because my bones would rub up on each other...
... or that I mostly slept on my chair to avoid heart burn in the middle of the night...
never mind the vomiting.

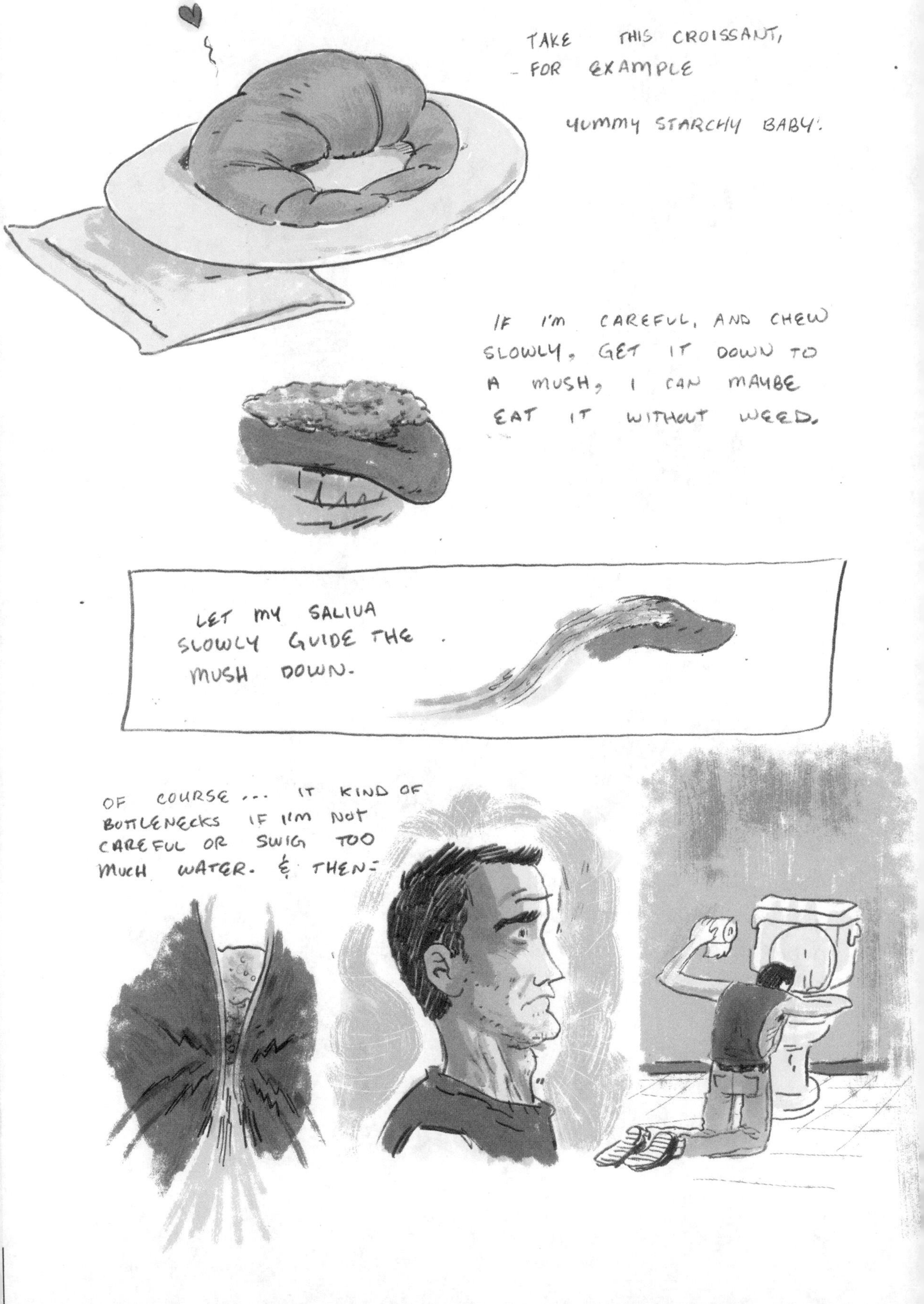
TAKE THIS CROISSANT, FOR EXAMPLE
YUMMY STARCHY BABY!
IF I'M CAREFUL, AND CHEW SLOWLY, GET IT DOWN TO A MUSH, I CAN MAYBE EAT IT WITHOUT WEED.
LET MY SALIVA SLOWLY GUIDE THE MUSH DOWN.
OF COURSE... IT KIND OF BOTTLENECKS IF I'M NOT CAREFUL OR SWIG TOO MUCH WATER. & THEN:

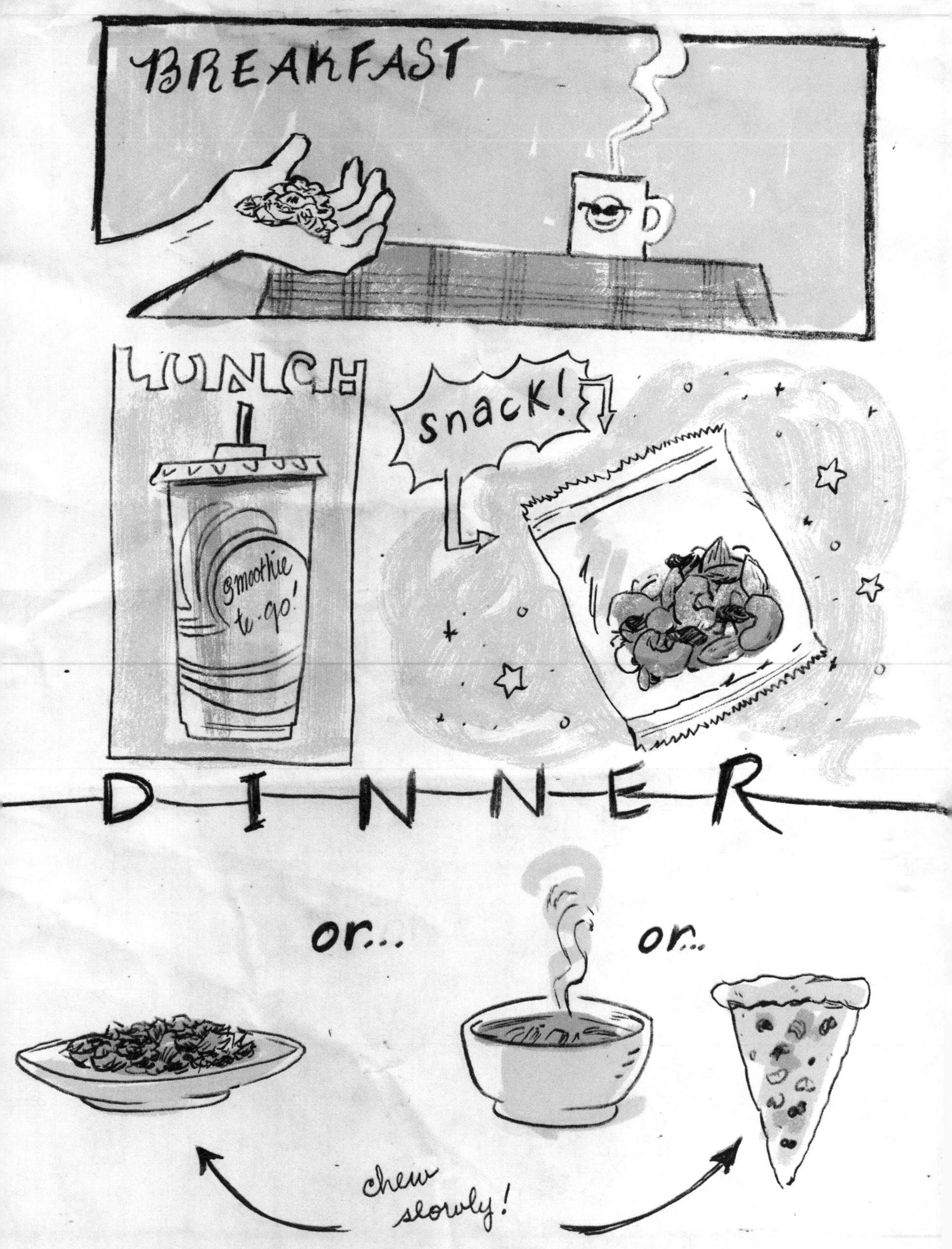

BREAKFAST
LUNCH
smoothie to-go!
snack!
DINNER
or...
or...
chew slowly!

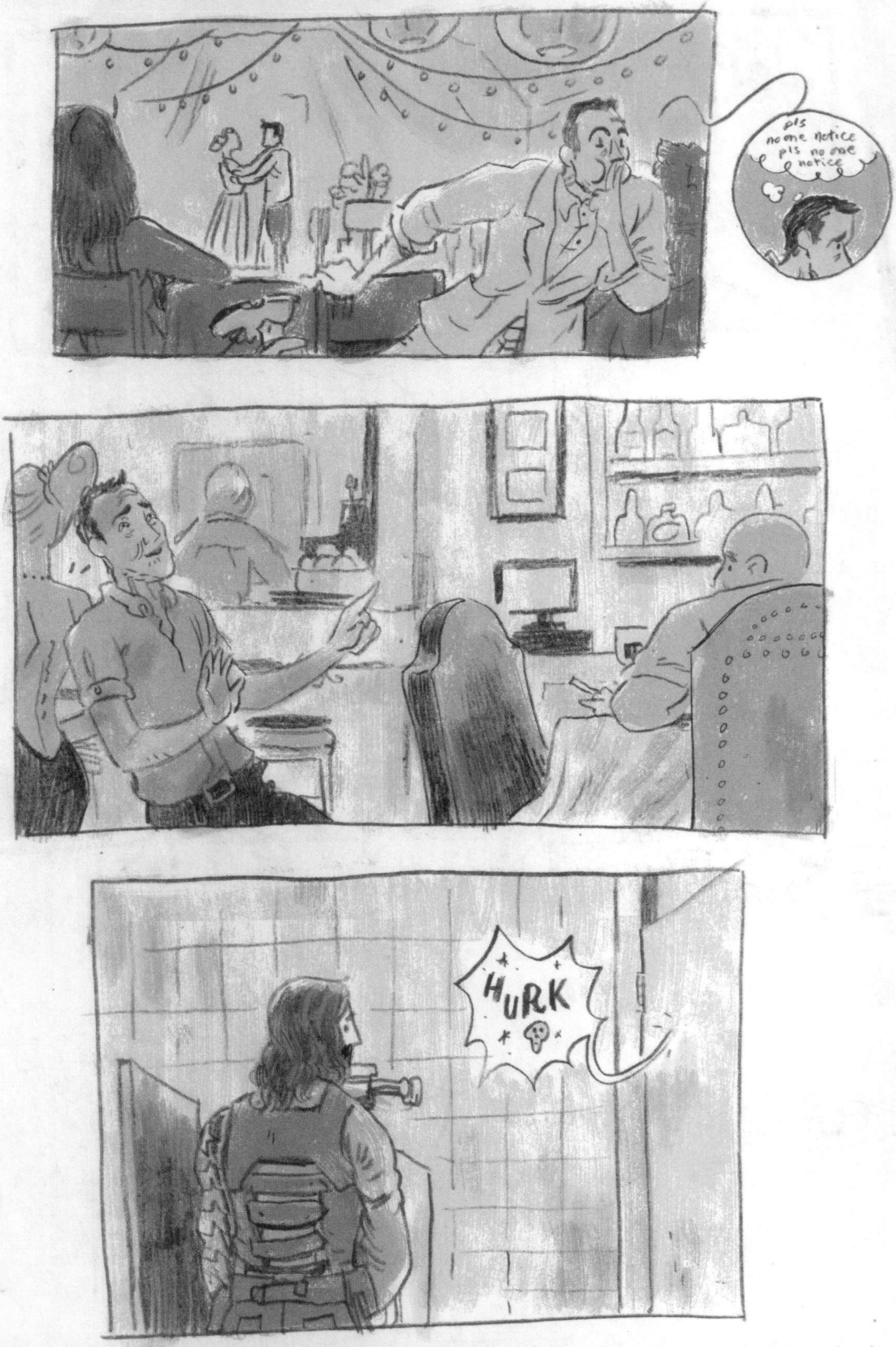
pls no one notice pls no one notice
HURK

The problem was keenly aware of "great timing"

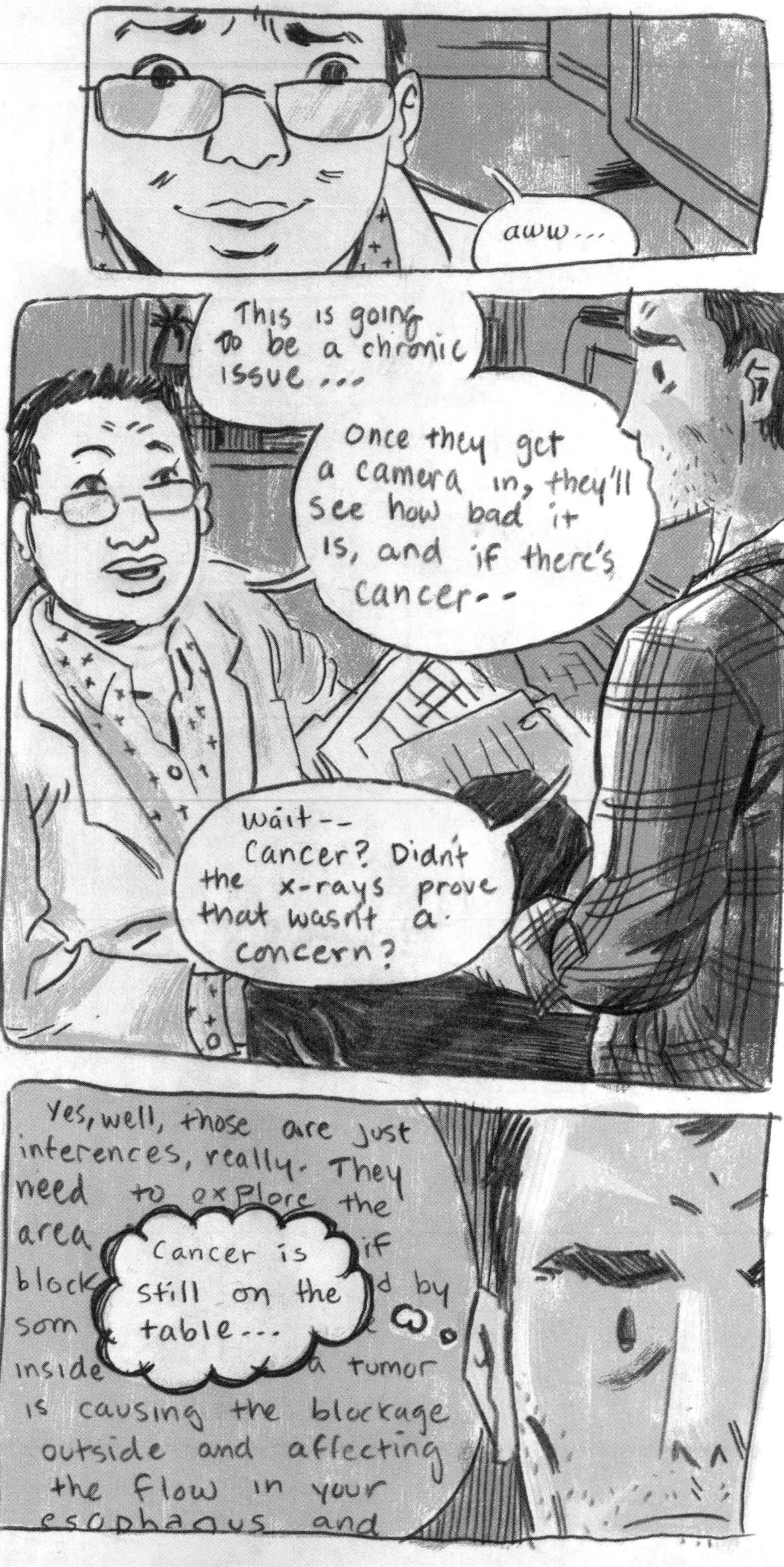
aww...
This is going to be a chronic issue...
Once they get a camera in, they'll see how bad it is, and if there's cancer--
Wait-- Cancer? Didn't the x-rays prove that wasn't a concern?
Yes, well, those are just inferences, really. They need to explore the area
if
block
d by
som
inside
a tumor is causing the blockage outside and affecting the flow in your esophagus and
Cancer is still on the table...

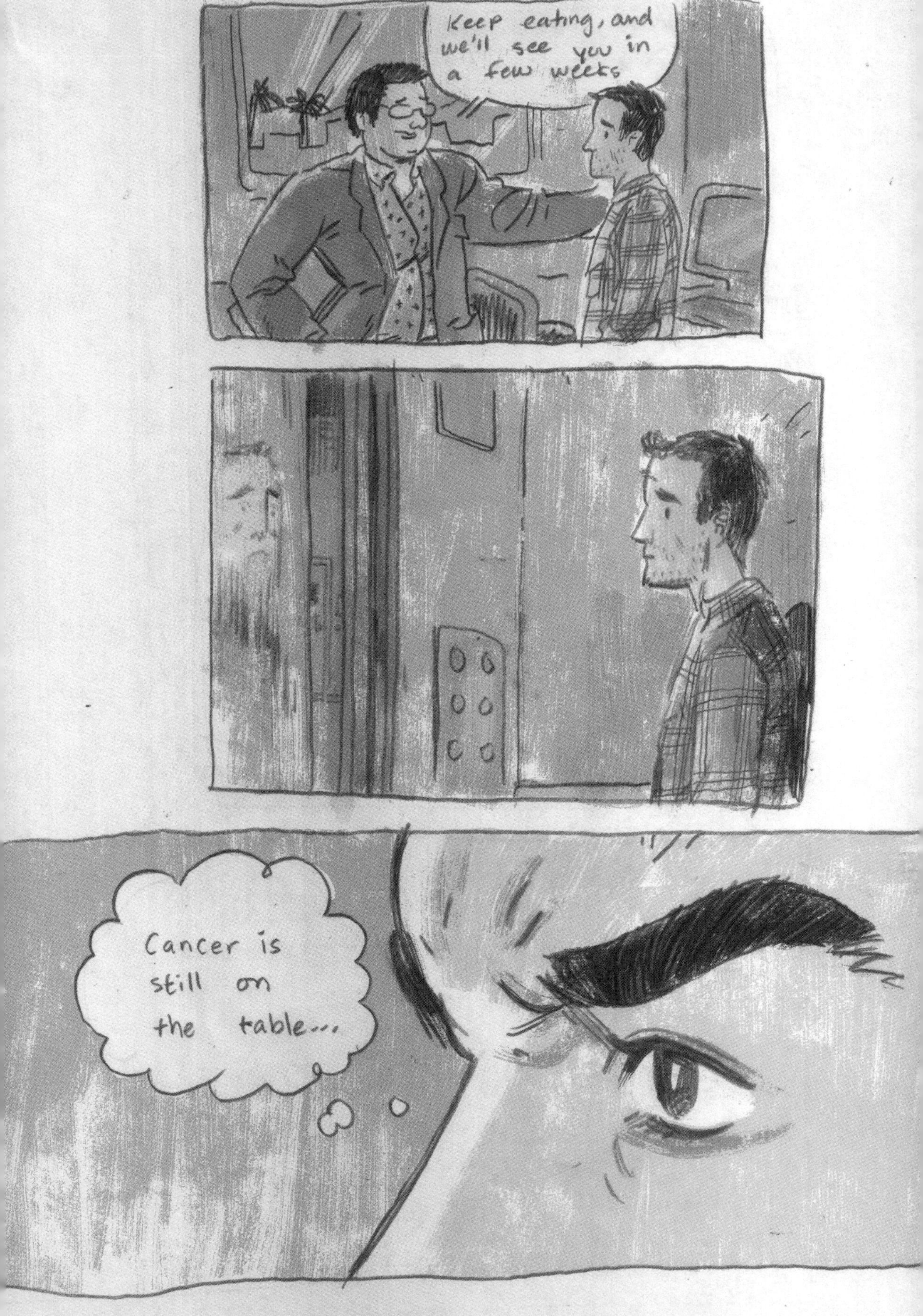
Keep eating, and we'll see you in a few weeks
Cancer is still on the table...

7.

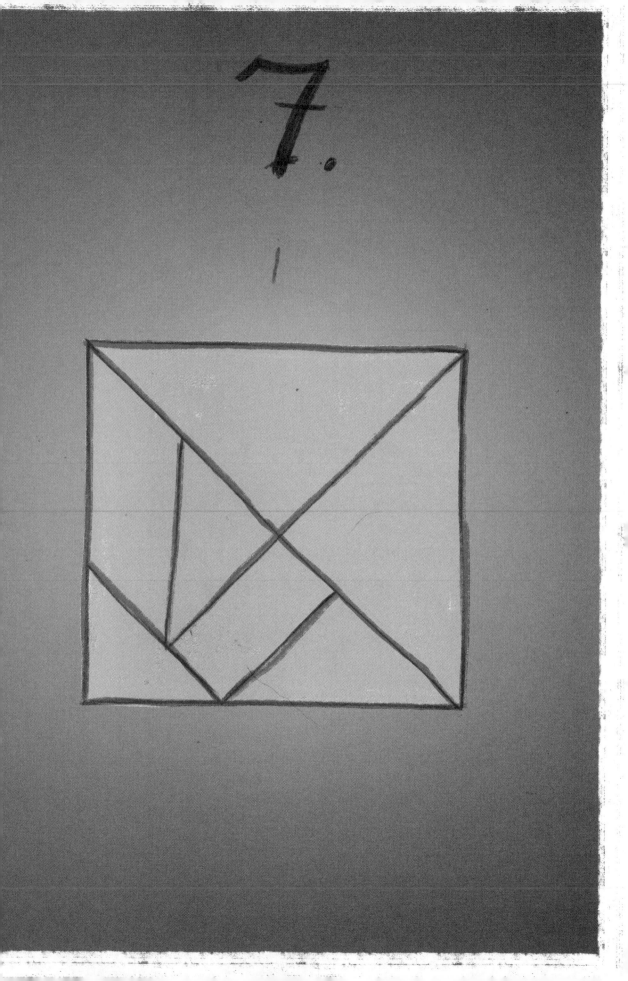

a memory (walking with Colleen Green)

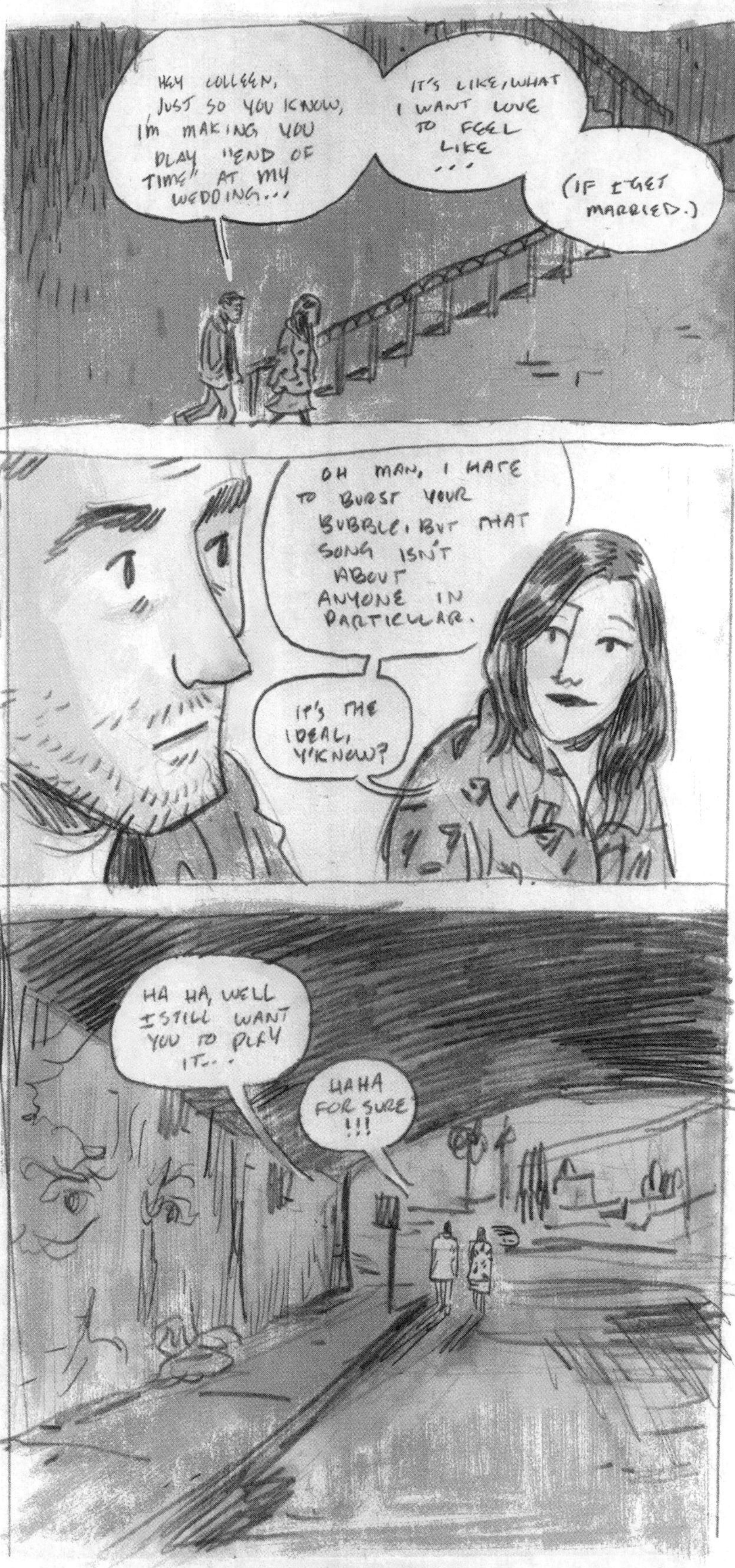
HEY COLLEEN, JUST SO YOU KNOW, I'M MAKING YOU PLAY "END OF TIME" AT MY WEDDING...
IT'S LIKE, WHAT I WANT LOVE TO FEEL LIKE ...
(IF I GET MARRIED.)
OH MAN, I HATE TO BURST YOUR BUBBLE, BUT THAT SONG ISN'T ABOUT ANYONE IN PARTICULAR.
IT'S THE IDEAL, Y'KNOW?
HA HA, WELL I STILL WANT YOU TO PLAY IT...
HAHA FOR SURE !!!

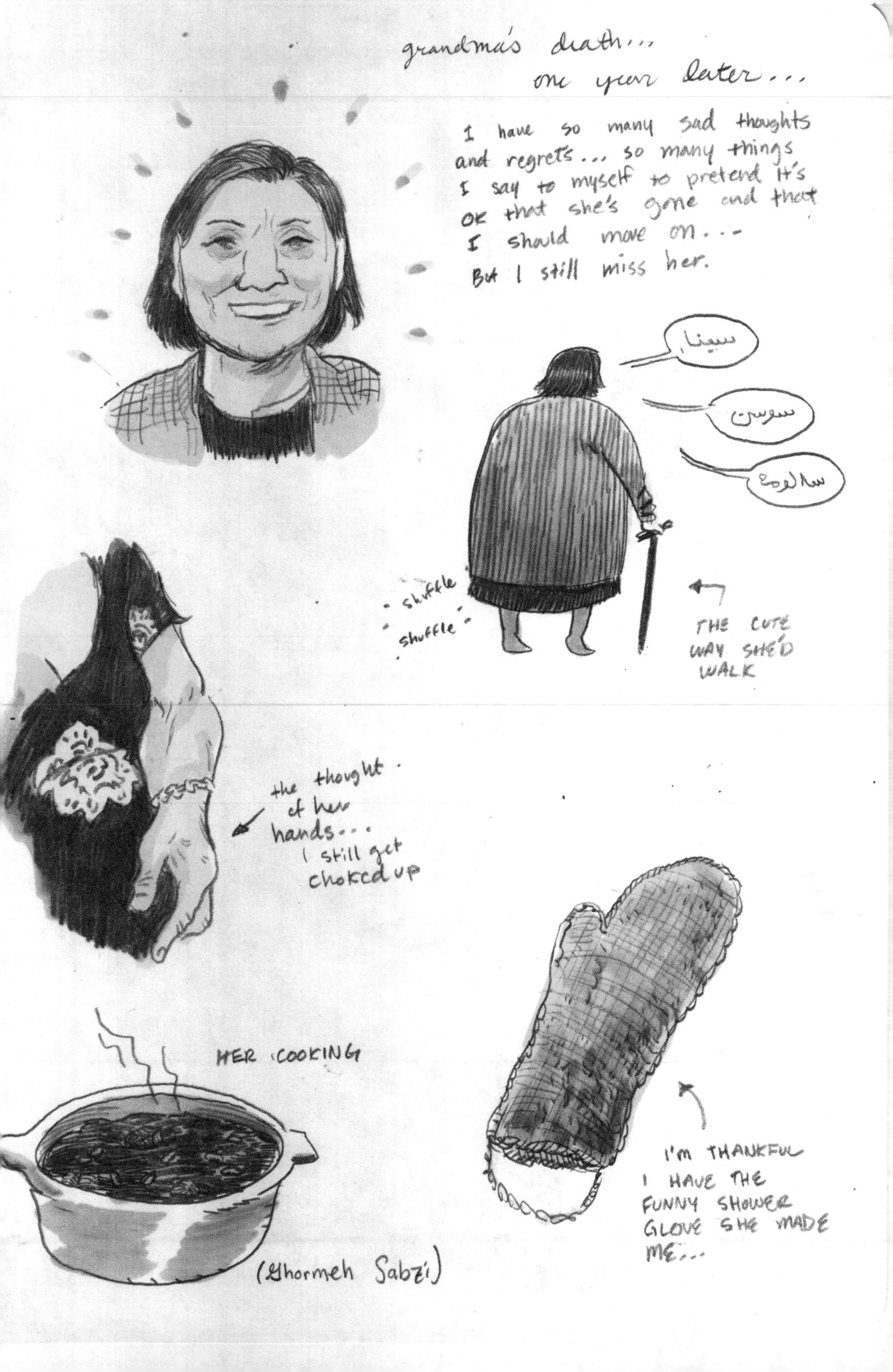
grandma's death...
one year later...
I have so many sad thoughts and regrets... so many things I say to myself to pretend it's OK that she's gone and that I should move on...
But I still miss her.
سینا
سوسن
سالومه
"shuffle"
"shuffle"
THE CUTE WAY SHE'D WALK
the thought of her hands... I still get choked up
HER COOKING
(Ghormeh Sabzi)
I'M THANKFUL I HAVE THE FUNNY SHOWER GLOVE SHE MADE ME...

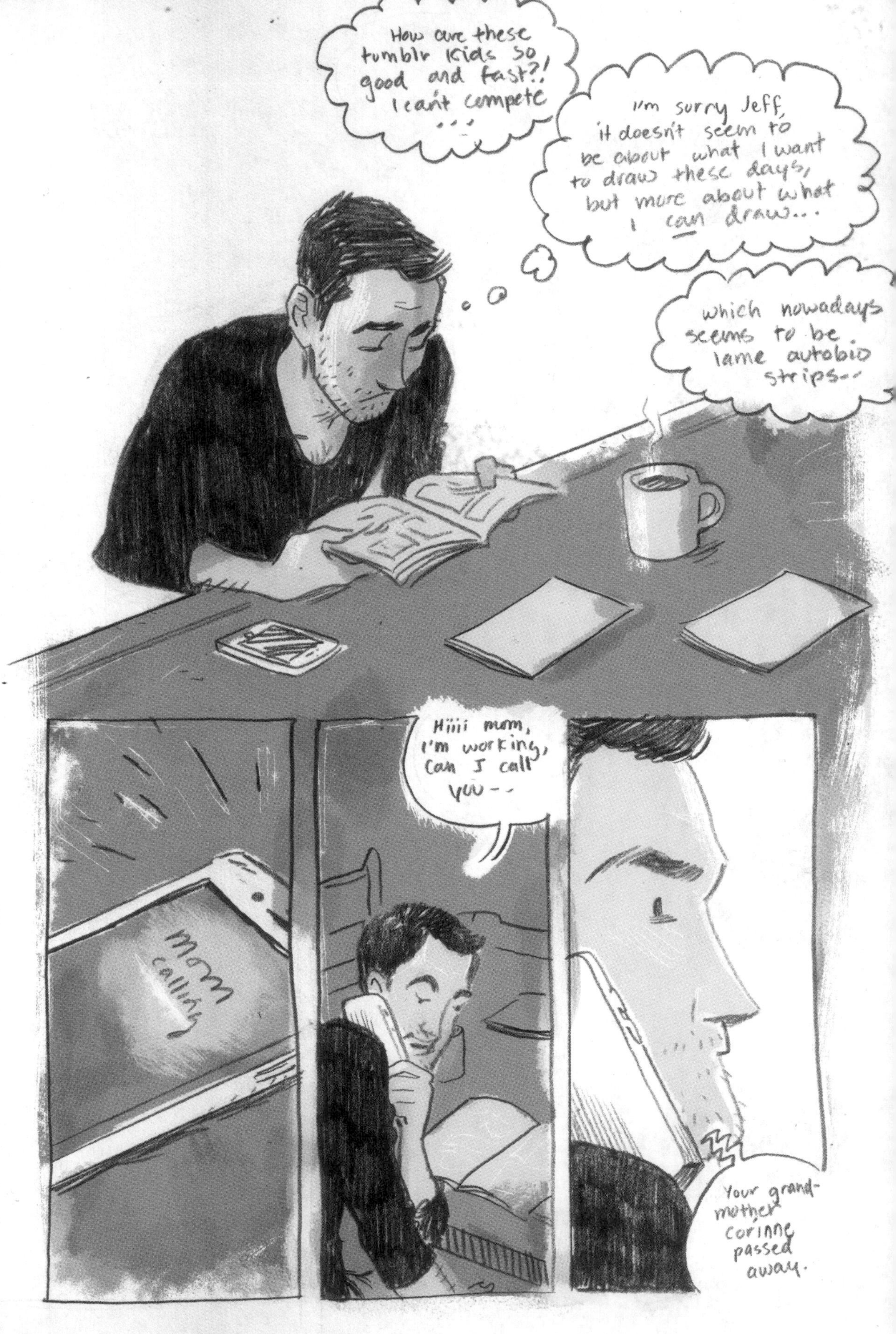
How are these tumblr kids so good and fast?! I can't compete ...
I'm sorry Jeff, it doesn't seem to be about what I want to draw these days, but more about what I can draw...
which nowadays seems to be lame autobio strips--
mom calling
Hiiii mom, I'm working, can I call you--
Your grand-mother Corinne passed away.

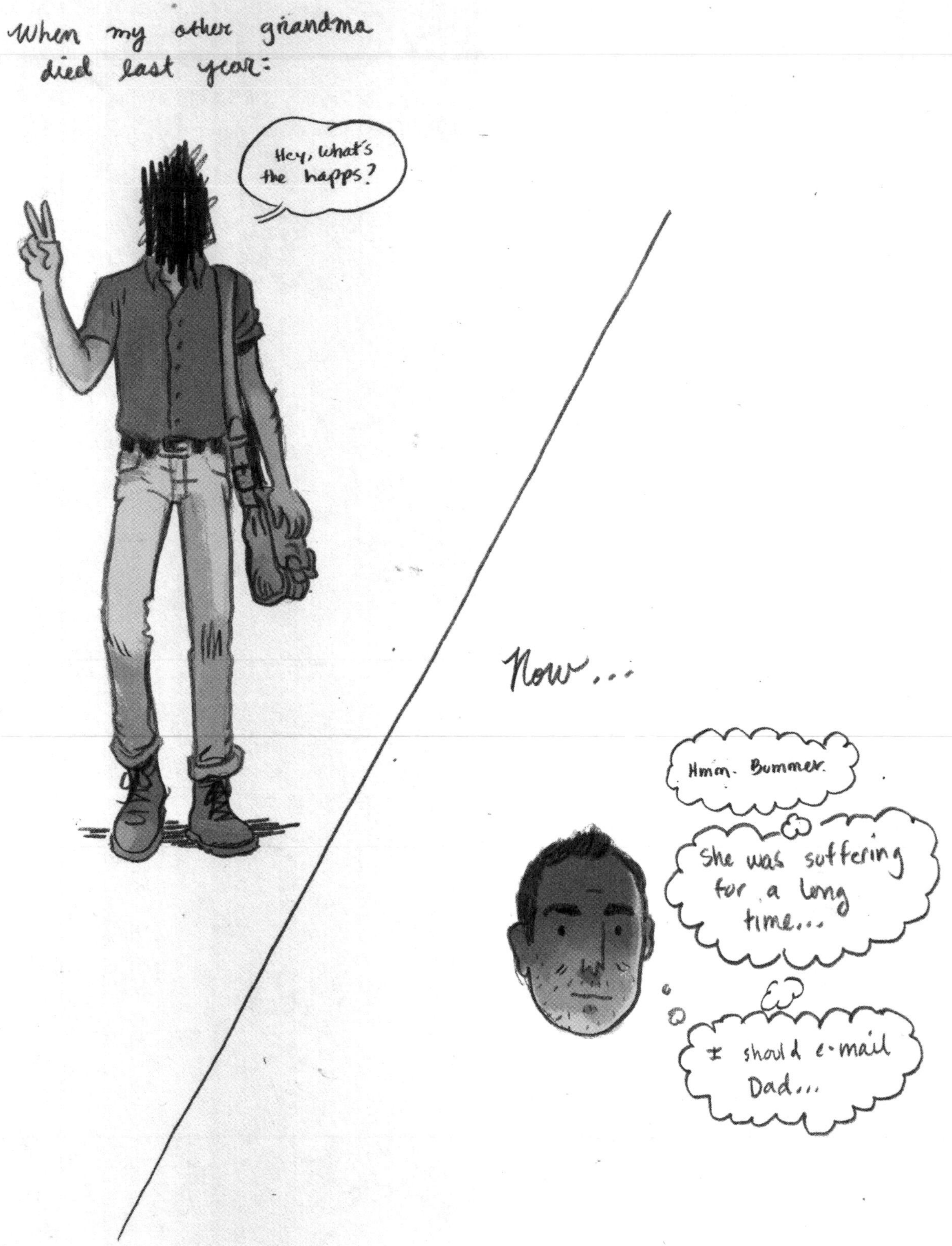
When my other grandma died last year:
Hey, what's the happs?
Now...
Hmm. Bummer.
She was suffering for a long time...
I should e-mail Dad...

maybe I'm just worn down from the weight loss...

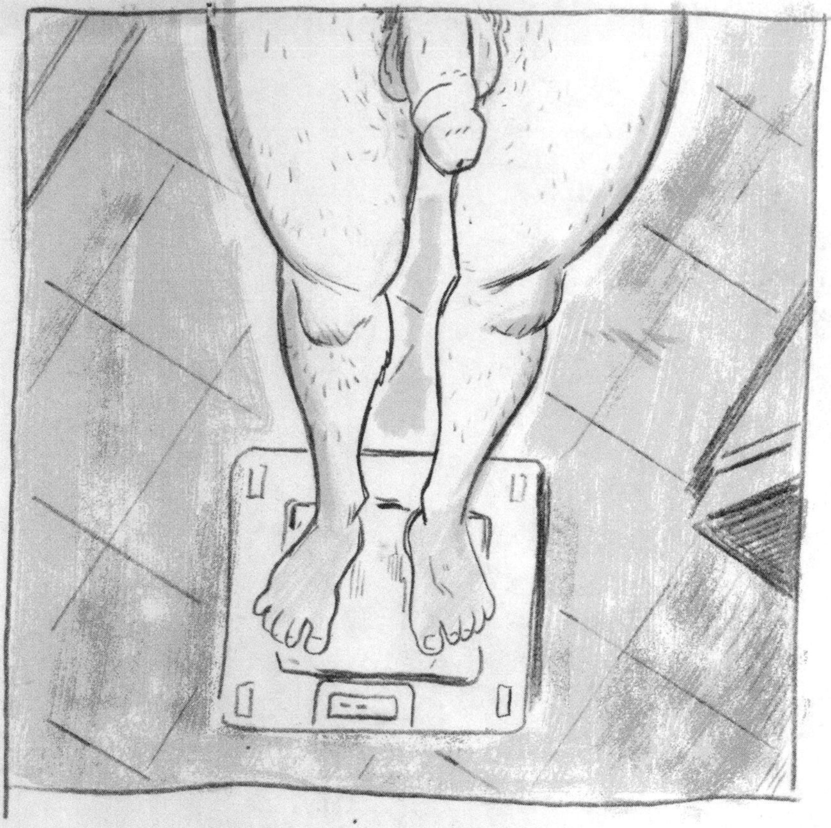

scale > 135 lbs

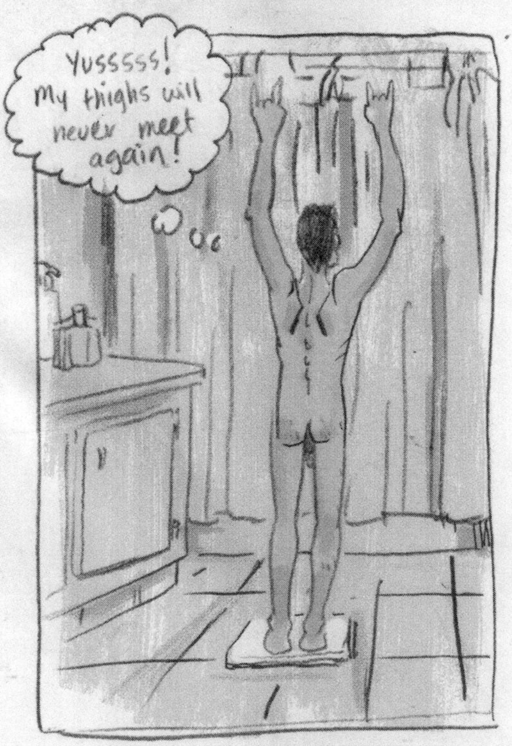
Yussssss! My thighs will never meet again!

scale < 135 lbs

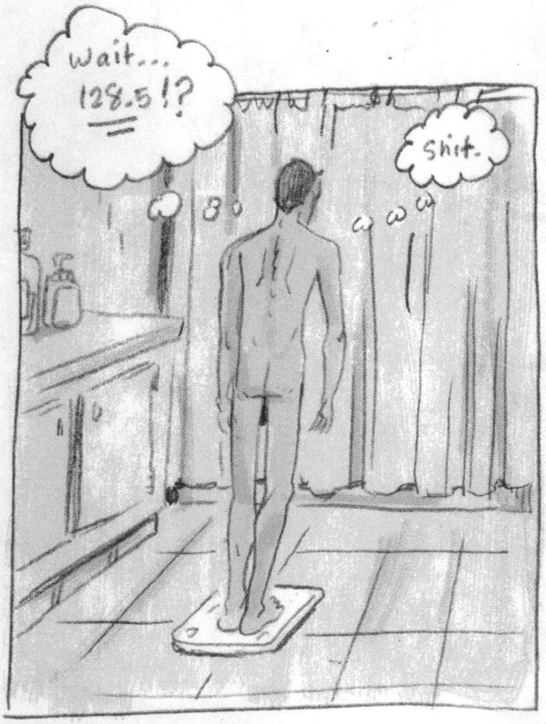
wait... 128.5!?
Shit.

Things the doctors did to me...

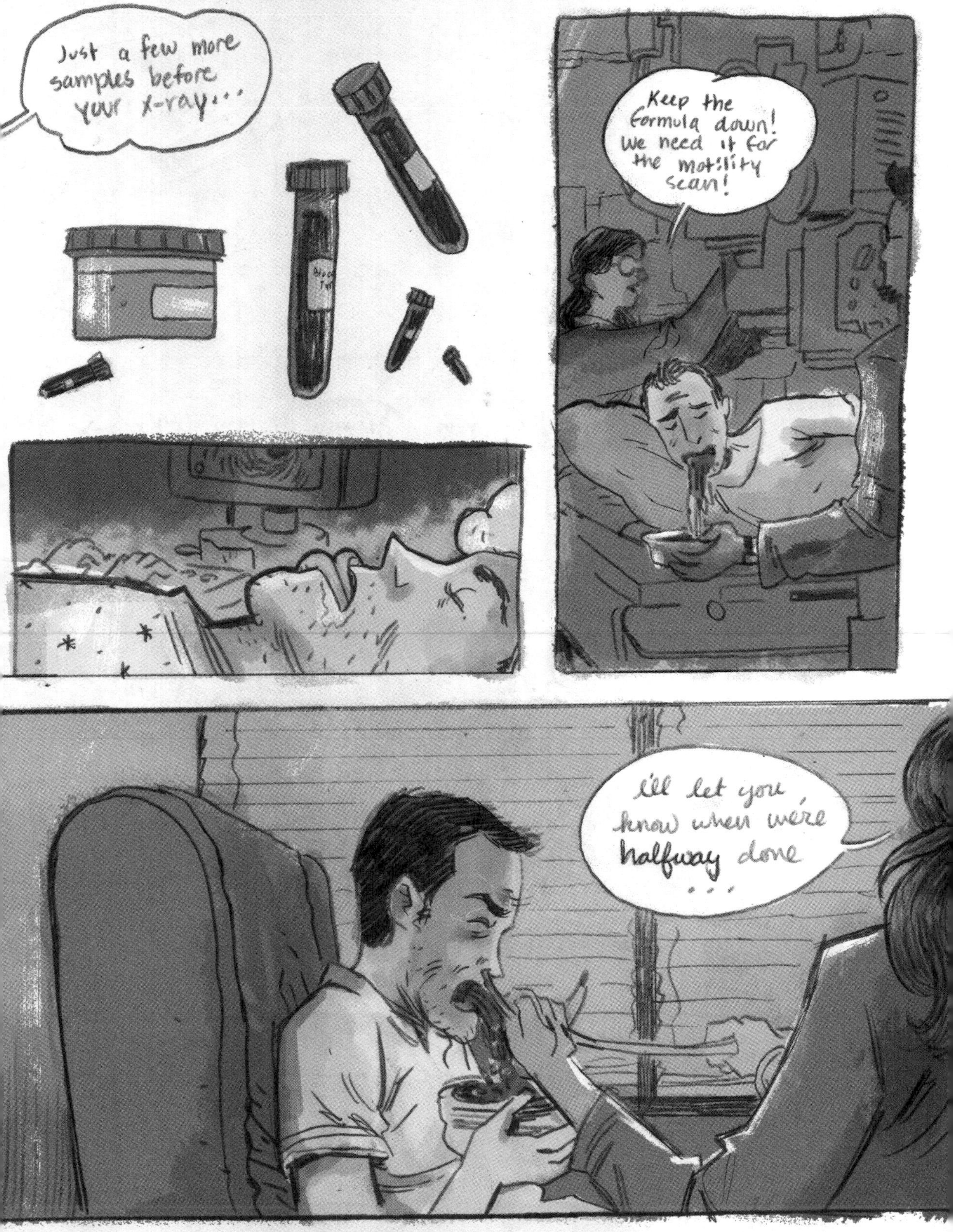
Just a few more samples before your x-ray...
Keep the formula down! We need it for the motility scan!
I'll let you know when we're halfway done ...

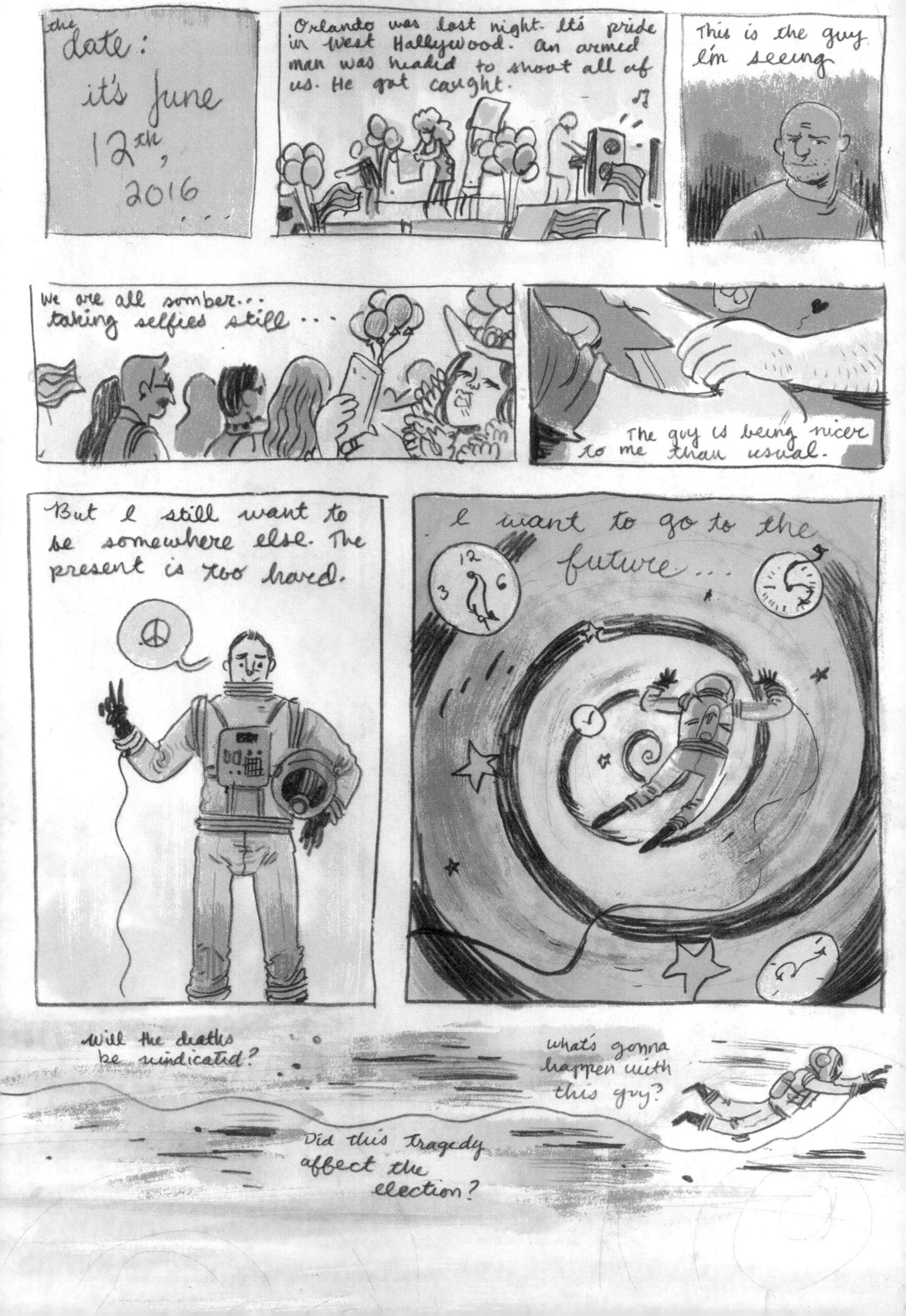

the date: it's June 12th, 2016 . . .
Orlando was last night. It's pride in West Hollywood. An armed man was headed to shoot all of us. He got caught.
This is the guy I'm seeing
We are all somber... taking selfies still...
The guy is being nicer to me than usual.
But I still want to be somewhere else. The present is too hard.
I want to go to the future...
Will the deaths be vindicated?
What's gonna happen with this guy?
Did this tragedy affect the election?

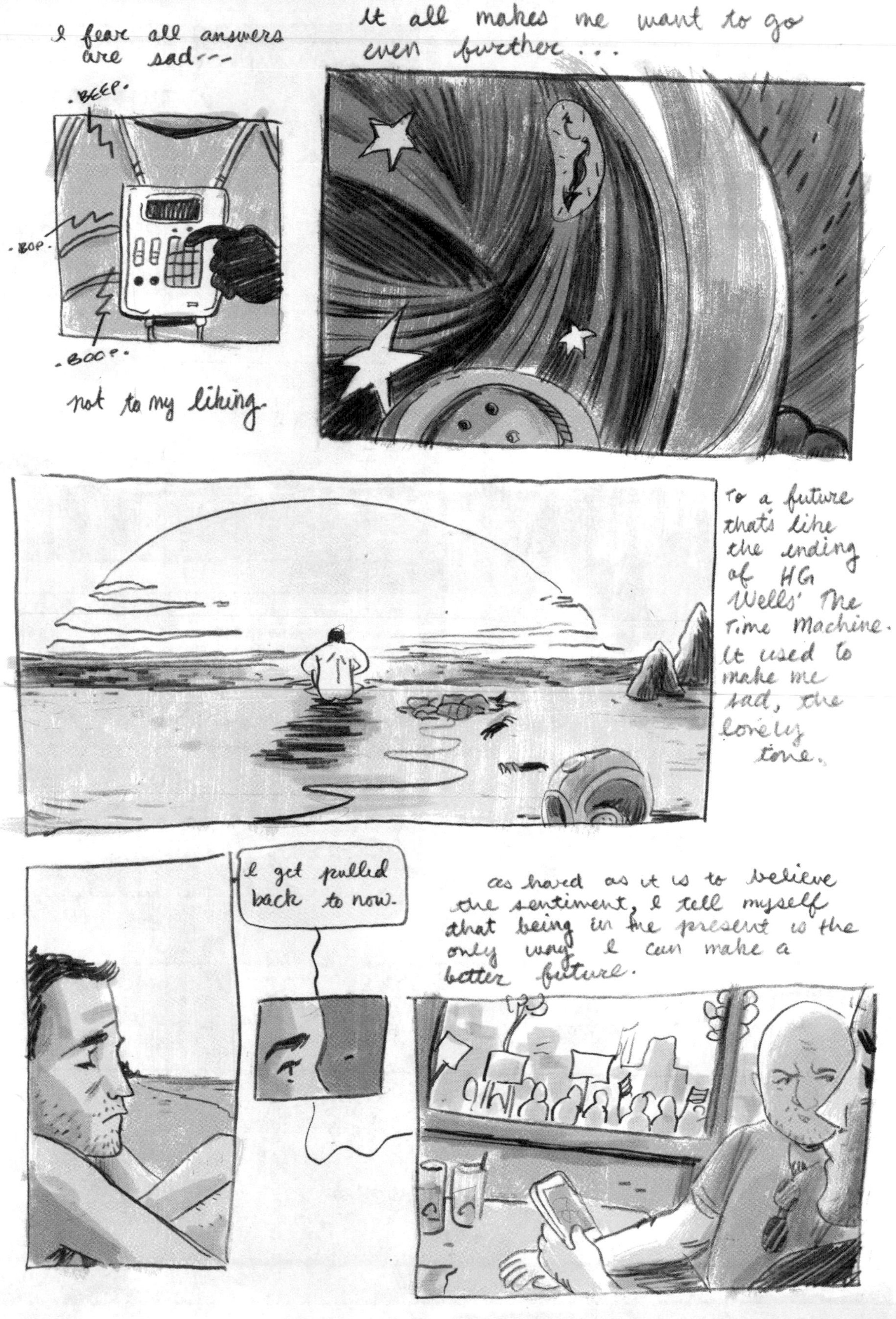
I fear all answers are sad---
-BEEP-
-BOP-
-BOOP-
not to my liking.
It all makes me want to go even further...
To a future that's like the ending of HG Wells' The Time Machine. It used to make me sad, the lonely tone.
I get pulled back to now.
as hard as it is to believe the sentiment, I tell myself that being in the present is the only way I can make a better future.

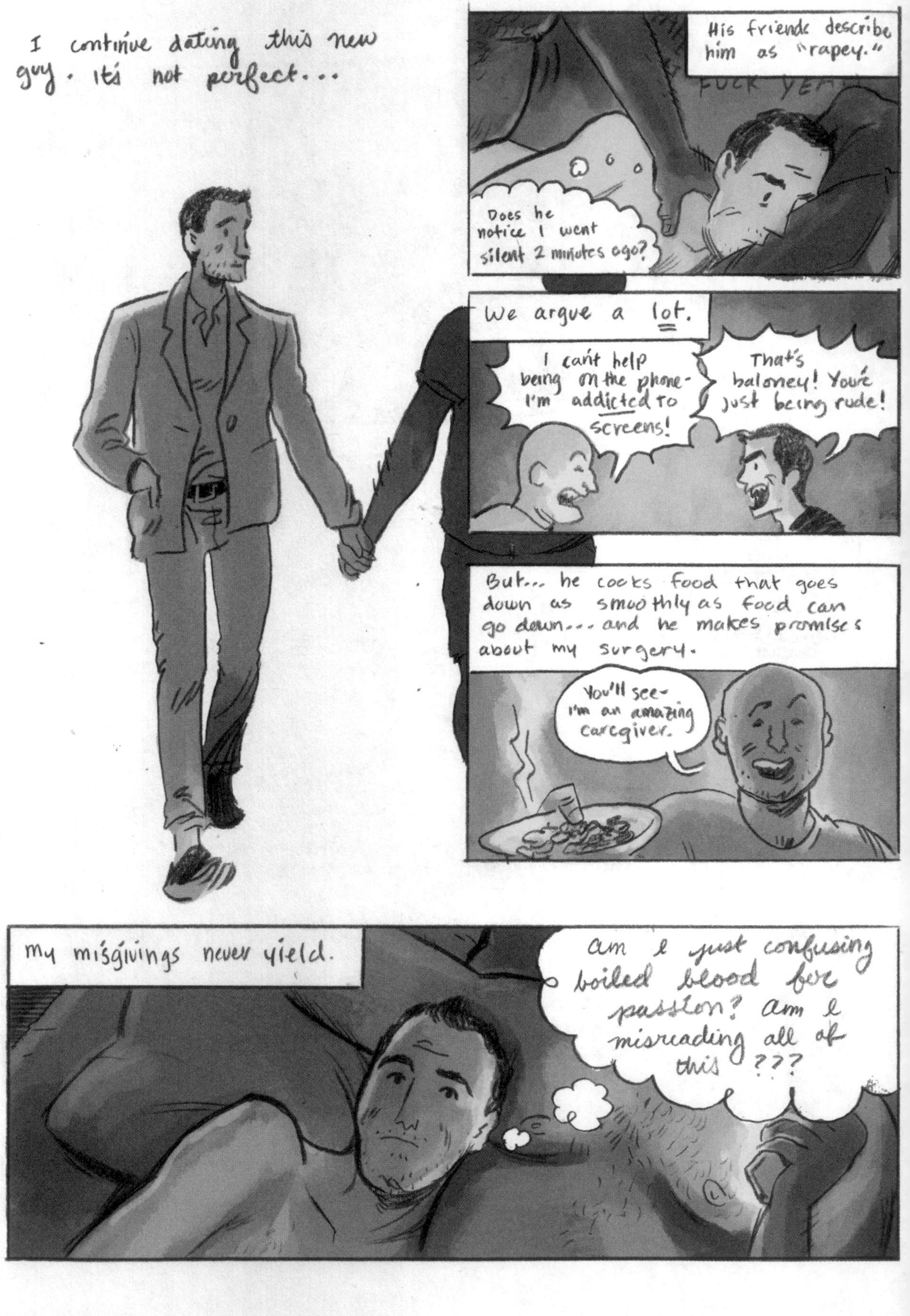
I continue dating this new guy. It's not perfect...
His friends describe him as "rapey."
Does he notice I went silent 2 minutes ago?
We argue a lot.
I can't help being on the phone- I'm addicted to screens!
That's baloney! You're just being rude!
But... he cooks food that goes down as smoothly as food can go down... and he makes promises about my surgery.
You'll see- I'm an amazing caregiver.
my misgivings never yield.
Am I just confusing boiled blood for passion? Am I misreading all of this???

And when he dumps me...

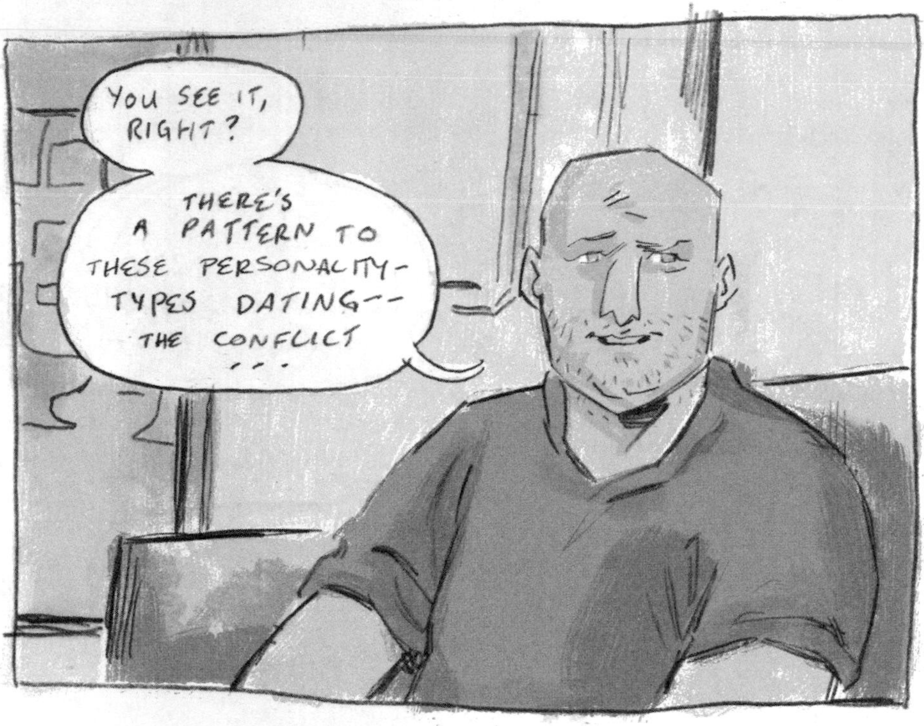
YOU SEE IT, RIGHT?
THERE'S A PATTERN TO THESE PERSONALITY-TYPES DATING-- THE CONFLICT ...

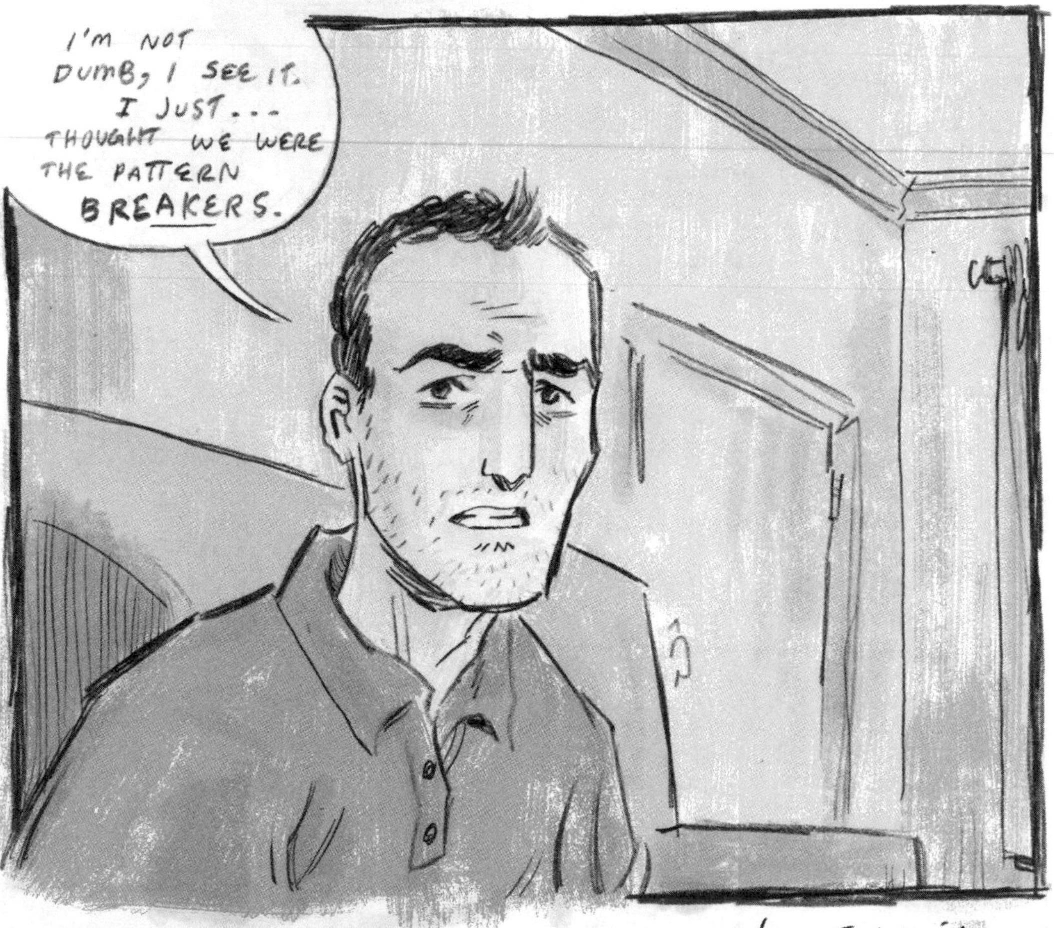
I'M NOT DUMB, I SEE IT. I JUST... THOUGHT WE WERE THE PATTERN BREAKERS.

I don't fight it too much.

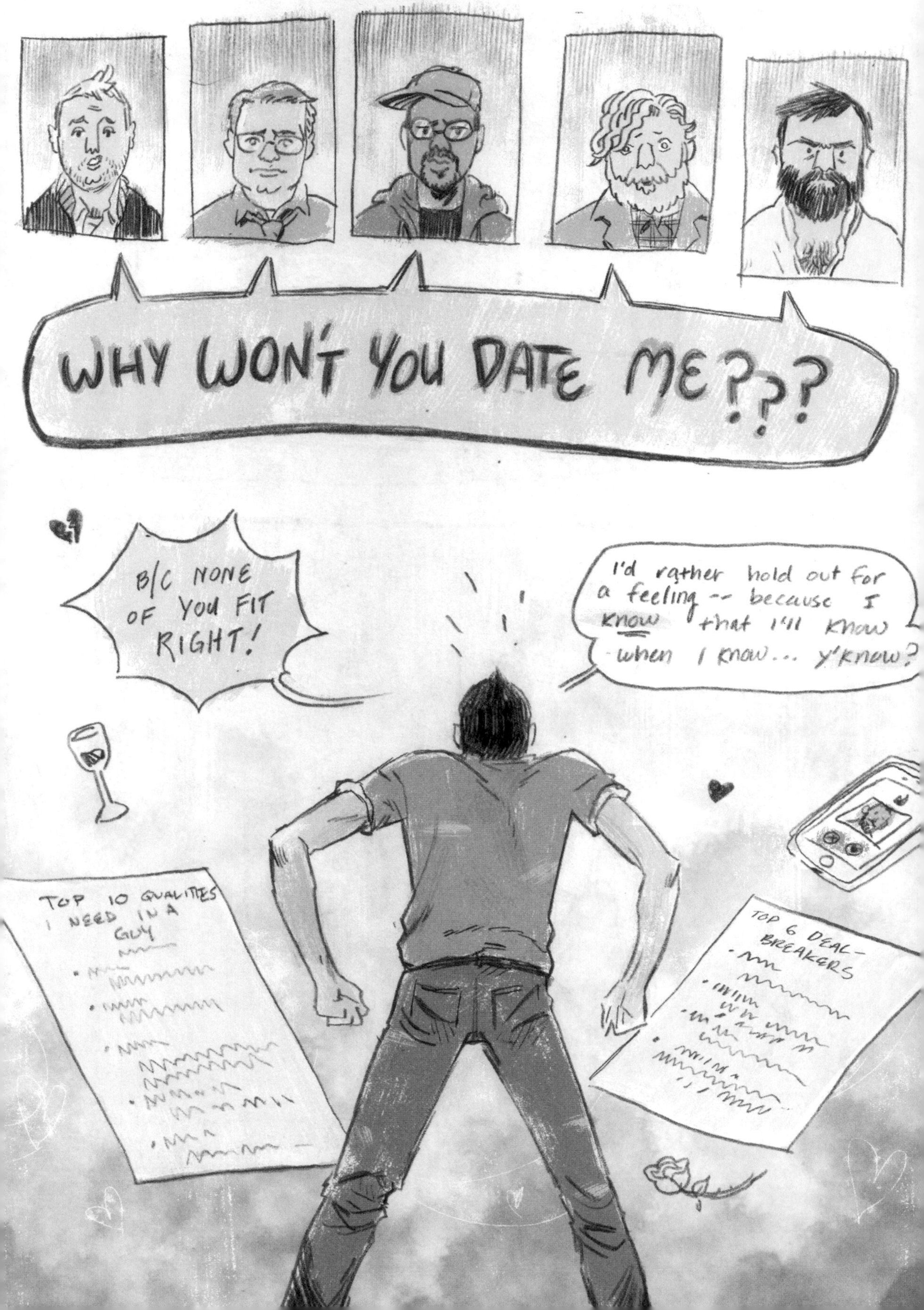
WHY WON'T YOU DATE ME???
B/C NONE OF YOU FIT RIGHT!
I'd rather hold out for a feeling -- because I KNOW that I'll know when I know... y'know?
TOP 10 QUALITIES I NEED IN A GUY
TOP 6 DEAL-BREAKERS

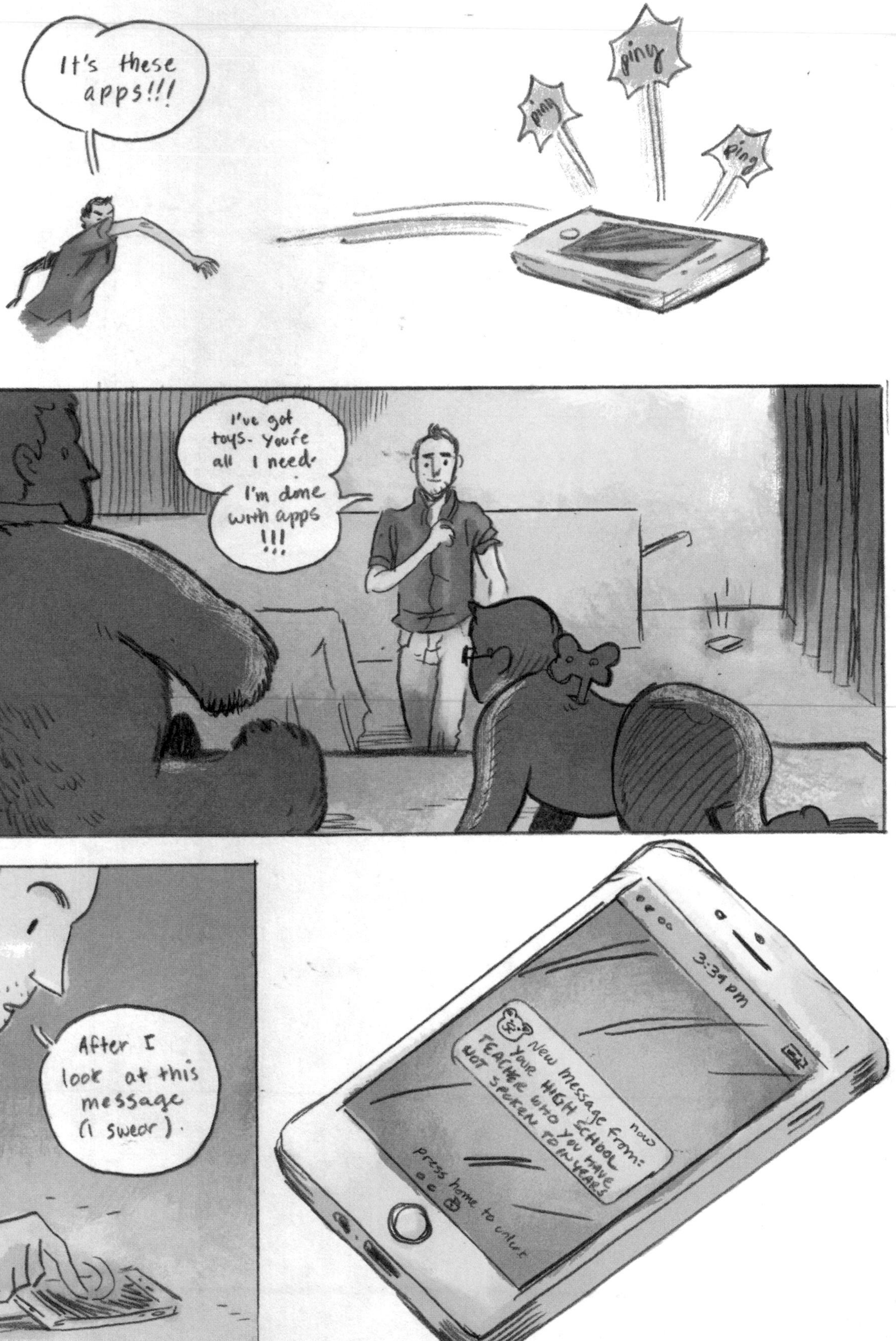
It's these apps!!!
ping
ping
ping
I've got toys. You're all I need.
I'm done with apps !!!
After I look at this message (I swear).
3:39 pm
now
New message from: YOUR HIGH SCHOOL TEACHER WHO YOU HAVE NOT SPOKEN TO IN YEARS
Press home to unlock

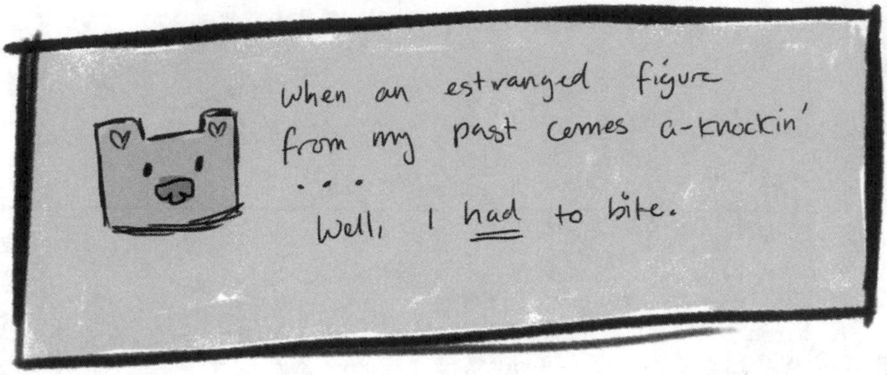
when an estranged figure from my past comes a-knockin'
. . .
Well, I had to bite.

8.

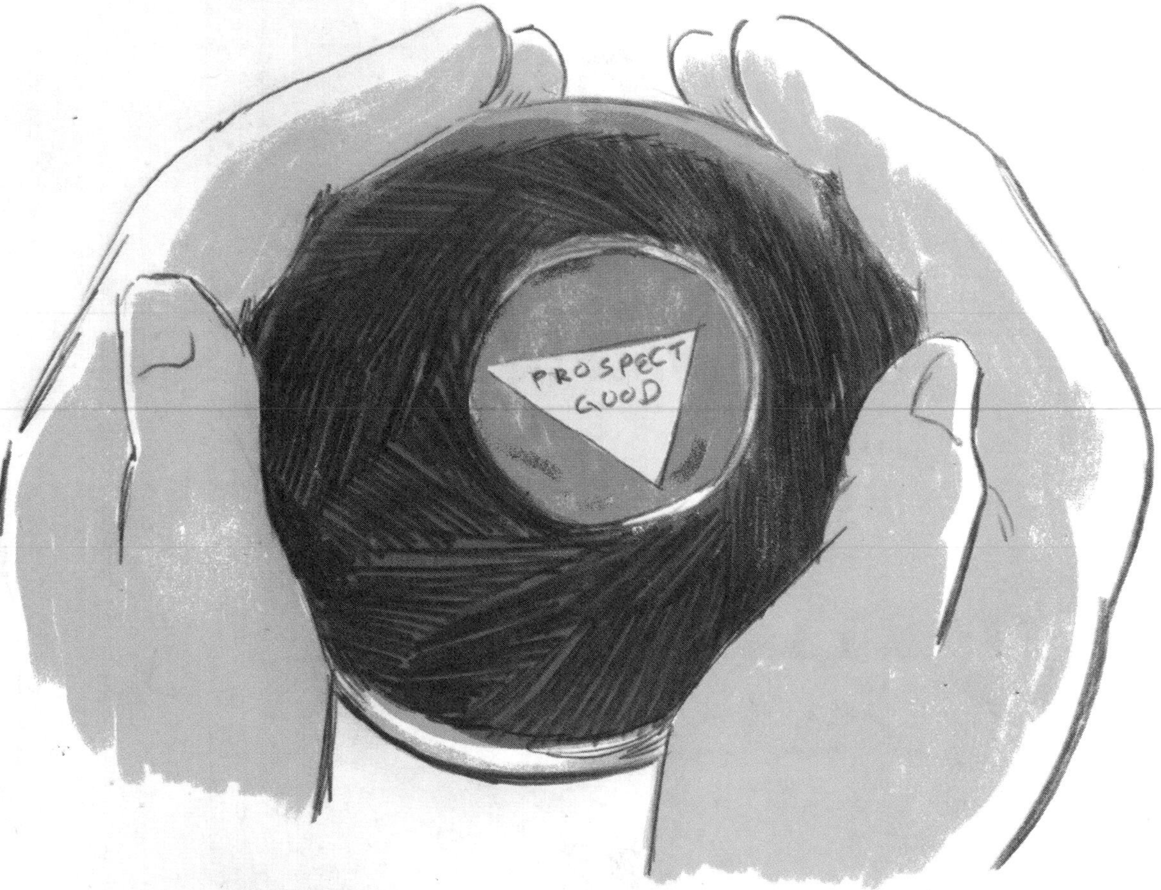
PROSPECT GOOD

I did this drawing
right after New York Comic-Con,
and right before lunch with
a Marvel editor

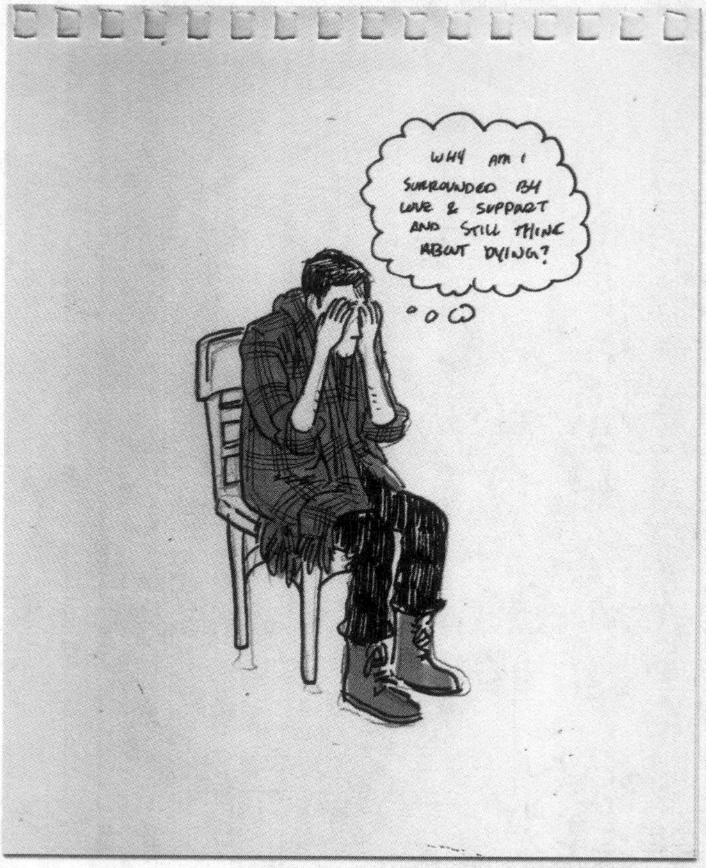
WHY AM I SURROUNDED BY LOVE & SUPPORT AND STILL THINK ABOUT DYING?

Later, I looked at the drawing,
and an awful feeling sank in...

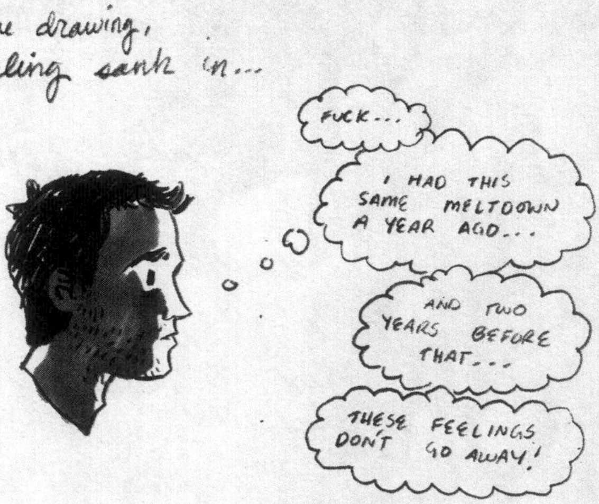
FUCK...
I HAD THIS SAME MELTDOWN A YEAR AGO...
AND TWO YEARS BEFORE THAT...
THESE FEELINGS DON'T GO AWAY!

When the feeling subsided,
I tried to write about it...

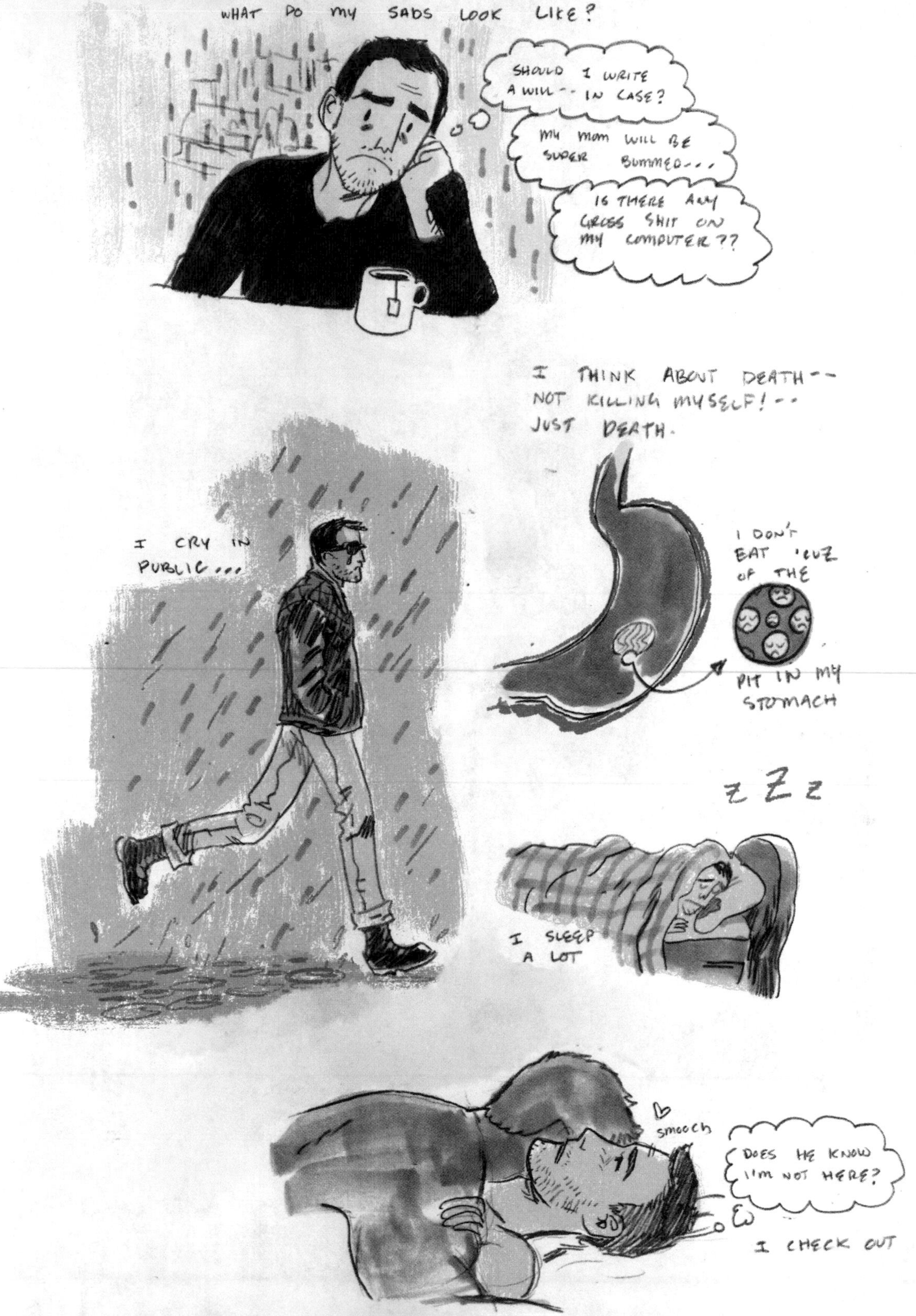
WHAT DO MY SADS LOOK LIKE?
SHOULD I WRITE A WILL-- IN CASE?
MY MOM WILL BE SUPER BUMMED...
IS THERE ANY GROSS SHIT ON MY COMPUTER??
I THINK ABOUT DEATH-- NOT KILLING MYSELF!-- JUST DEATH.
I CRY IN PUBLIC...
I DON'T EAT 'CUZ OF THE
PIT IN MY STOMACH
Z Z Z
I SLEEP A LOT
smooch
DOES HE KNOW I'M NOT HERE?
I CHECK OUT

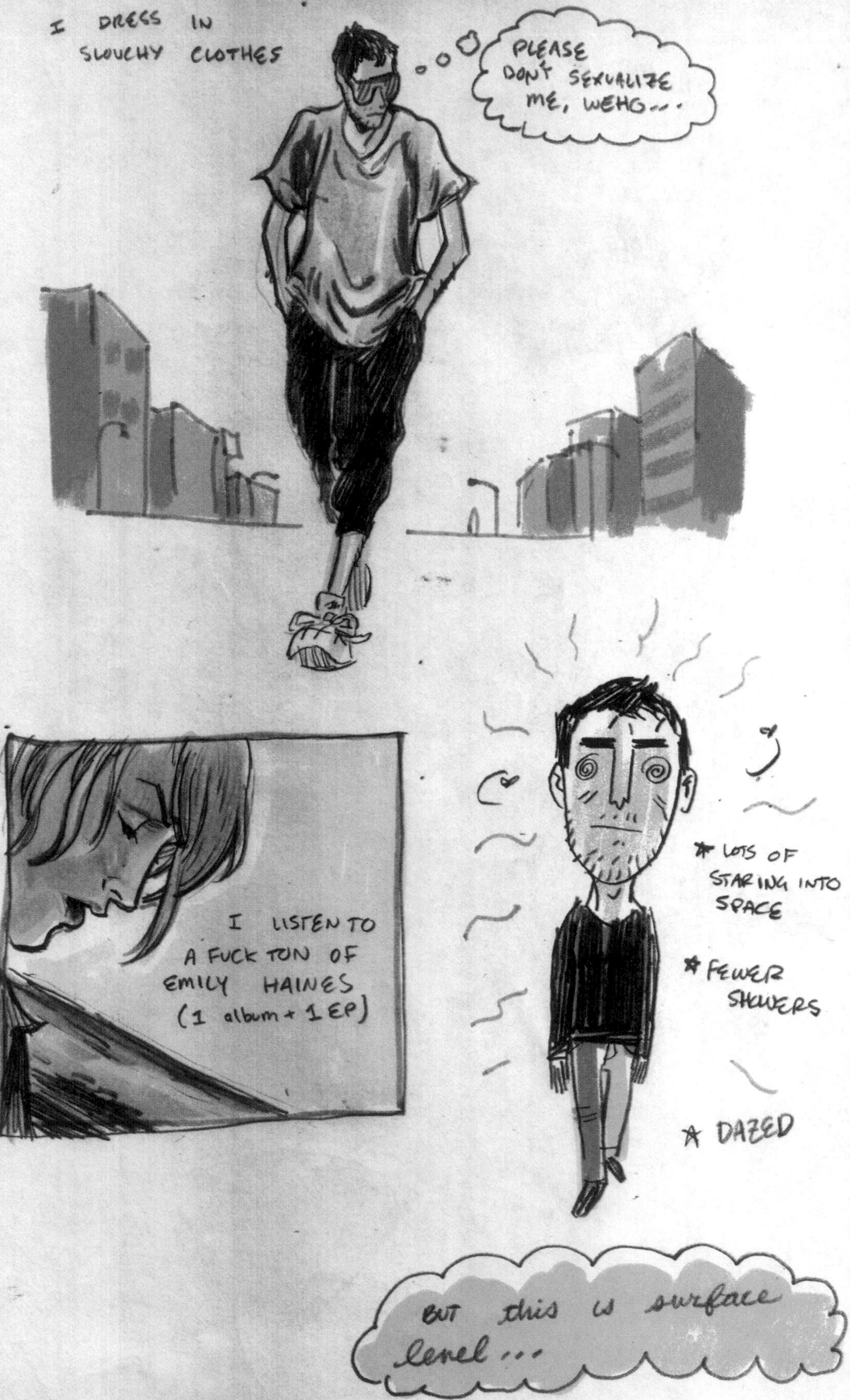

I DRESS IN SLOUCHY CLOTHES
PLEASE DON'T SEXUALIZE ME, WEHO...
I LISTEN TO A FUCK TON OF EMILY HAINES (1 album + 1 EP)
* LOTS OF STARING INTO SPACE
* FEWER SHOWERS
* DAZED
BUT this is surface level...

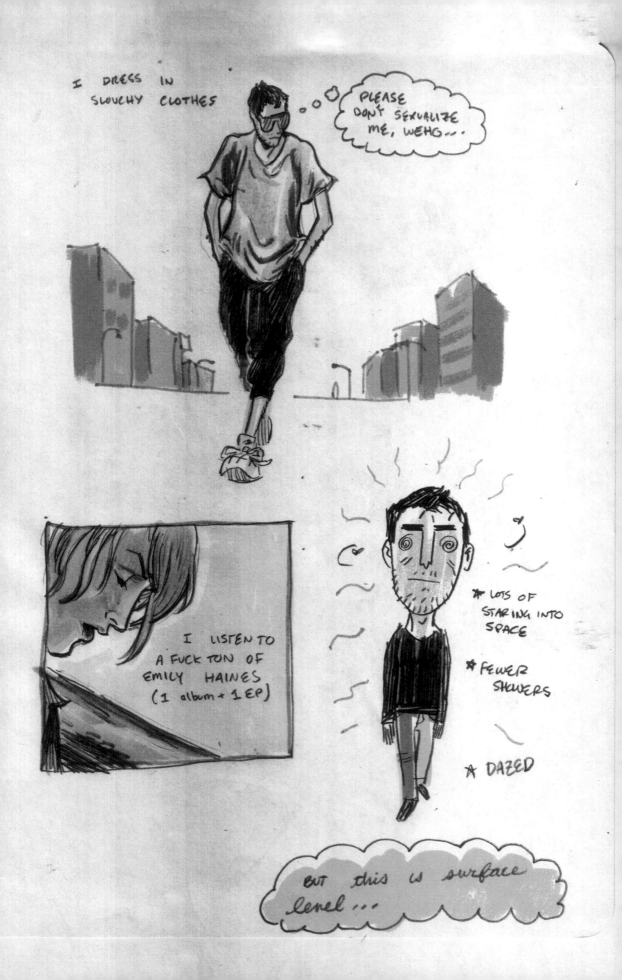

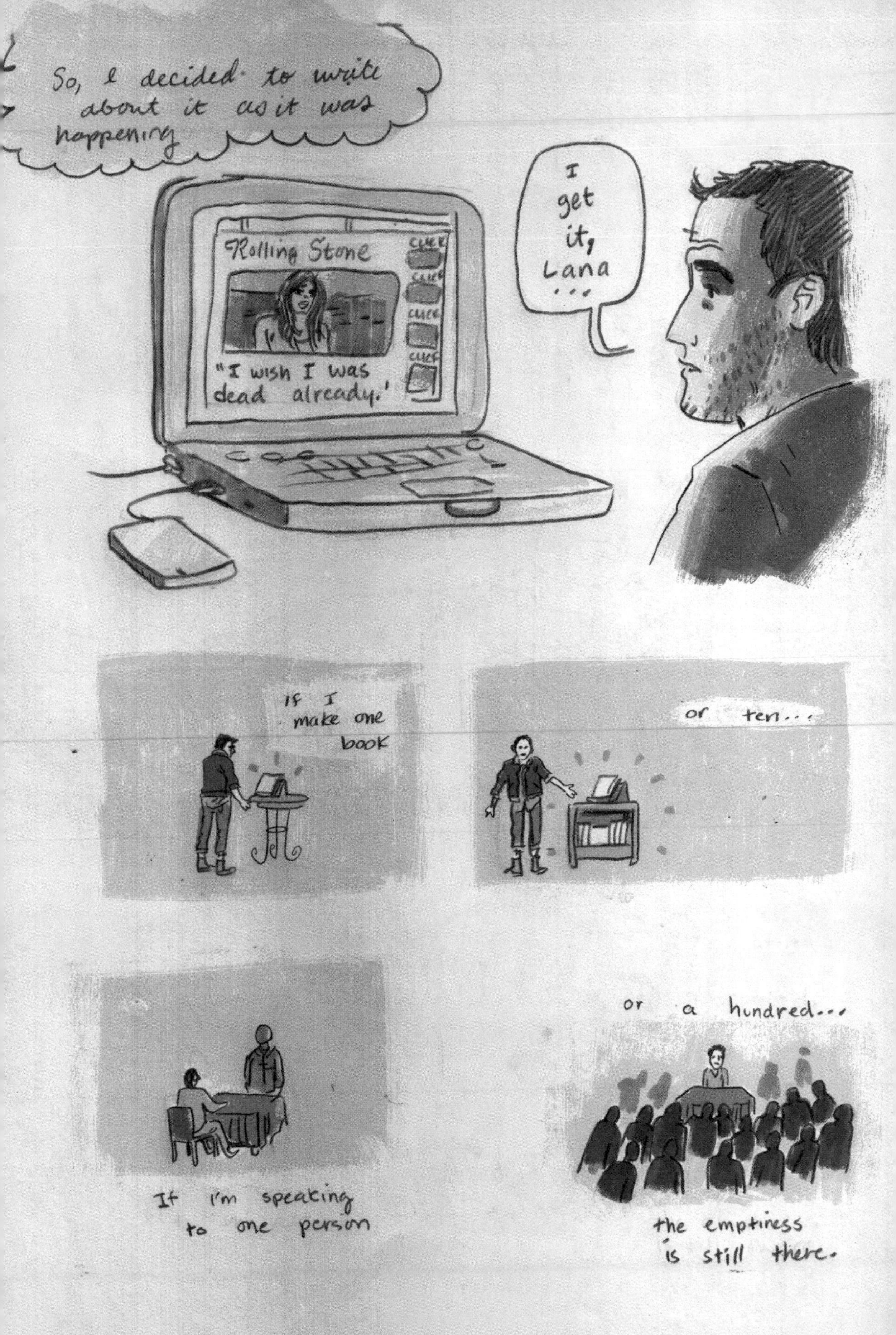
So, I decided to write about it as it was happening
Rolling Stone
CLICK
CLICK
CLICK
CLICK
"I wish I was dead already.'
I get it, Lana . . .
If I make one book
or ten . . .
If I'm speaking to one person
or a hundred . . .
the emptiness is still there.

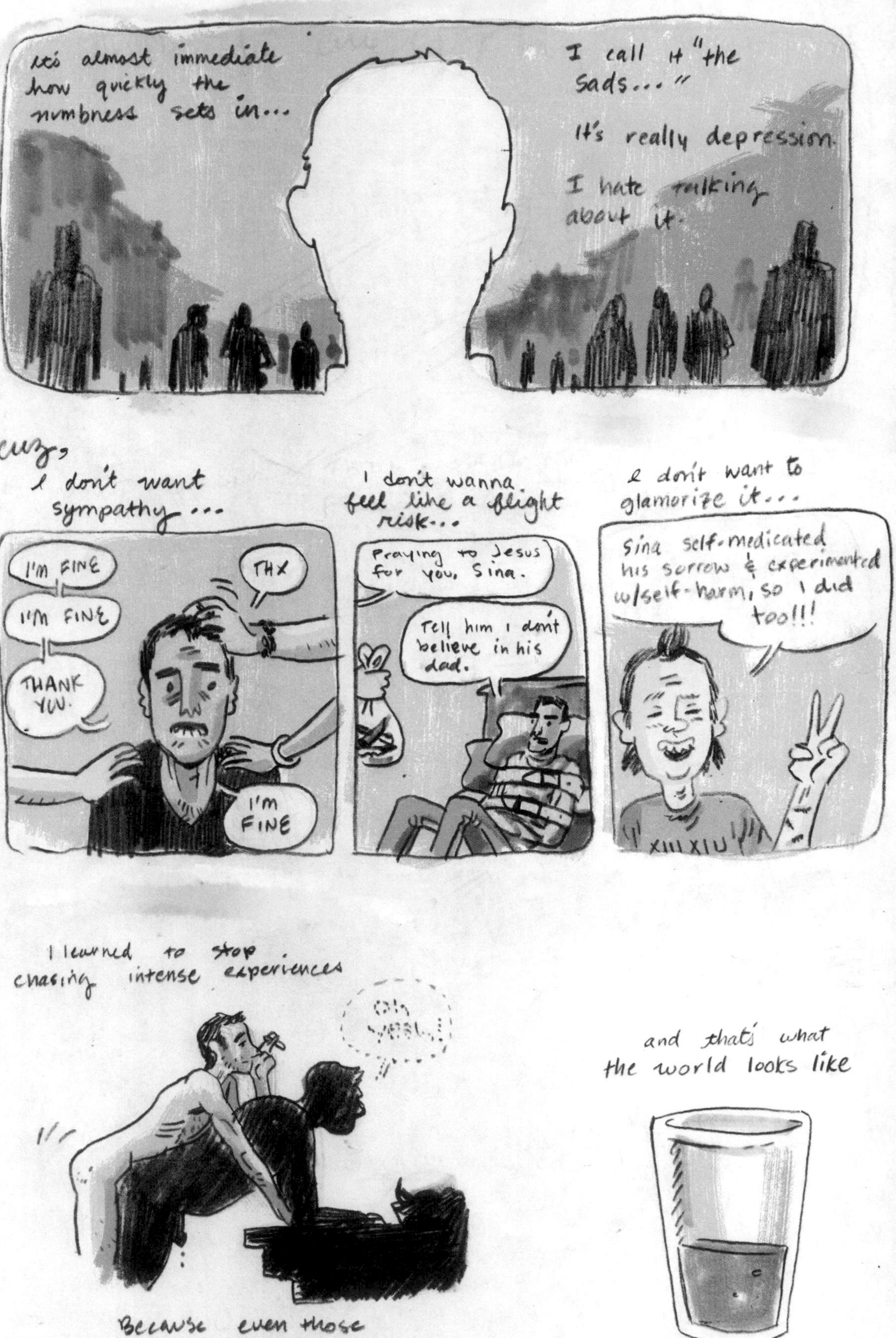
it's almost immediate how quickly the numbness sets in...
I call it "the sads..."
It's really depression.
I hate talking about it.
cuz,
I don't want sympathy...
I'M FINE
I'M FINE
THANK YOU.
THX
I'M FINE
I don't wanna feel like a flight risk...
Praying to Jesus for you, Sina.
Tell him I don't believe in his dad.
I don't want to glamorize it...
Sina self-medicated his sorrow & experimented w/self-harm, so I did too!!!
XIII XIV
I learned to stop chasing intense experiences
OH YEAH!
Because even those began to feel hollow
and that's what the world looks like
on a good day

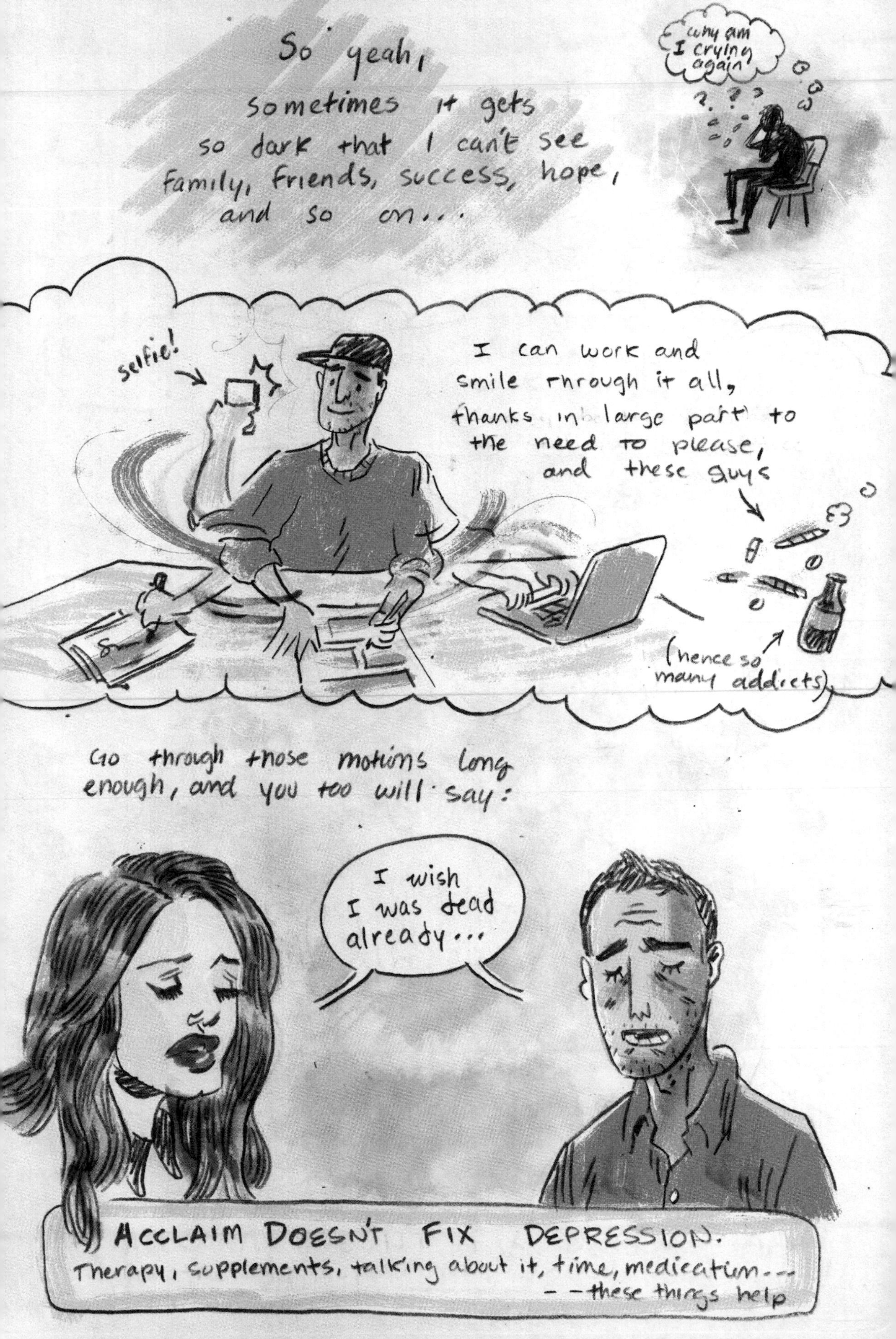
So yeah,
sometimes it gets so dark that I can't see family, friends, success, hope, and so on...
why am I crying again
I can work and smile through it all, thanks in large part to the need to please, and these guys
selfie!
(hence so many addicts)
Go through those motions long enough, and you too will say:
I wish I was dead already...
ACCLAIM DOESN'T FIX DEPRESSION.
Therapy, supplements, talking about it, time, medication...
--these things help

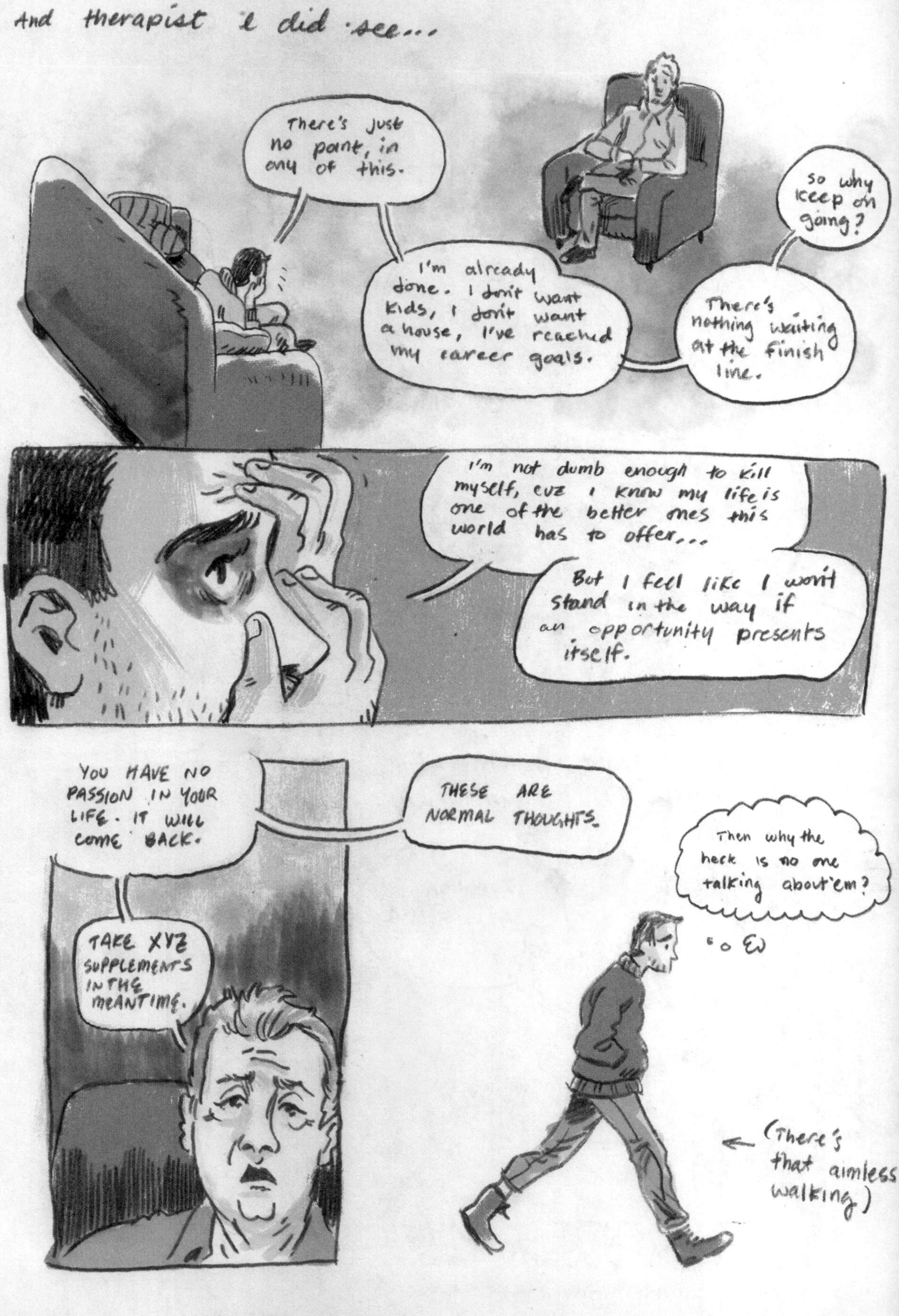
And therapist I did see...
There's just no point, in any of this.
I'm already done. I don't want kids, I don't want a house, I've reached my career goals.
There's nothing waiting at the finish line.
So why keep on going?
I'm not dumb enough to kill myself, cuz I know my life is one of the better ones this world has to offer...
But I feel like I won't stand in the way if an opportunity presents itself.
YOU HAVE NO PASSION IN YOUR LIFE. IT WILL COME BACK.
THESE ARE NORMAL THOUGHTS.
TAKE XYZ SUPPLEMENTS IN THE MEANTIME.
Then why the heck is no one talking about 'em?
(There's that aimless walking)

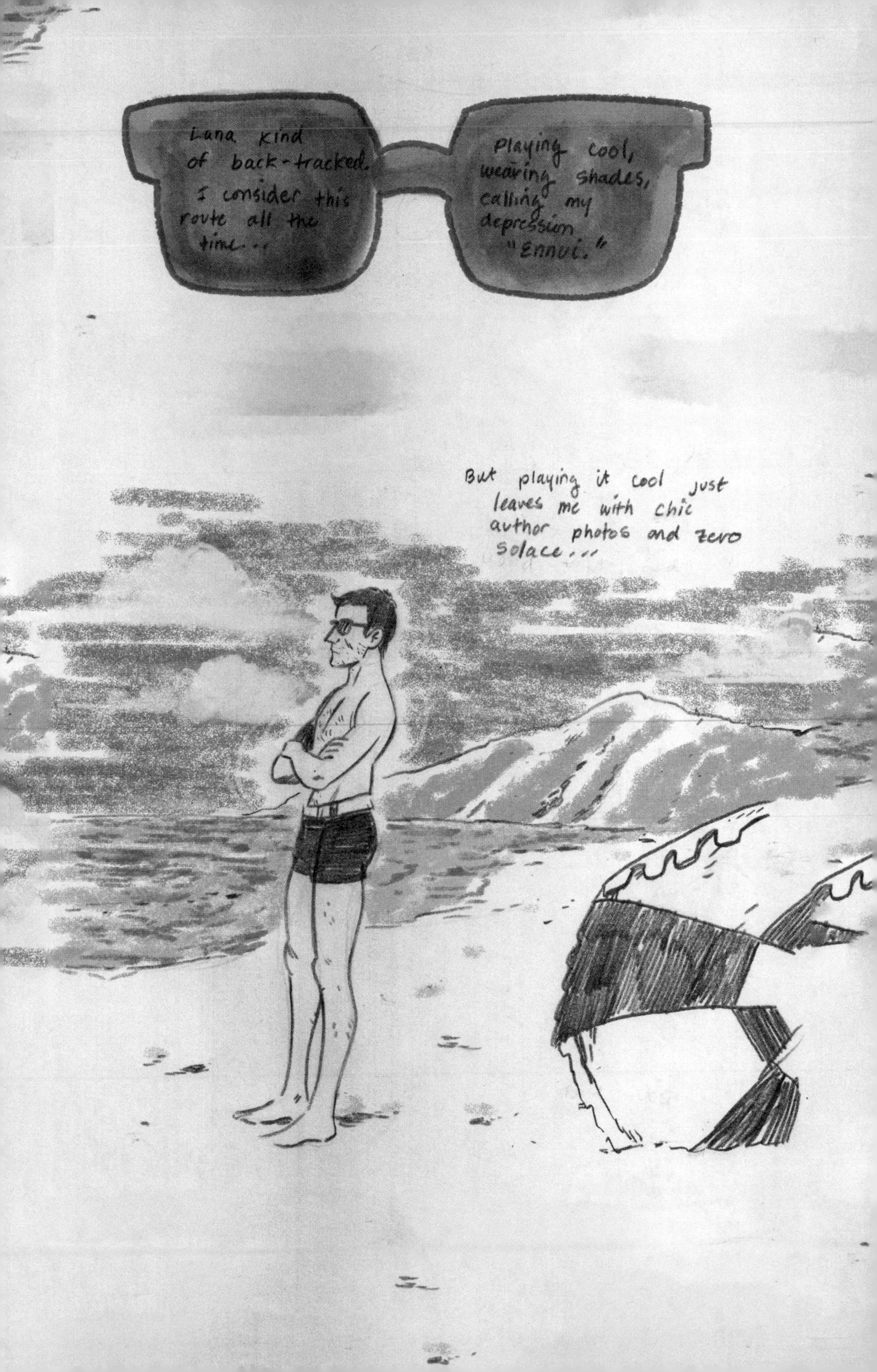
Lana kind of back-tracked. I consider this route all the time...
Playing cool, wearing shades, calling my depression "Ennui."
But playing it cool just leaves me with chic author photos and zero solace...

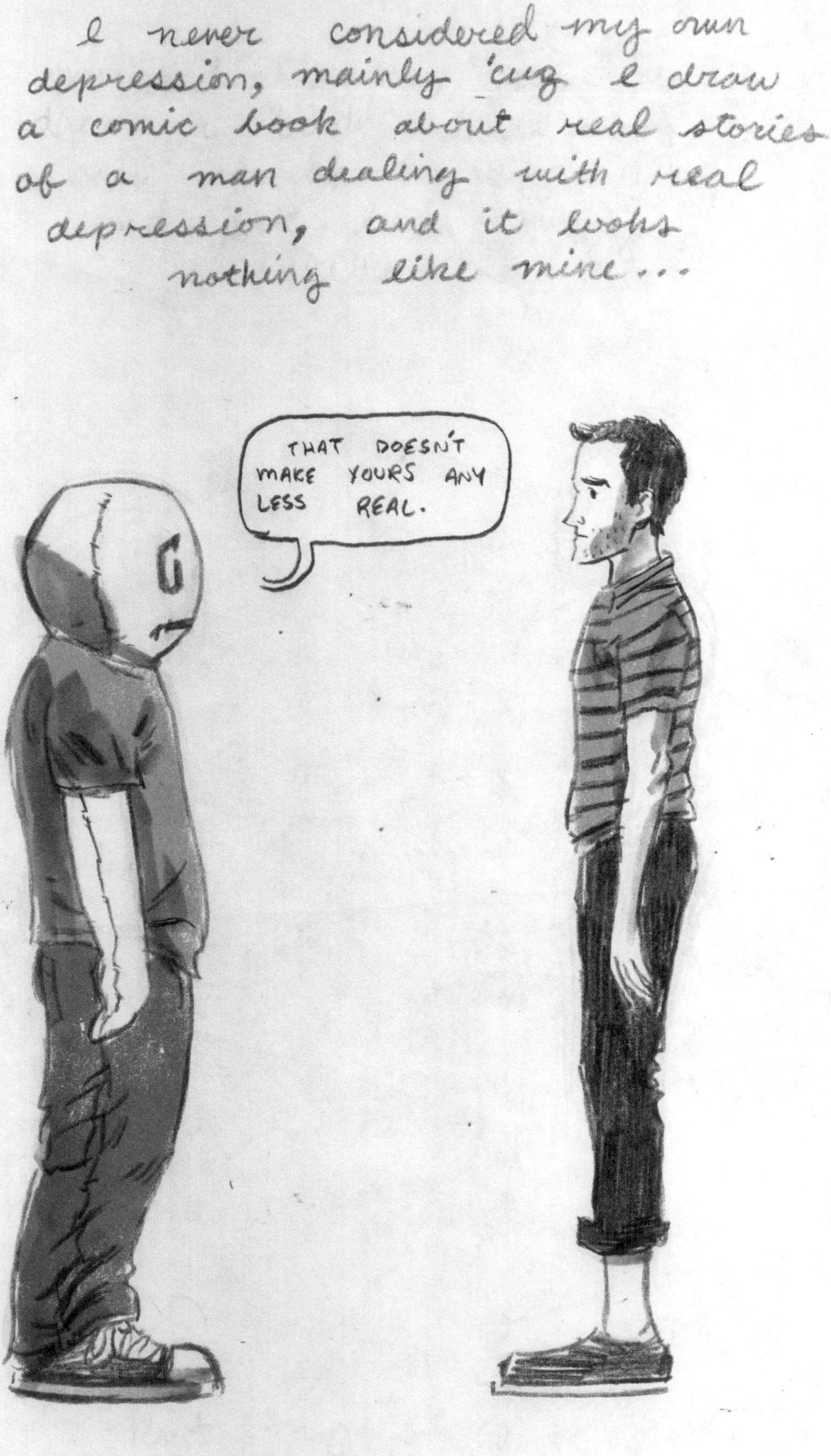
I never considered my own depression, mainly 'cuz I draw a comic book about real stories of a man dealing with real depression, and it looks nothing like mine...
THAT DOESN'T MAKE YOURS ANY LESS REAL.

when the sads fade away, it's easy
to swipe them under the rug...

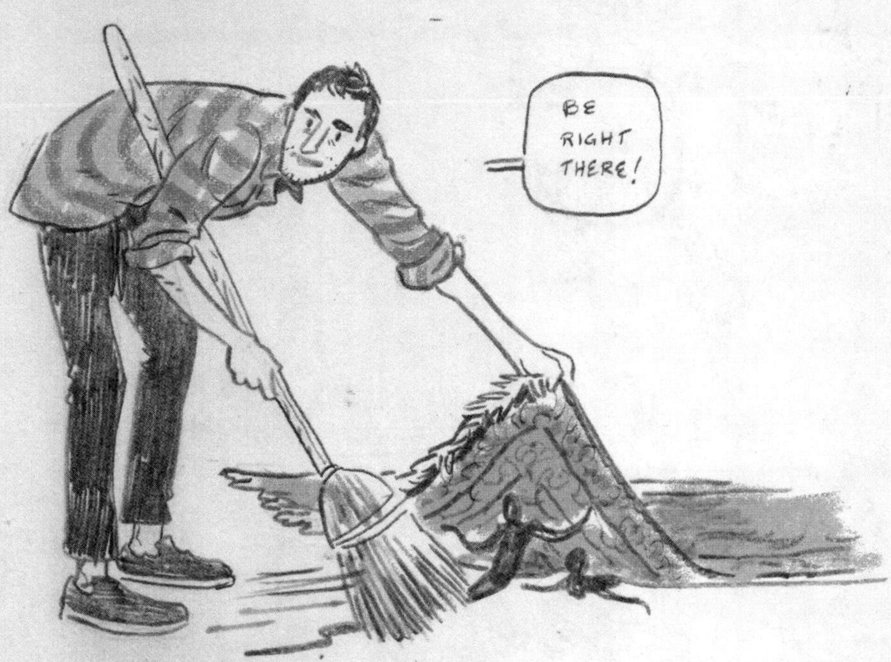
BE RIGHT THERE!

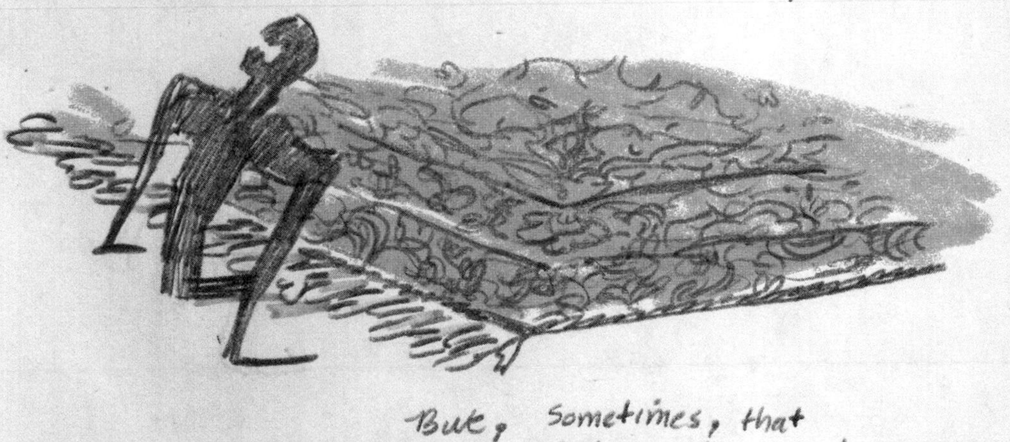

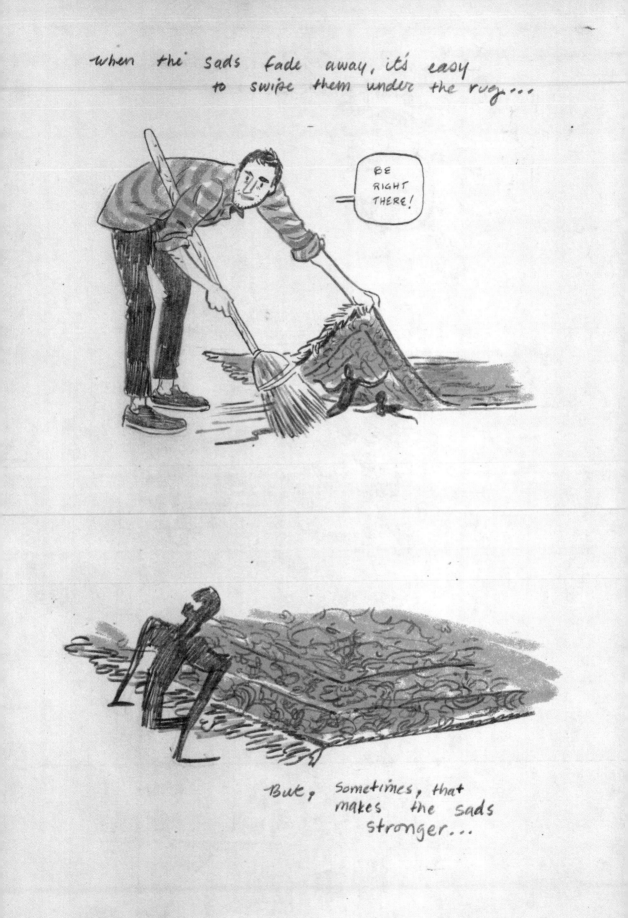

But, sometimes, that
makes the sads
stronger...

which leads to...

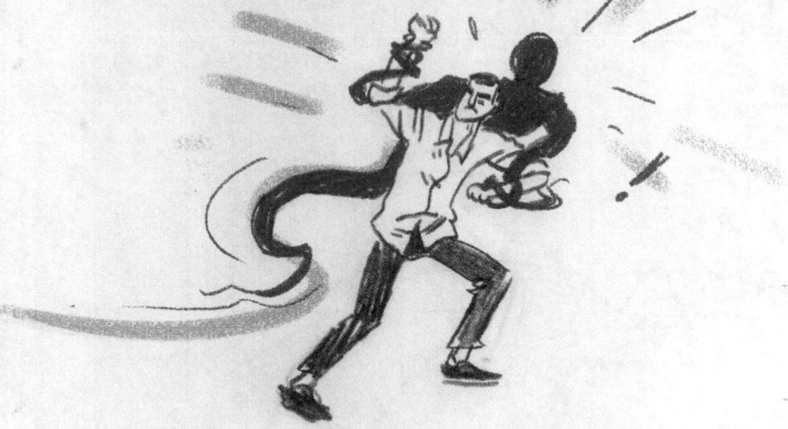

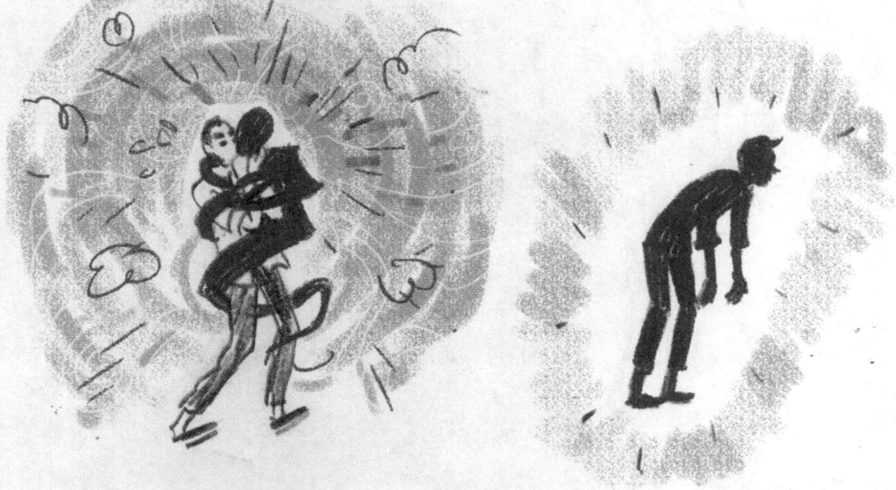

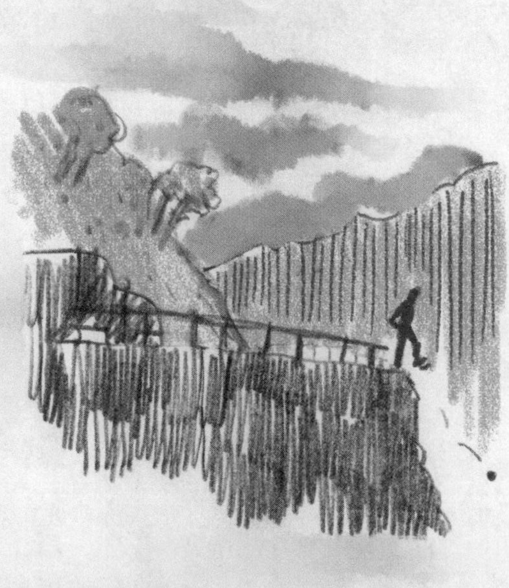

and you end up here.

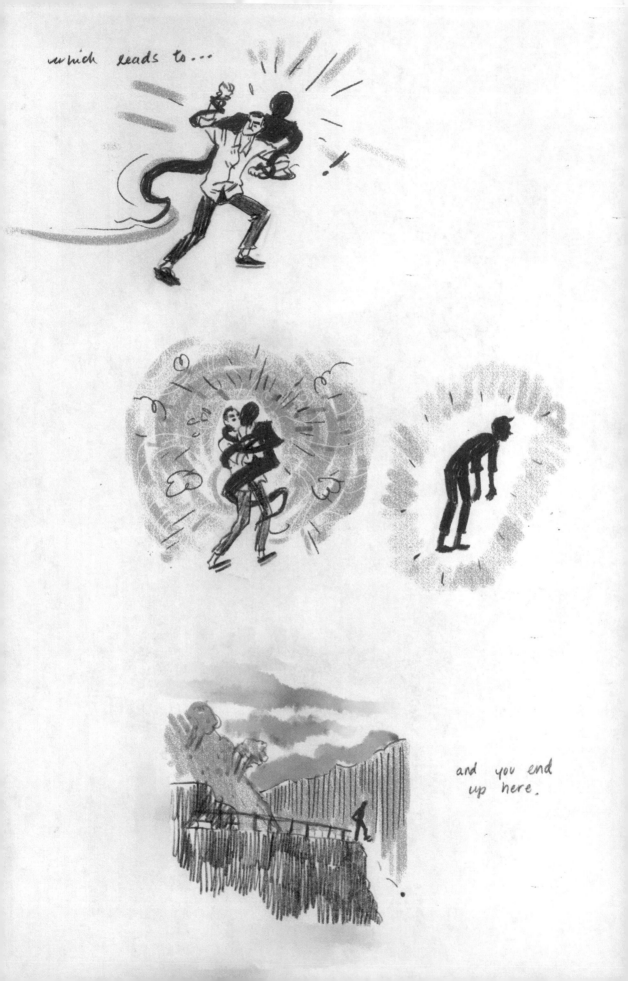

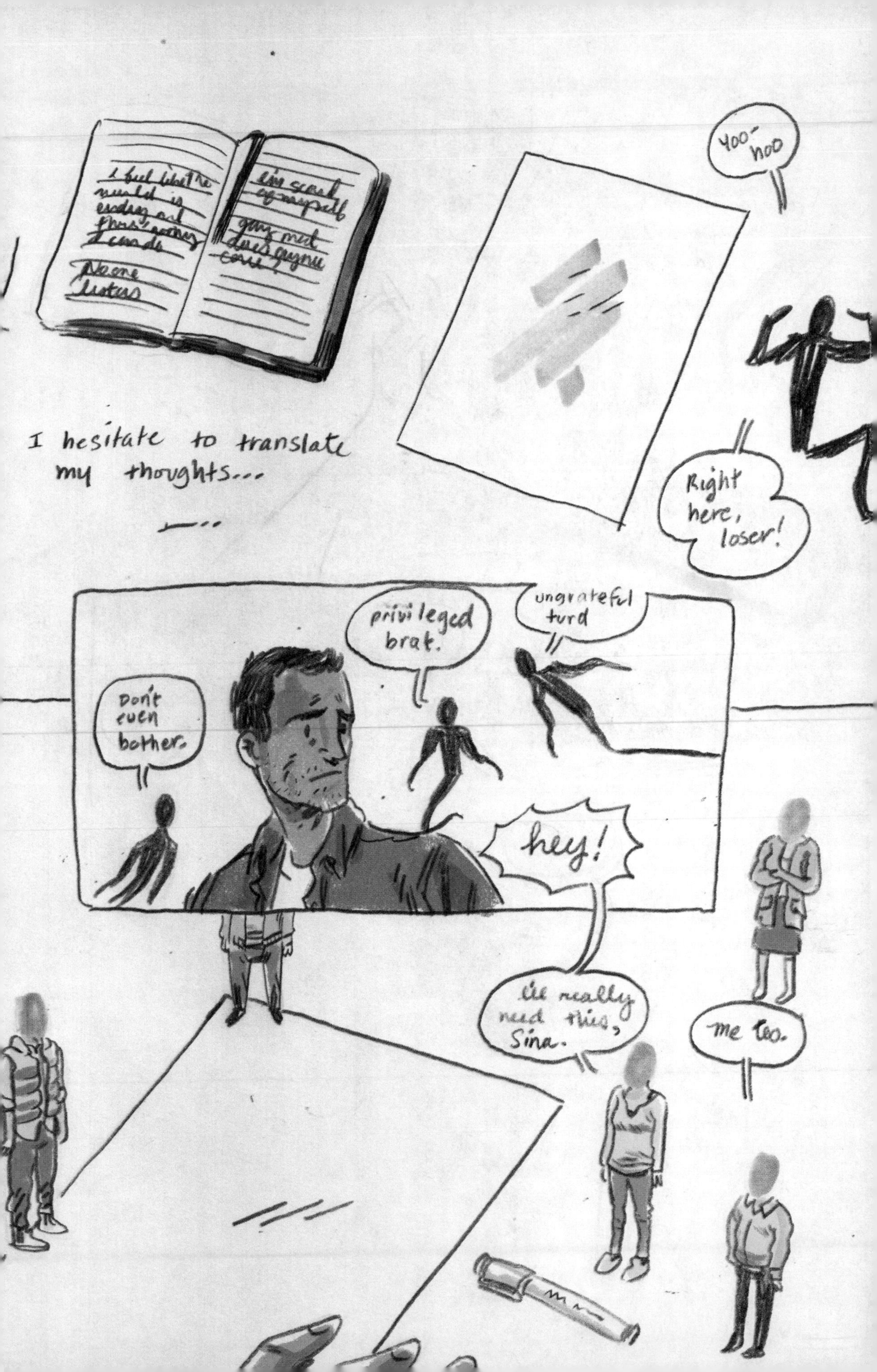

I hesitate to translate my thoughts...
Yoo-hoo
Right here, loser!
privileged brat.
ungrateful turd
Don't even bother.
hey!
We really need this, Sina.
me too.

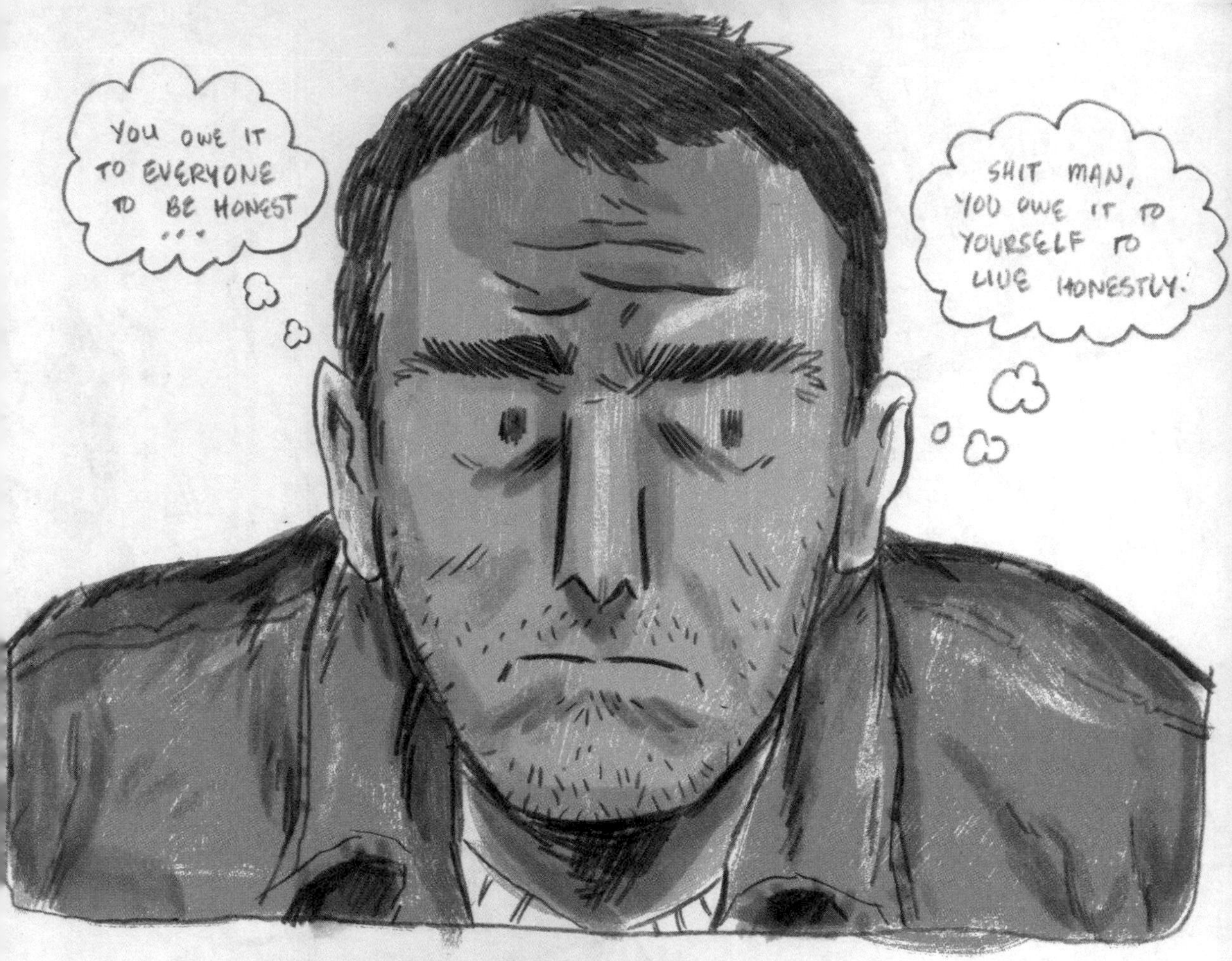
YOU OWE IT TO EVERYONE TO BE HONEST ...
SHIT MAN, YOU OWE IT TO YOURSELF TO LIVE HONESTLY.

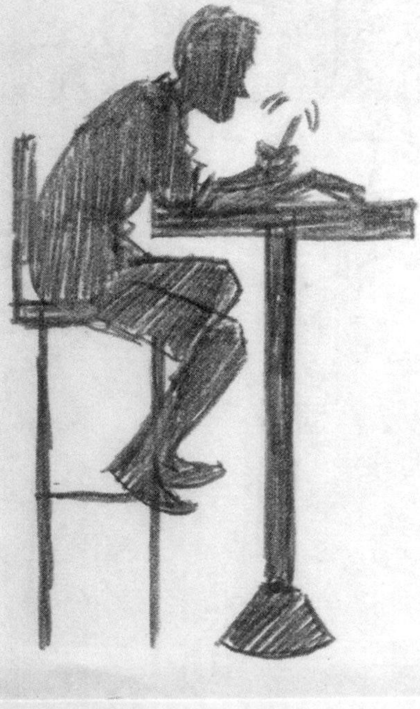

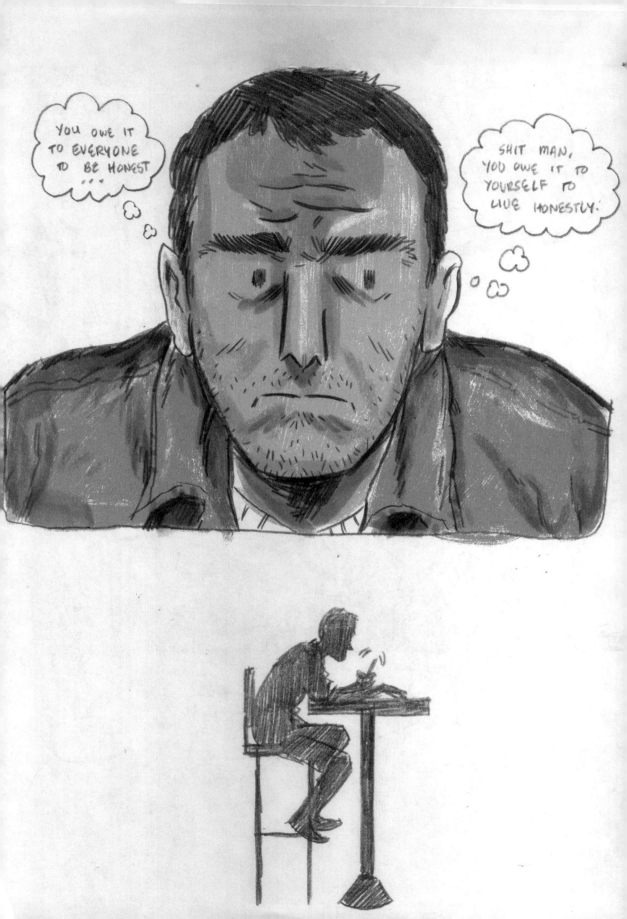

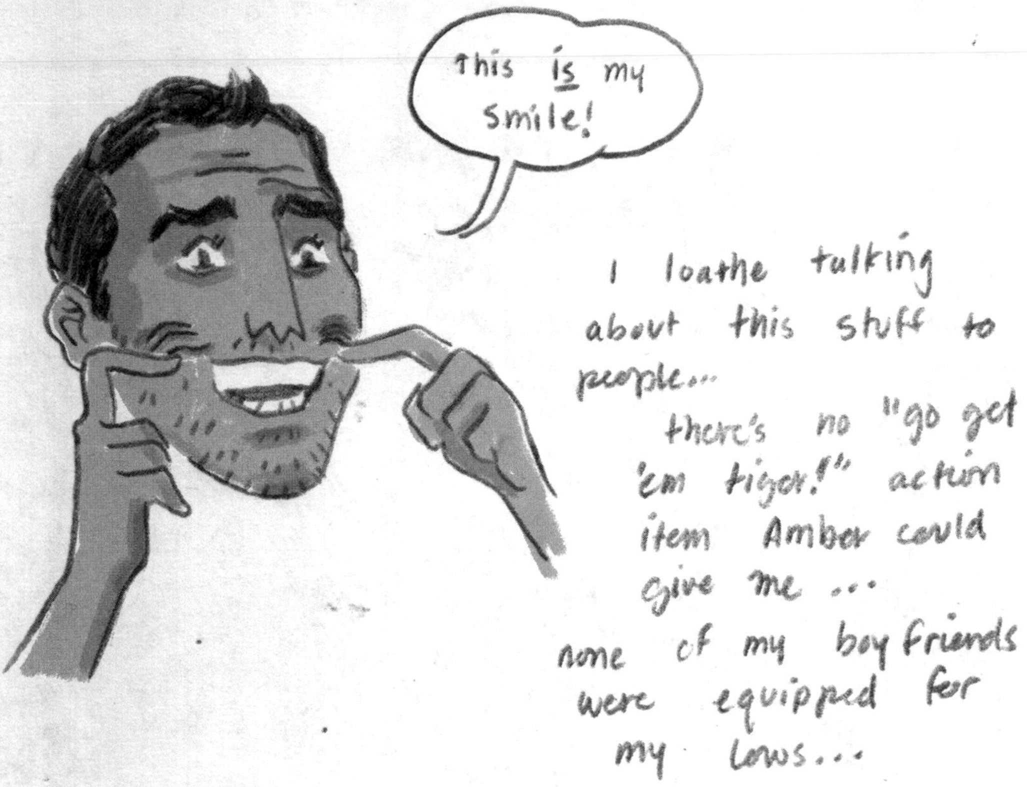
This is my smile!
I loathe talking about this stuff to people... there's no "go get 'em tiger!" action item Amber could give me... none of my boyfriends were equipped for my lows...

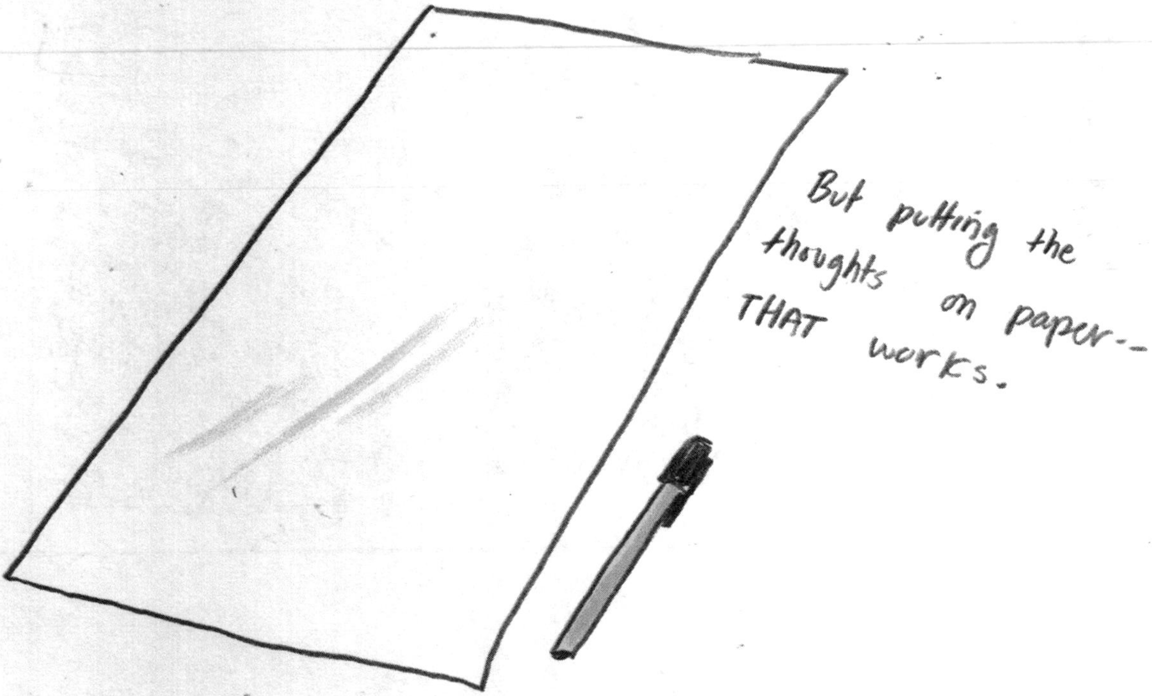
But putting the thoughts on paper-- THAT works.

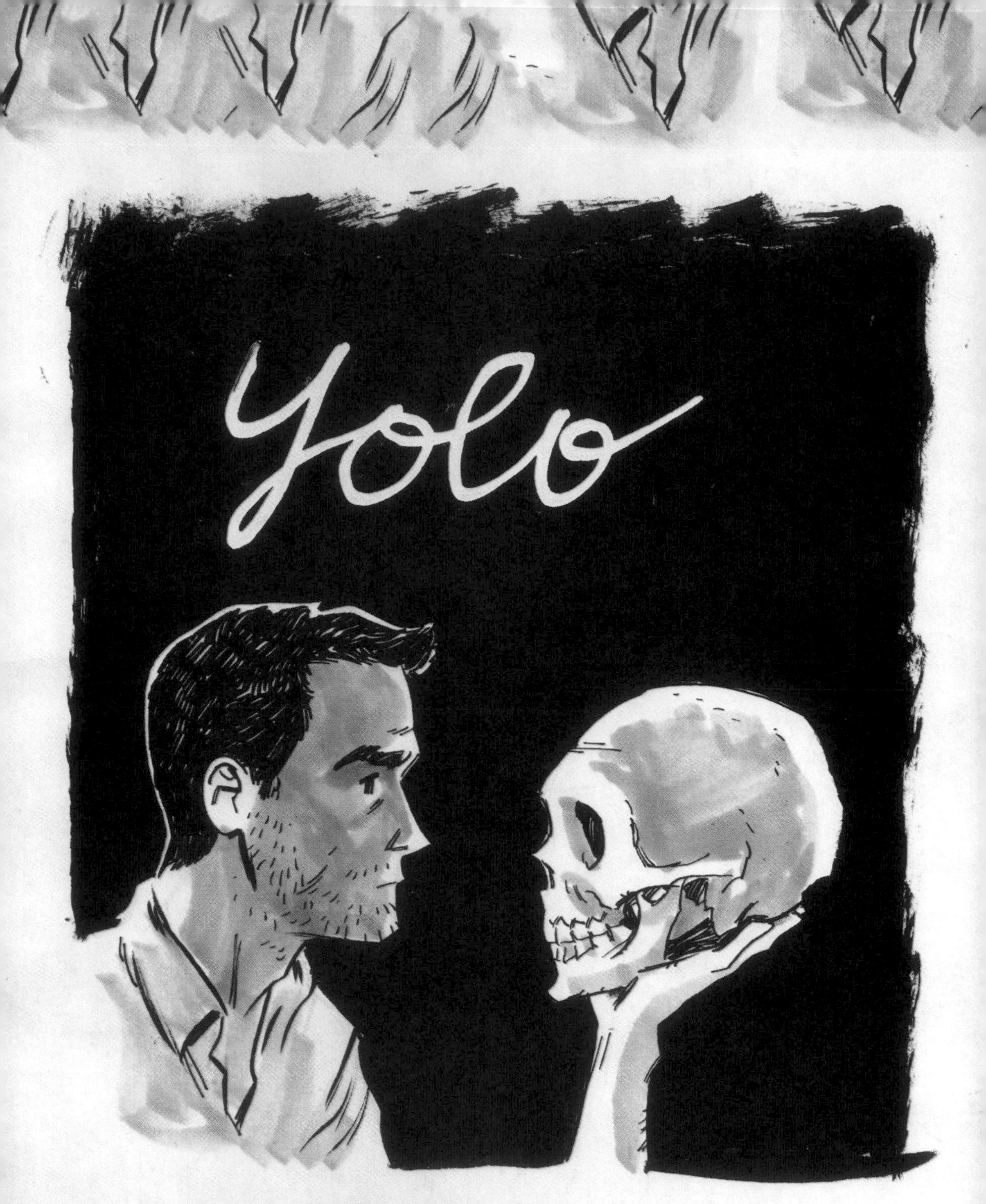
Yolo

9.

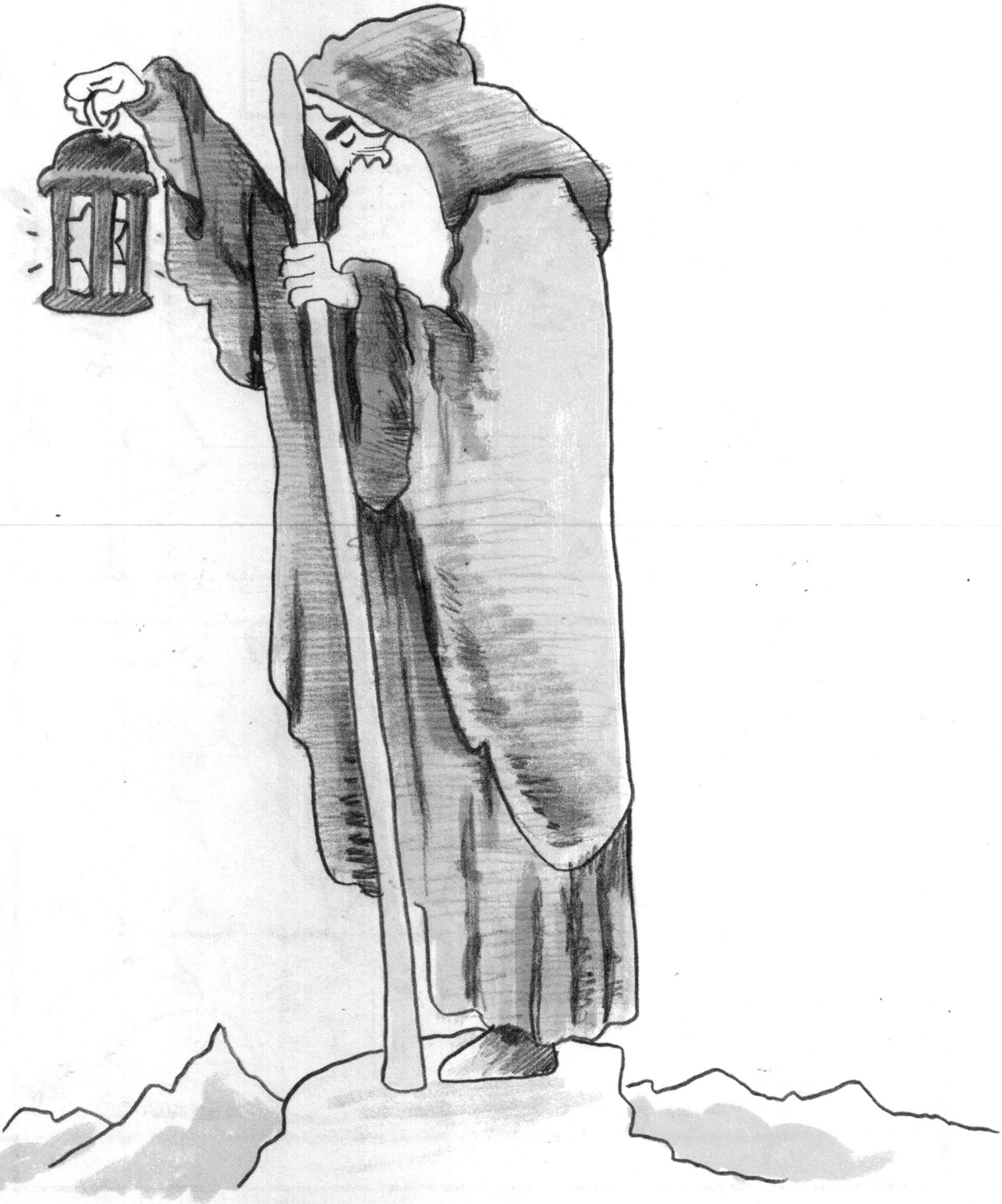

A SIDEBAR...

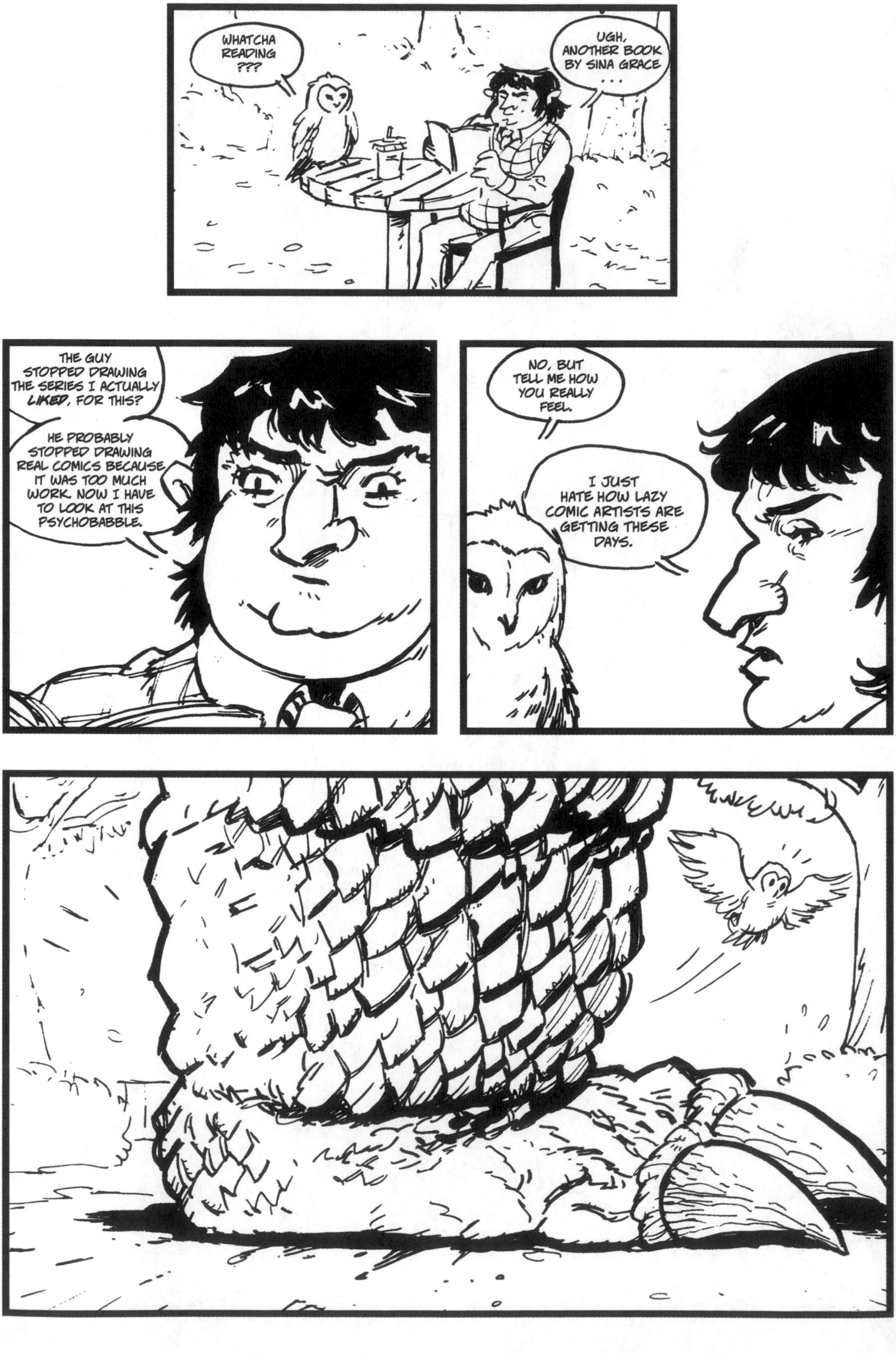
WHATCHA READING ???
UGH, ANOTHER BOOK BY SINA GRACE . . .
THE GUY STOPPED DRAWING THE SERIES I ACTUALLY *LIKED*, FOR THIS?
HE PROBABLY STOPPED DRAWING REAL COMICS BECAUSE IT WAS TOO MUCH WORK. NOW I HAVE TO LOOK AT THIS PSYCHOBABBLE.
NO, BUT TELL ME HOW YOU REALLY FEEL.
I JUST HATE HOW LAZY COMIC ARTISTS ARE GETTING THESE DAYS.

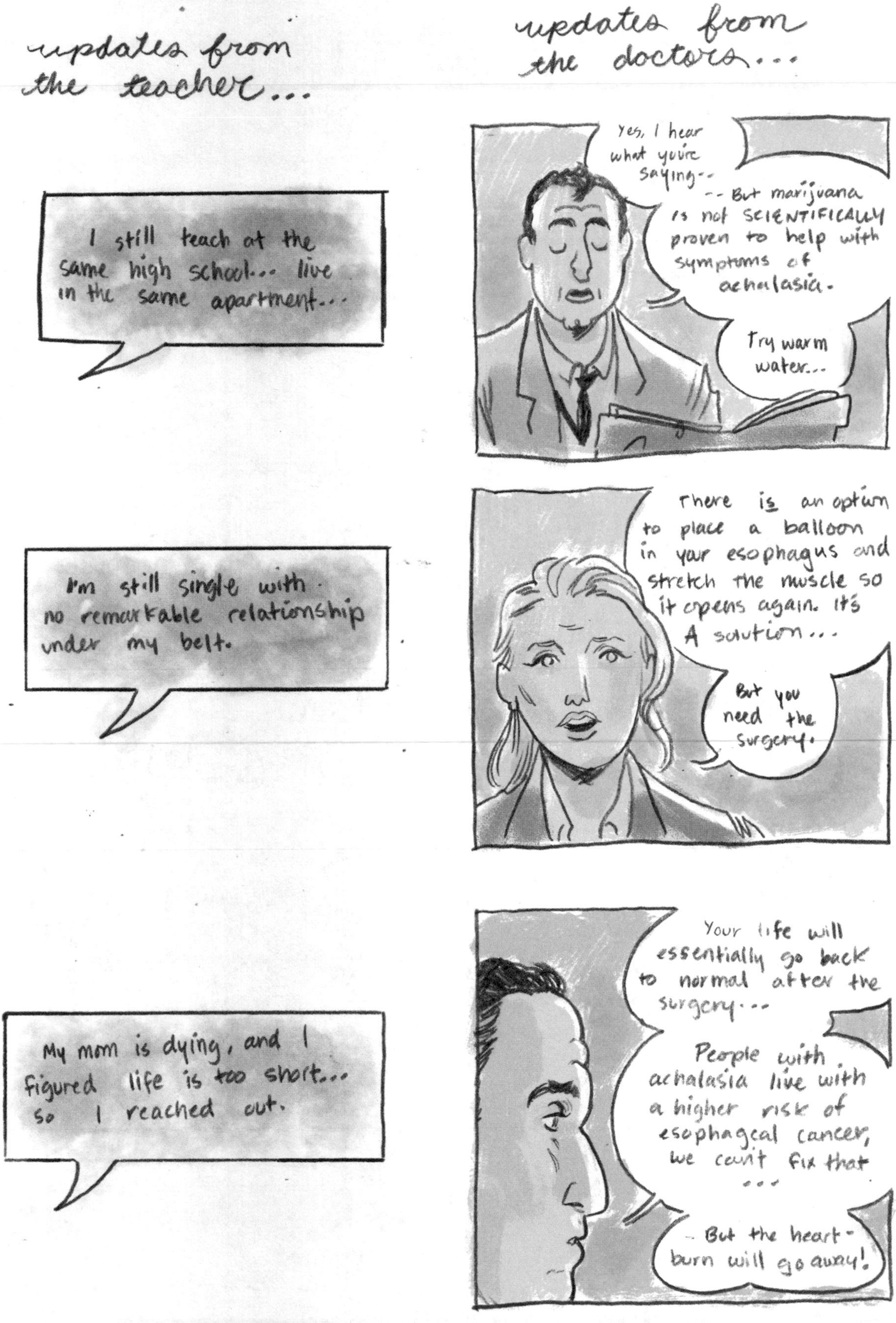
updates from the teacher...
updates from the doctors...
I still teach at the same high school... live in the same apartment...
Yes, I hear what you're saying--
--But marijuana is not SCIENTIFICALLY proven to help with symptoms of achalasia.
Try warm water...
I'm still single with no remarkable relationship under my belt.
There is an option to place a balloon in your esophagus and stretch the muscle so it opens again. It's A solution...
But you need the surgery.
My mom is dying, and I figured life is too short... so I reached out.
Your life will essentially go back to normal after the surgery...
People with achalasia live with a higher risk of esophageal cancer, we can't fix that...
-But the heart-burn will go away!

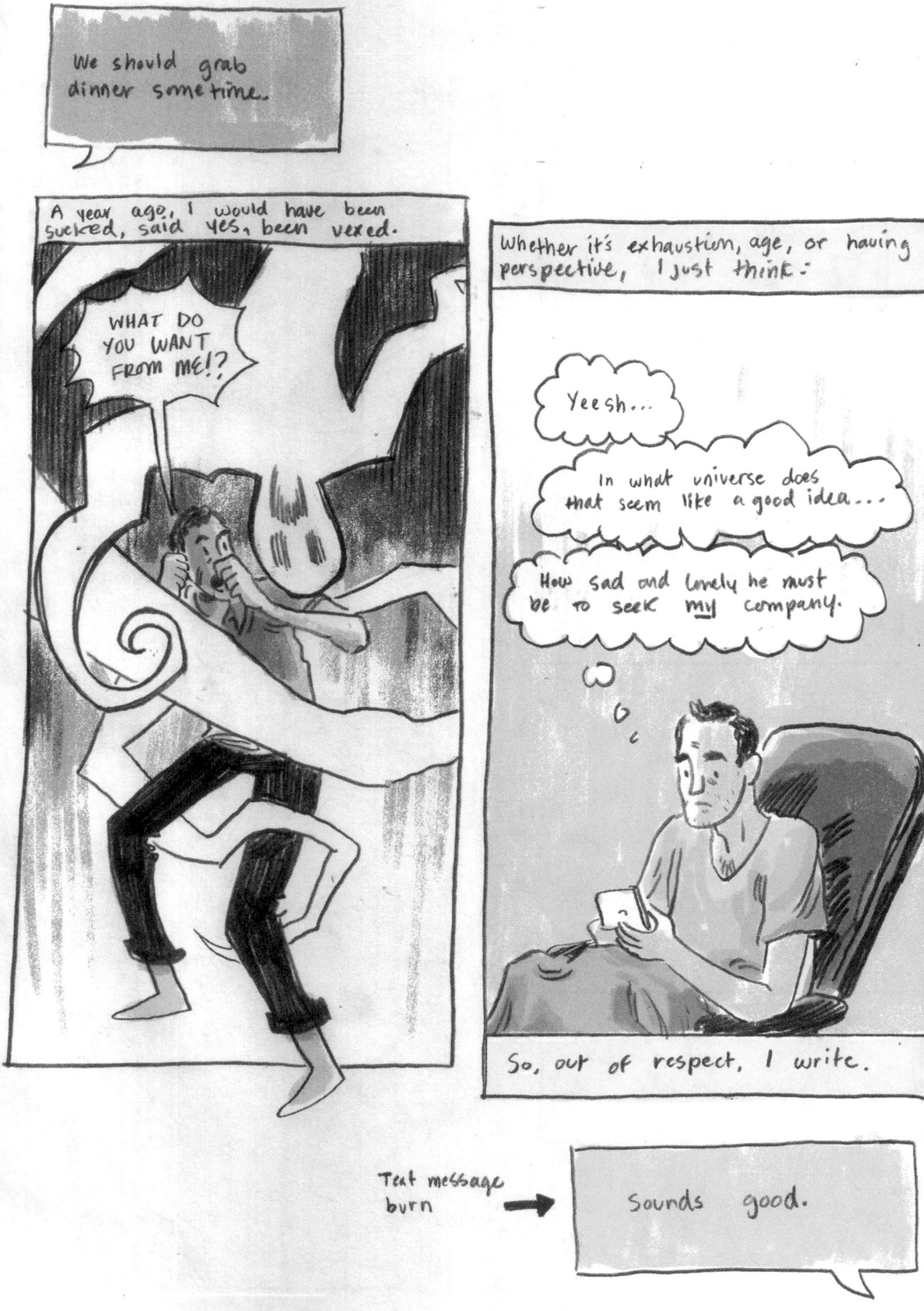

We should grab dinner sometime.
A year ago, I would have been sucked, said yes, been vexed.
WHAT DO YOU WANT FROM ME!?
Whether it's exhaustion, age, or having perspective, I just think:
Yeesh...
In what universe does that seem like a good idea...
How sad and lonely he must be to seek my company.
So, out of respect, I write.
Text message burn
Sounds good.

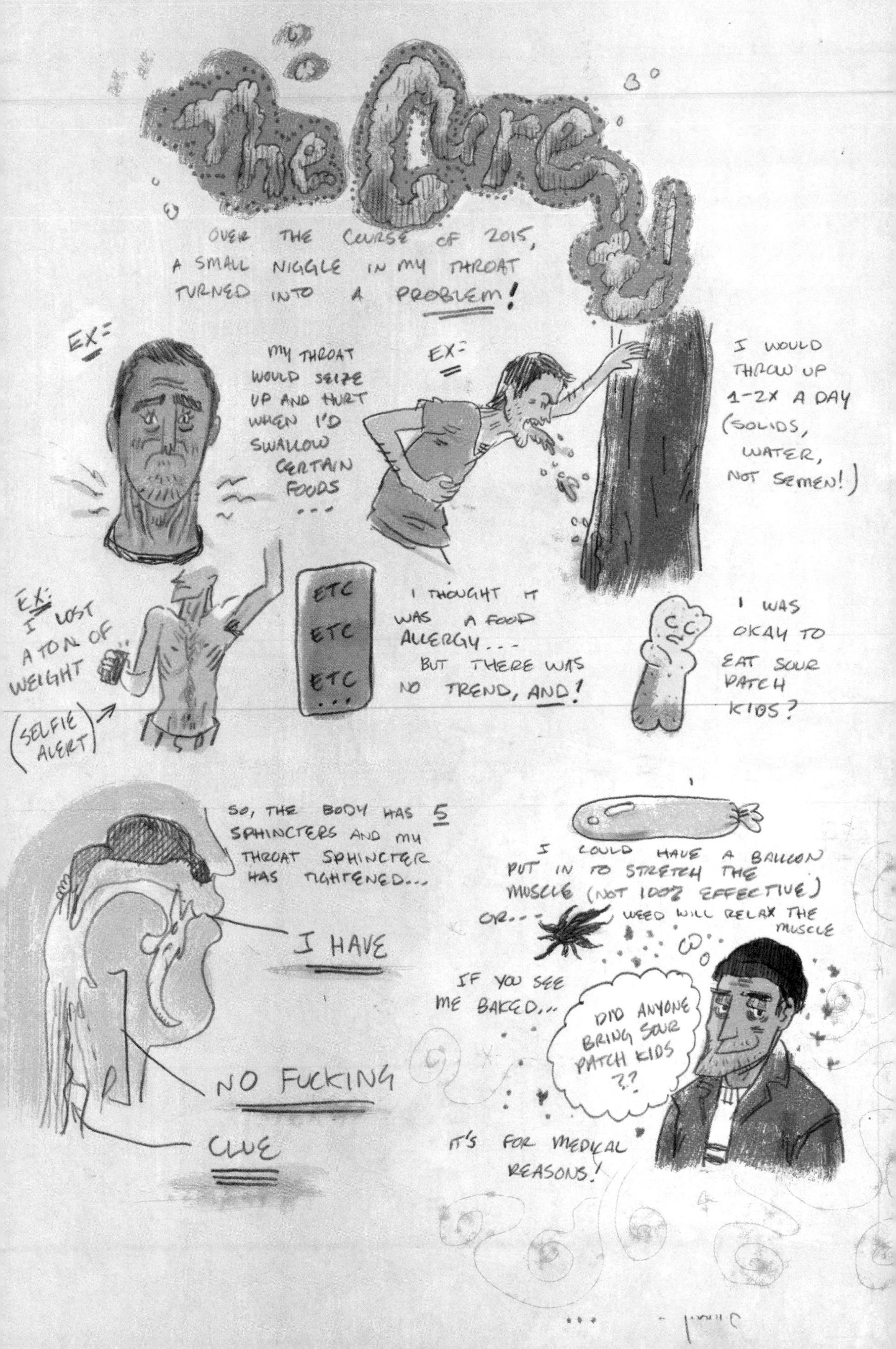
OVER THE COURSE OF 2015, A SMALL NIGGLE IN MY THROAT TURNED INTO A PROBLEM!
EX:
MY THROAT WOULD SEIZE UP AND HURT WHEN I'D SWALLOW CERTAIN FOODS...
EX:
I WOULD THROW UP 1-2X A DAY (SOLIDS, WATER, NOT SEMEN!)
EX: I LOST A TON OF WEIGHT
(SELFIE ALERT)
ETC
ETC
ETC...
I THOUGHT IT WAS A FOOD ALLERGY... BUT THERE WAS NO TREND, AND!
I WAS OKAY TO EAT SOUR PATCH KIDS?
SO, THE BODY HAS 5 SPHINCTERS AND MY THROAT SPHINCTER HAS TIGHTENED...
I HAVE
NO FUCKING
CLUE
I COULD HAVE A BALLOON PUT IN TO STRETCH THE MUSCLE (NOT 100% EFFECTIVE)
OR...
WEED WILL RELAX THE MUSCLE
IF YOU SEE ME BAKED...
DID ANYONE BRING SOUR PATCH KIDS ??
IT'S FOR MEDICAL REASONS!

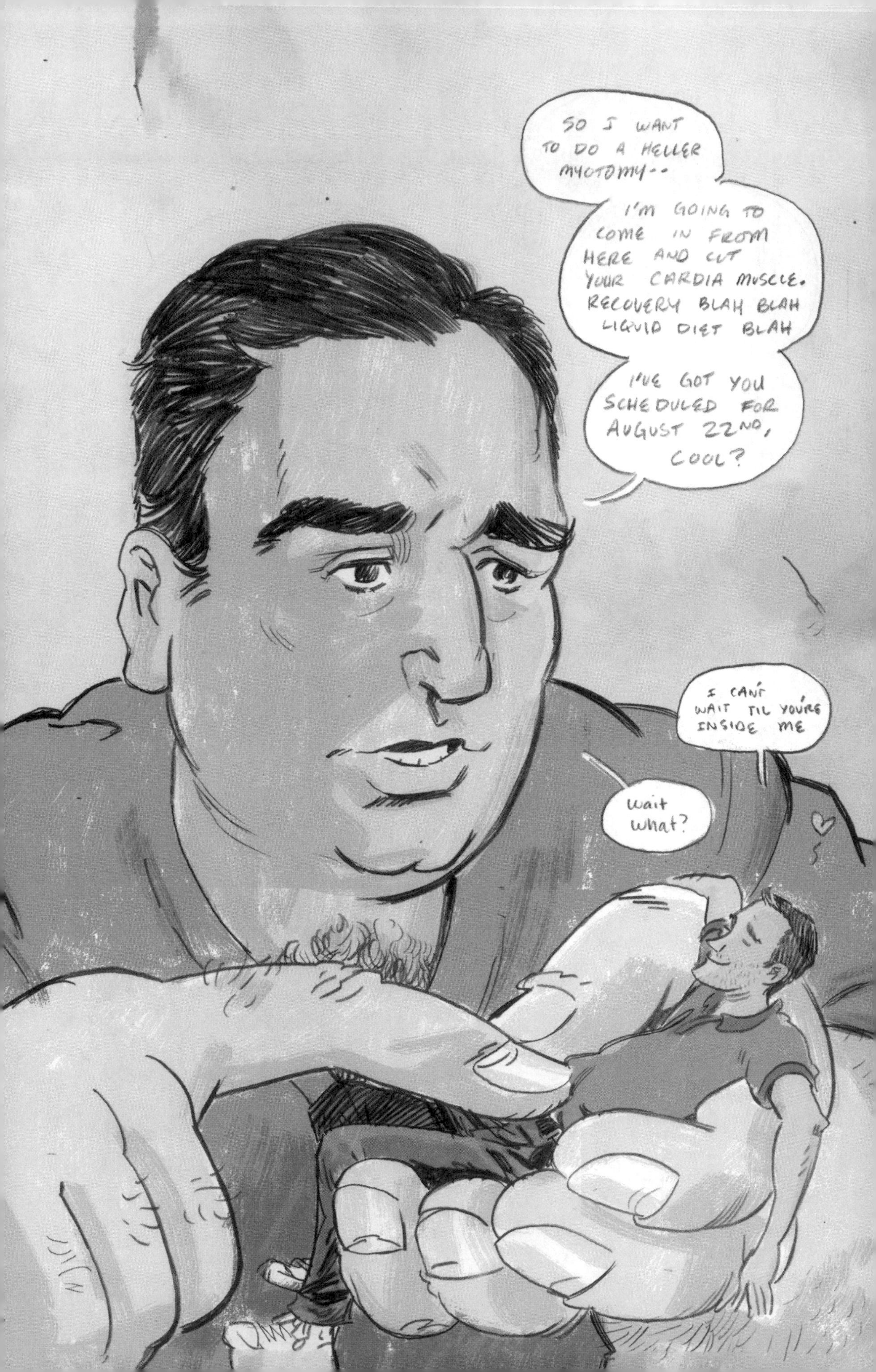
SO I WANT TO DO A HELLER MYOTOMY--
I'M GOING TO COME IN FROM HERE AND CUT YOUR CARDIA MUSCLE. RECOVERY BLAH BLAH LIQUID DIET BLAH
I'VE GOT YOU SCHEDULED FOR AUGUST 22ND, COOL?
I CAN'T WAIT TIL YOU'RE INSIDE ME
Wait what?

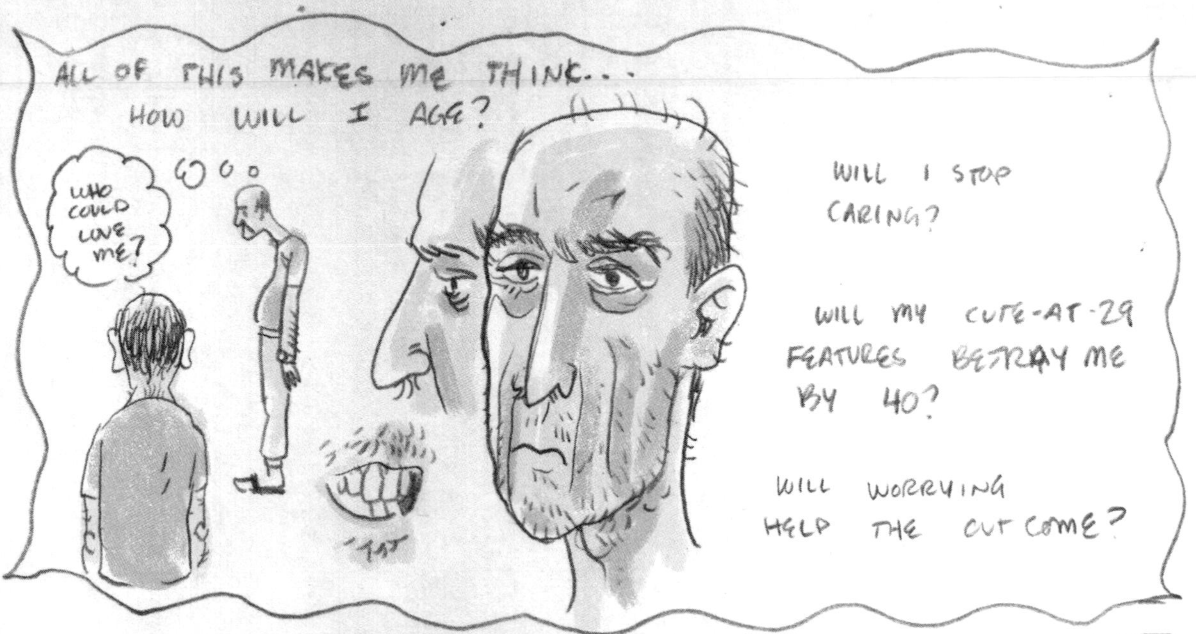
ALL OF THIS MAKES ME THINK...
HOW WILL I AGE?
WHO COULD LOVE ME?
WILL I STOP CARING?
WILL MY CUTE-AT-29 FEATURES BETRAY ME BY 40?
WILL WORRYING HELP THE OUTCOME?

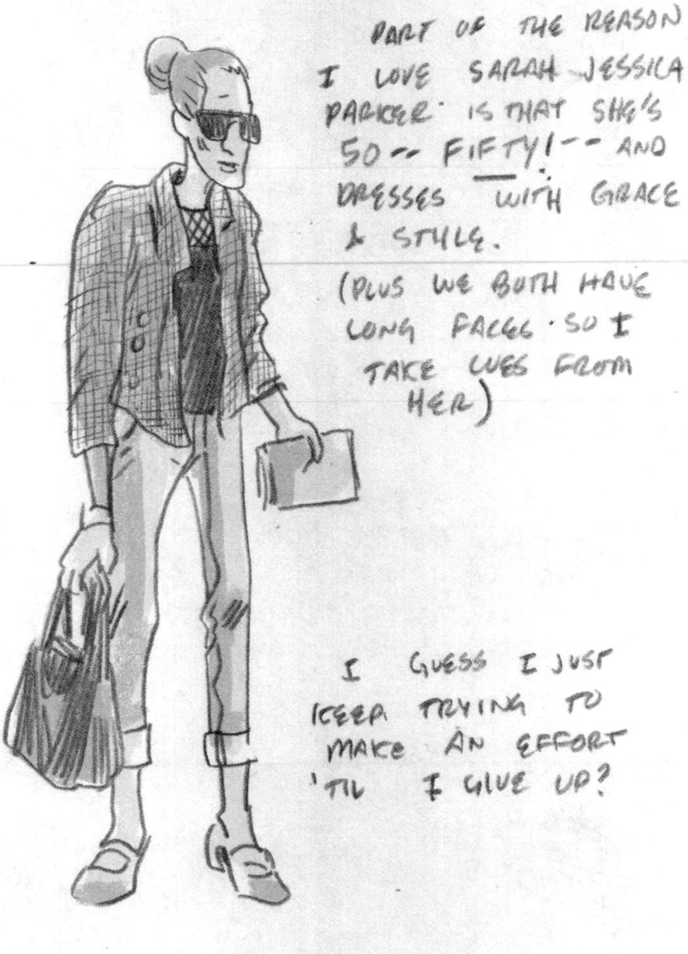
PART OF THE REASON I LOVE SARAH JESSICA PARKER IS THAT SHE'S 50 -- FIFTY! -- AND DRESSES WITH GRACE & STYLE.
(PLUS WE BOTH HAVE LONG FACES SO I TAKE CUES FROM HER)
I GUESS I JUST KEEP TRYING TO MAKE AN EFFORT 'TIL I GIVE UP?

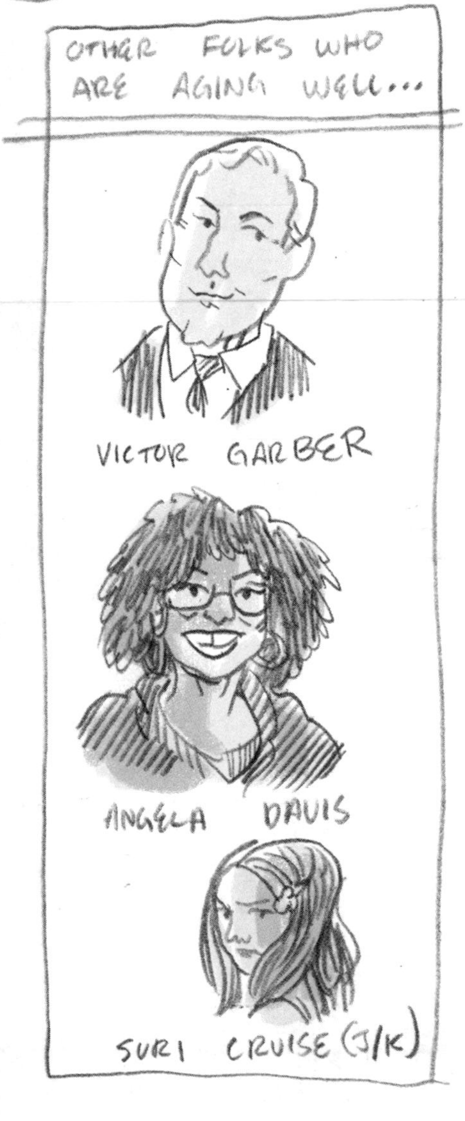
OTHER FOLKS WHO ARE AGING WELL...
VICTOR GARBER
ANGELA DAVIS
SURI CRUISE (J/K)

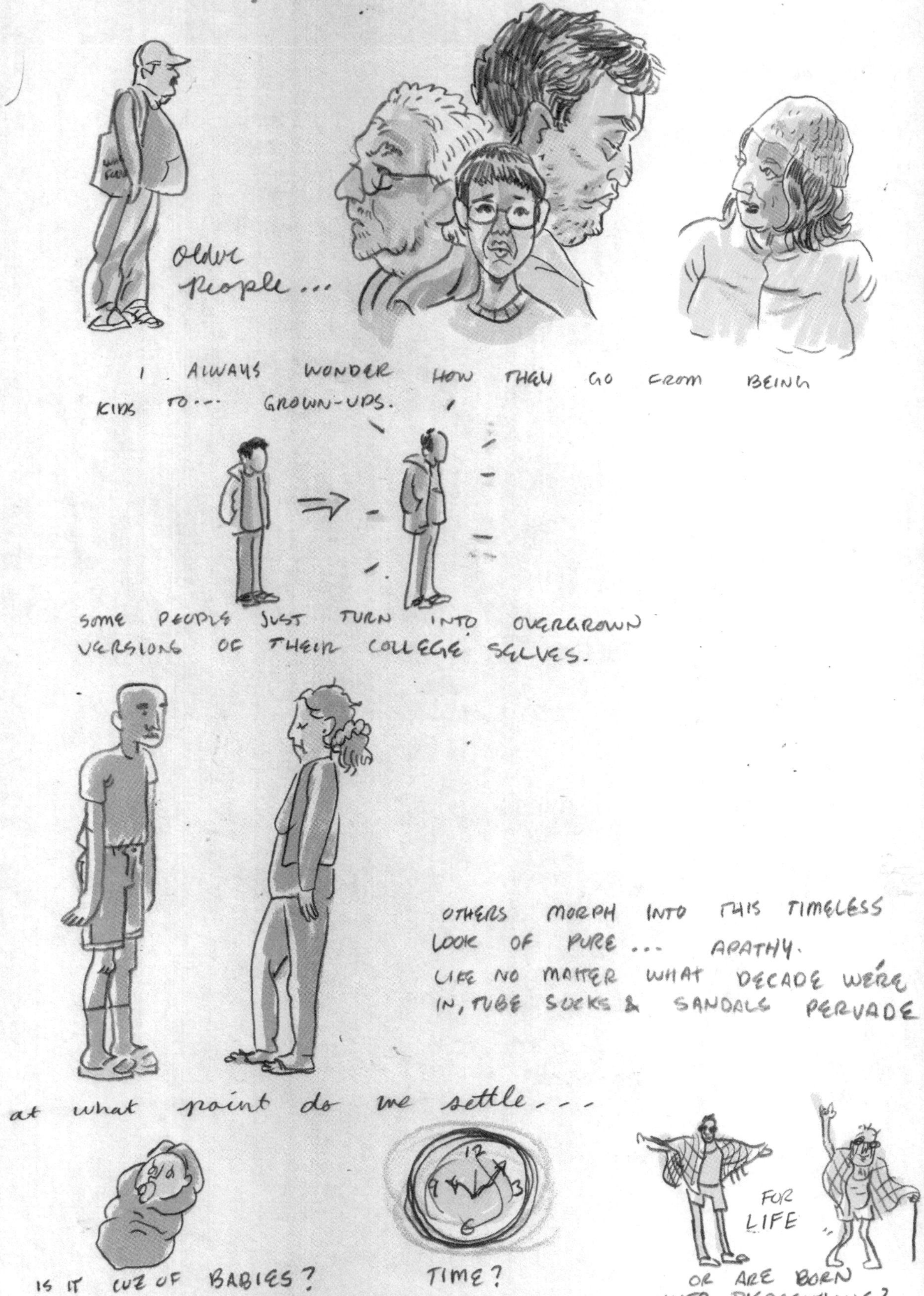
Older People...
I ALWAYS WONDER HOW THEY GO FROM BEING KIDS TO... GROWN-UPS.
SOME PEOPLE JUST TURN INTO OVERGROWN VERSIONS OF THEIR COLLEGE SELVES.
OTHERS MORPH INTO THIS TIMELESS LOOK OF PURE... APATHY.
LIFE NO MATTER WHAT DECADE WE'RE IN, TUBE SOCKS & SANDALS PERVADE
at what point do we settle...
IS IT CUZ OF BABIES?
12
9
3
6
TIME?
FOR LIFE
OR ARE BORN INTO DISPOSITIONS?

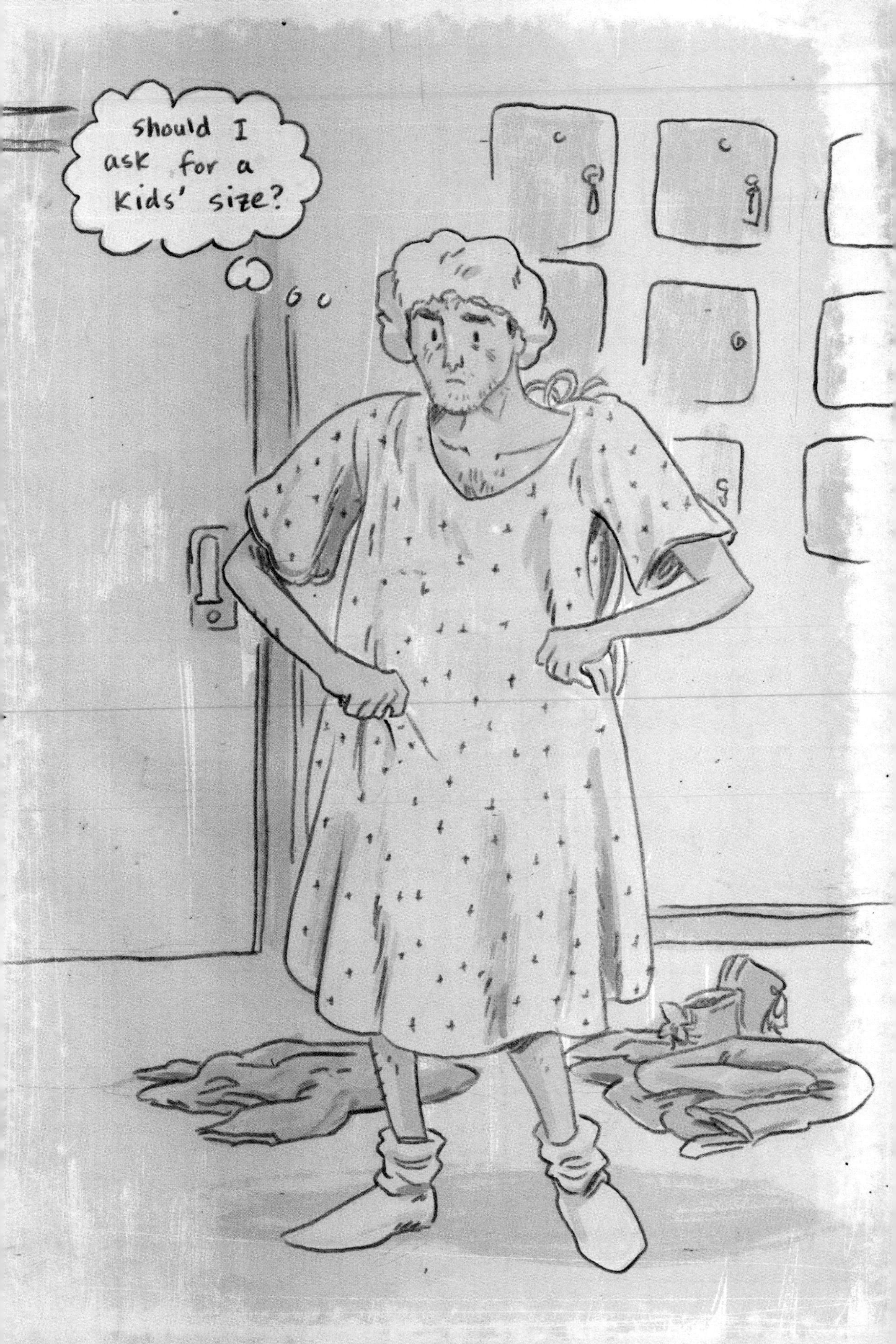
Should I ask for a kids' size?

the big day!

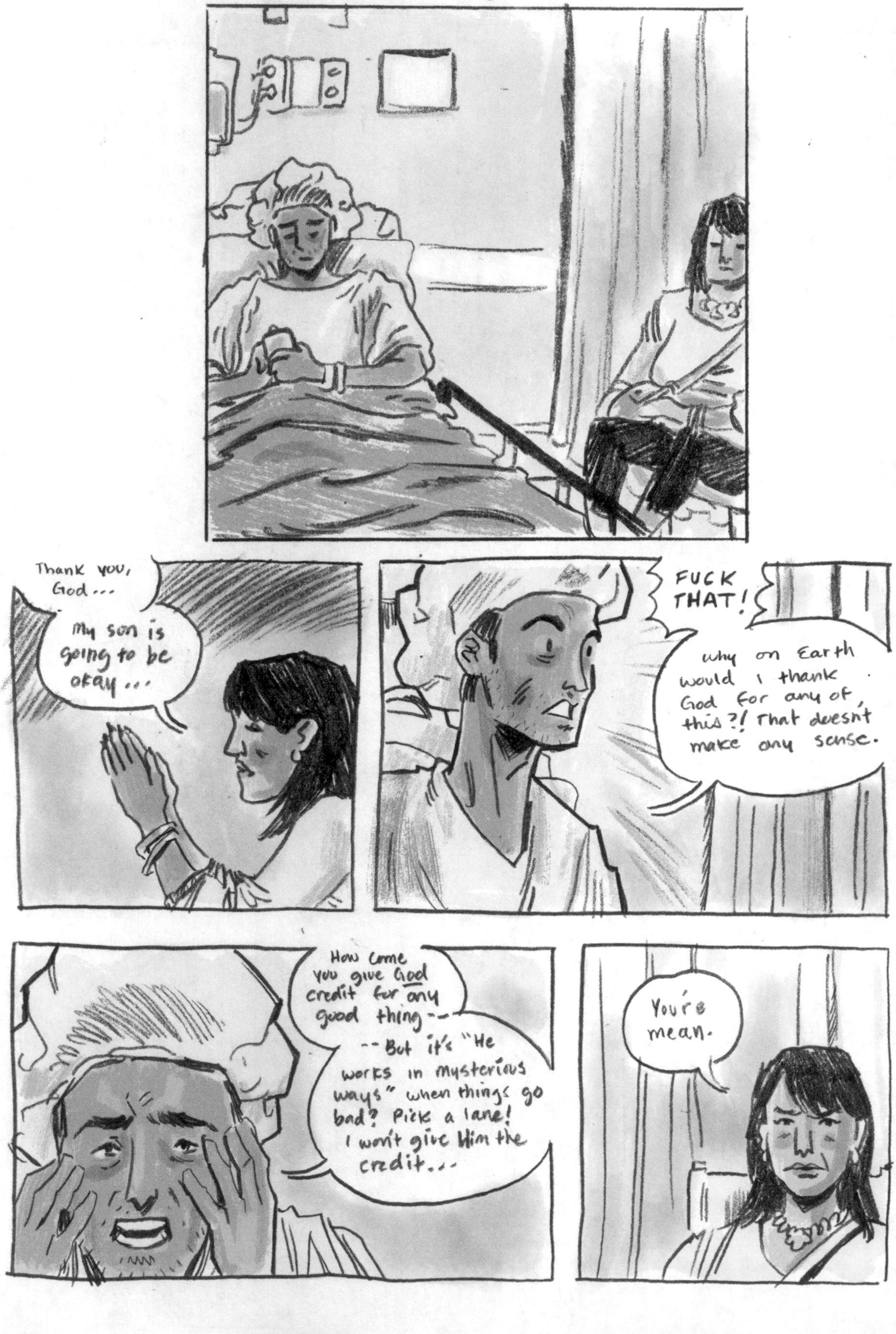
Thank you, God...
My son is going to be okay...
FUCK THAT!
why on Earth would I thank God for any of this?! That doesn't make any sense.
How come you give God credit for any good thing--
--But it's "He works in mysterious ways" when things go bad? Pick a lane! I won't give Him the credit...
You're mean.

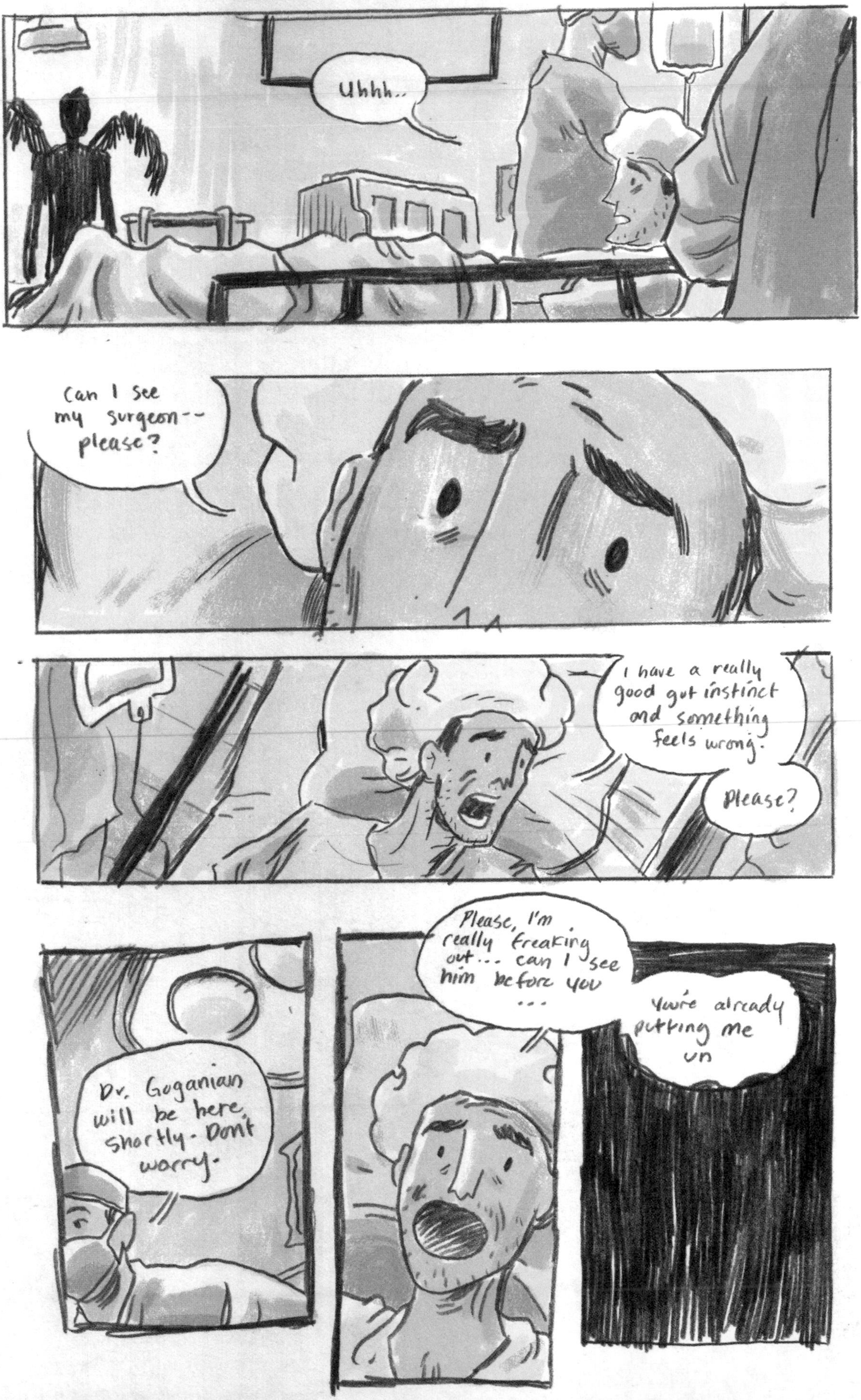
Uhhh..
Can I see my surgeon-- please?
I have a really good gut instinct and something feels wrong.
Please?
Dr. Goganian will be here shortly. Don't worry.
Please, I'm really freaking out... can I see him before you ...
You're already putting me un

You don't need to see
the recovery...

The epidural-sized needles
used to block my nerves, so
the pain could go from a
9 to a 4...

The catheter...

The two weeks of liquid
and broth...

The night I sobbed in my chair
because I ate a bowl of pasta
without weed...

The night Cash brought
me soup and popsicles...

The month it took to finally
remember what "normal" feels like...

I got better.

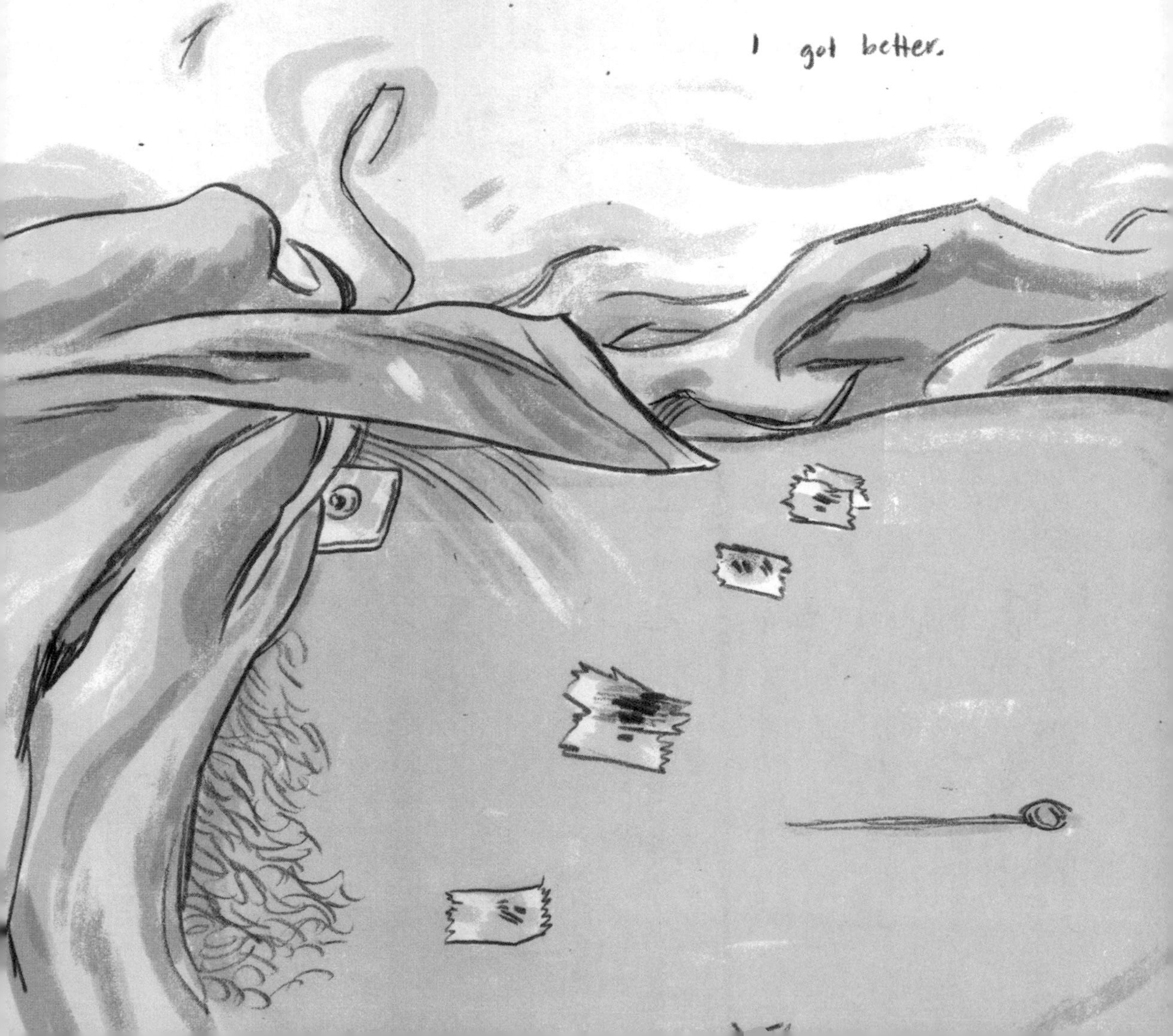

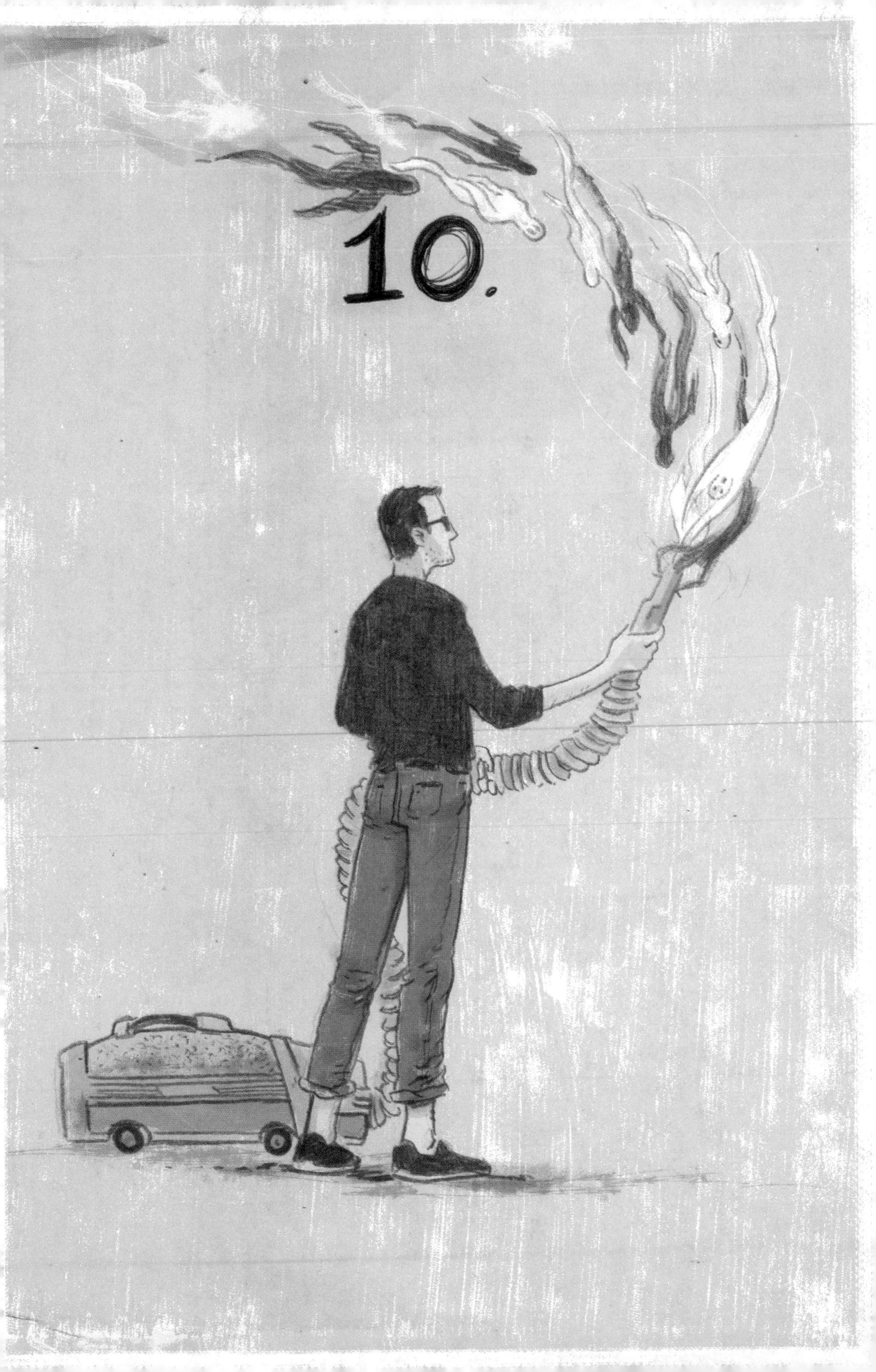
10.

a memory (shopping with an unnamed pal)

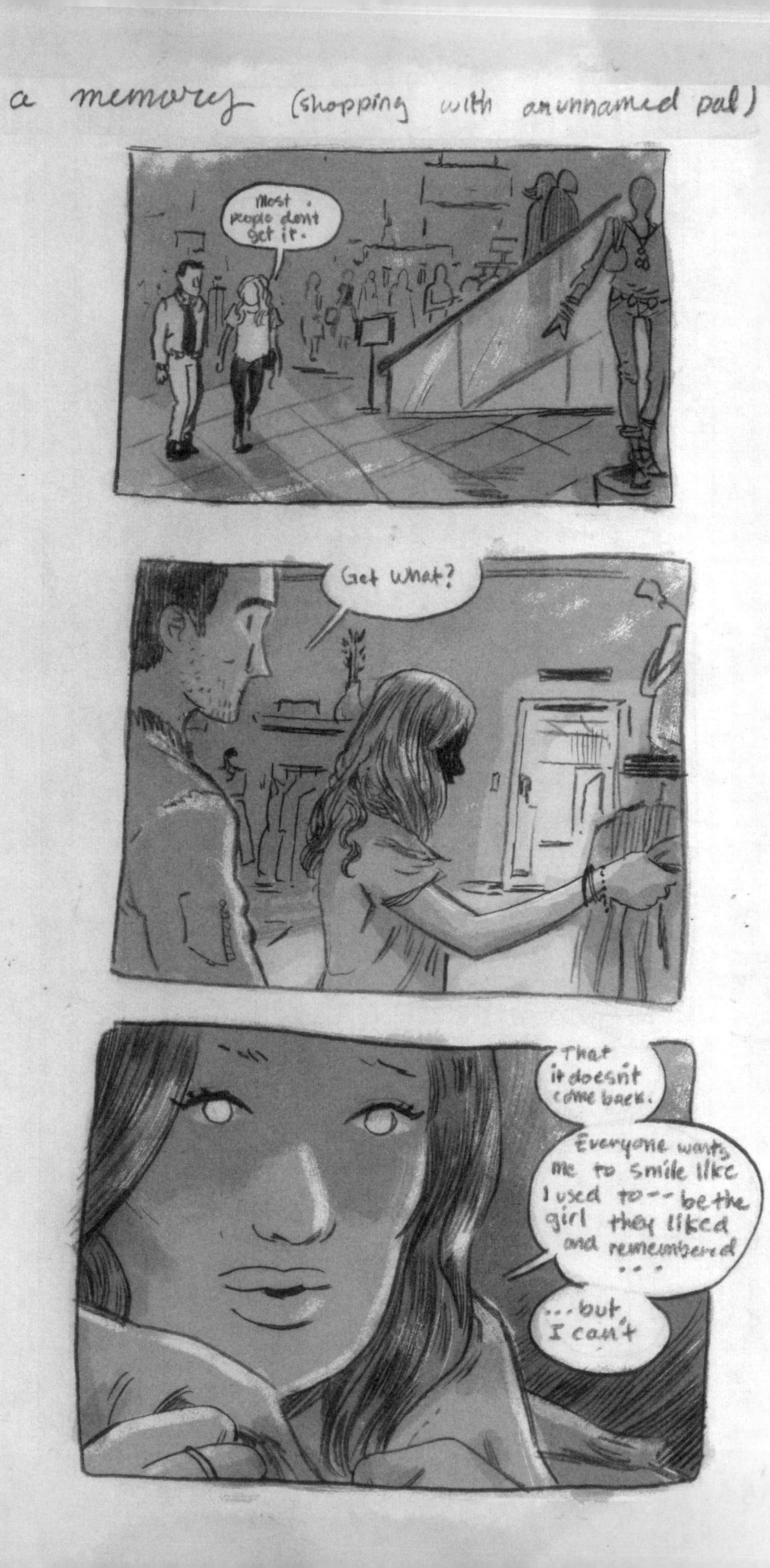

Most people dont get it.
Get what?
That it doesn't come back.
Everyone wants me to smile like I used to -- be the girl they liked and remembered . . .
. . . but, I can't

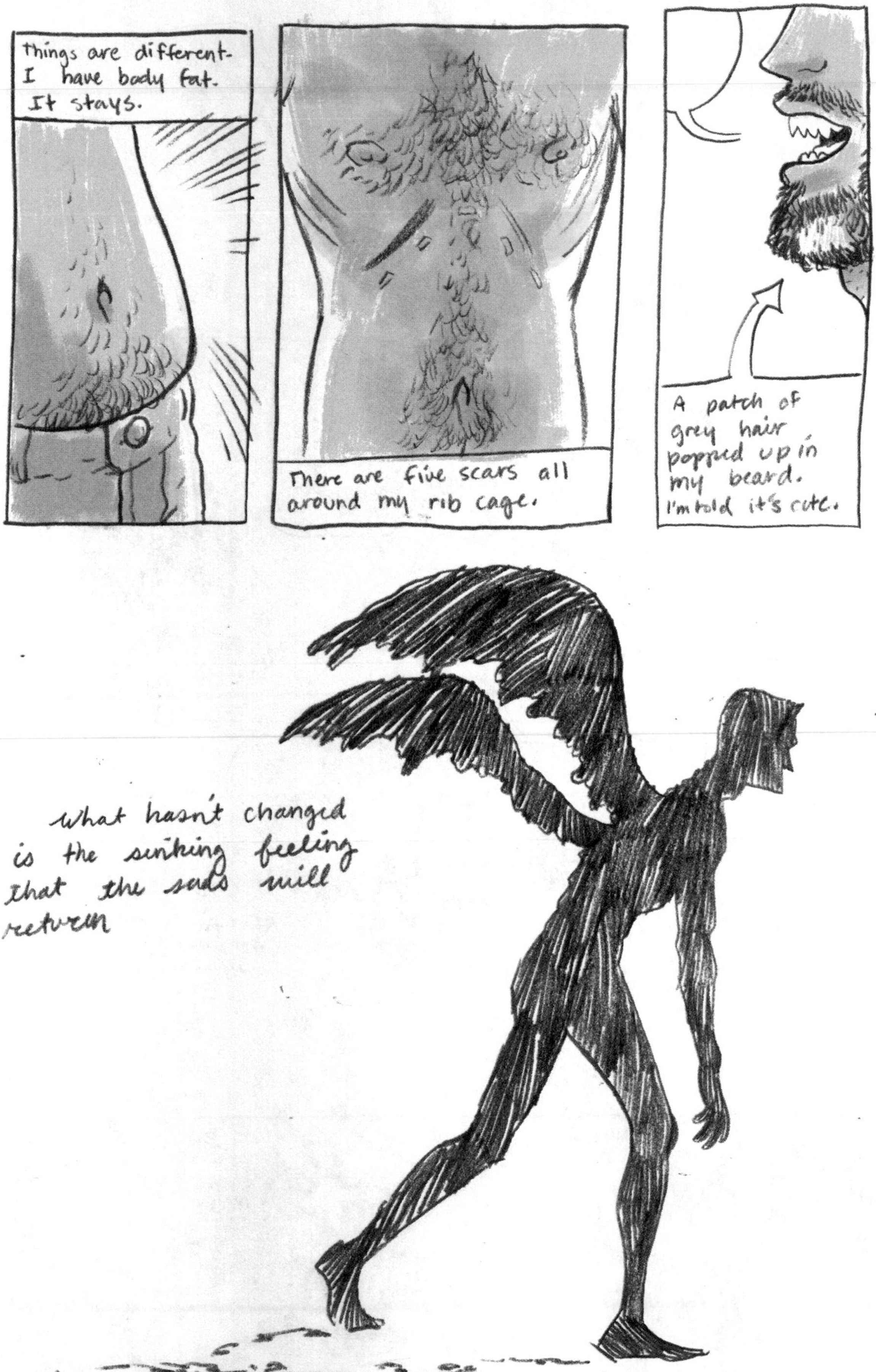
things are different-
I have body fat.
It stays.
There are five scars all
around my rib cage.
A patch of
grey hair
popped up in
my beard.
I'm told it's cute.
What hasn't changed
is the sinking feeling
that the sads will
return

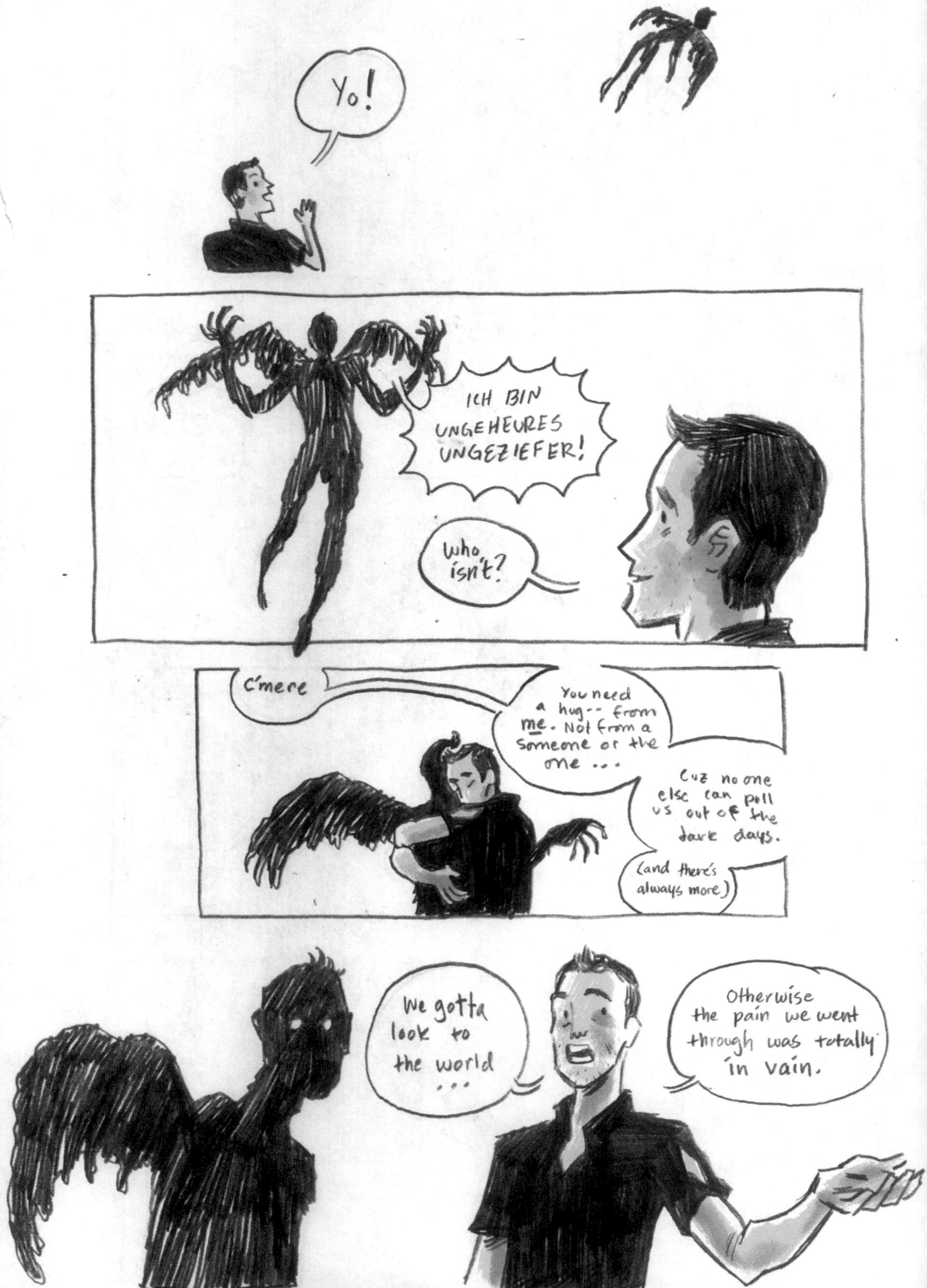
Yo!
ICH BIN UNGEHEURES UNGEZIEFER!
Who isn't?
C'mere
You need a hug-- from me. Not from a someone or the one...
Cuz no one else can pull us out of the dark days.
(and there's always more)
We gotta look to the world...
Otherwise the pain we went through was totally in vain.

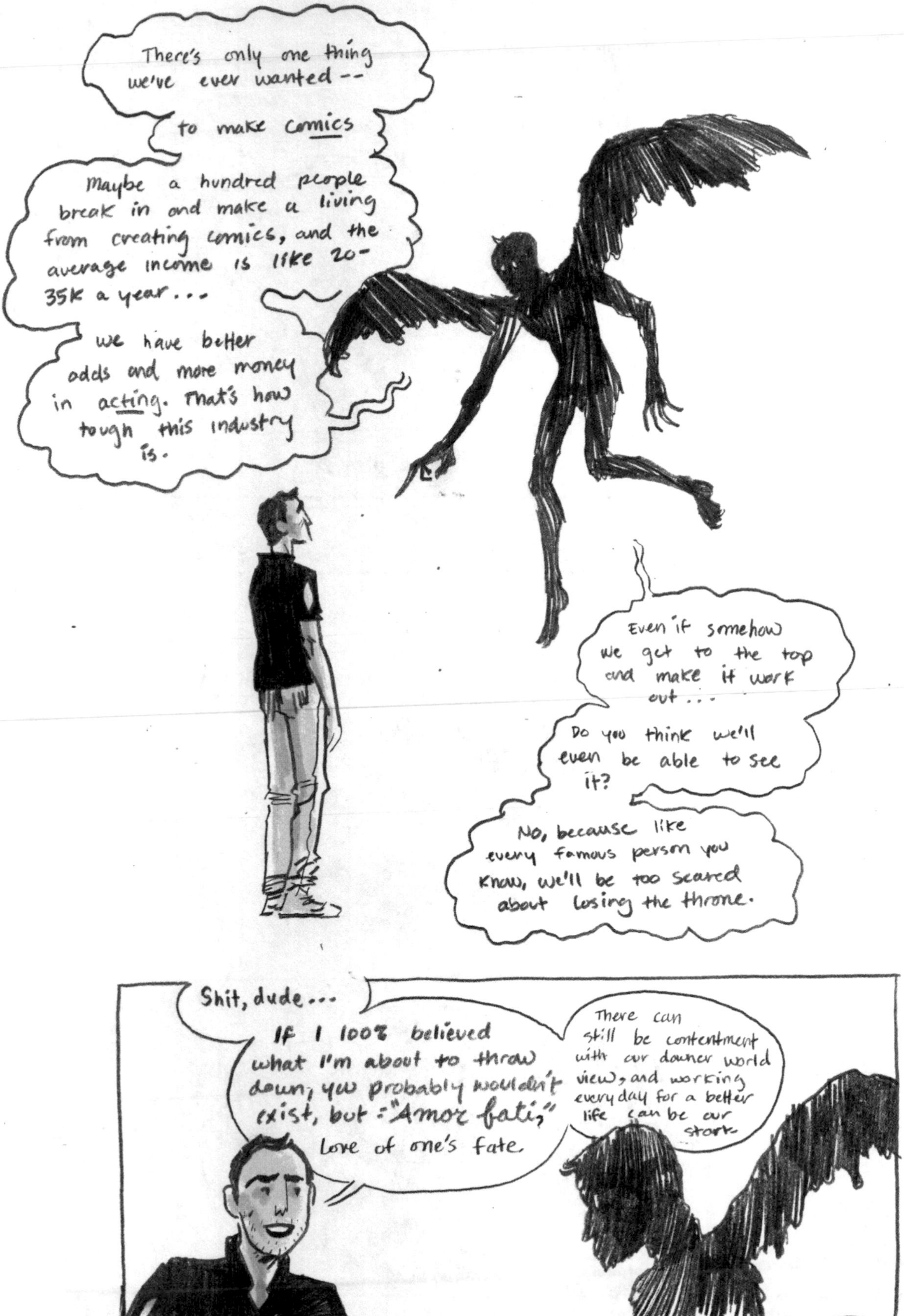
There's only one thing we've ever wanted --
to make comics
Maybe a hundred people break in and make a living from creating comics, and the average income is like 20-35K a year...
we have better odds and more money in acting. That's how tough this industry is.
Even if somehow we get to the top and make it work out...
Do you think we'll even be able to see it?
No, because like every famous person you know, we'll be too scared about losing the throne.
Shit, dude...
If I 100% believed what I'm about to throw down, you probably wouldn't exist, but: "Amor fati," love of one's fate.
There can still be contentment with our downer world view, and working every day for a better life can be our stork

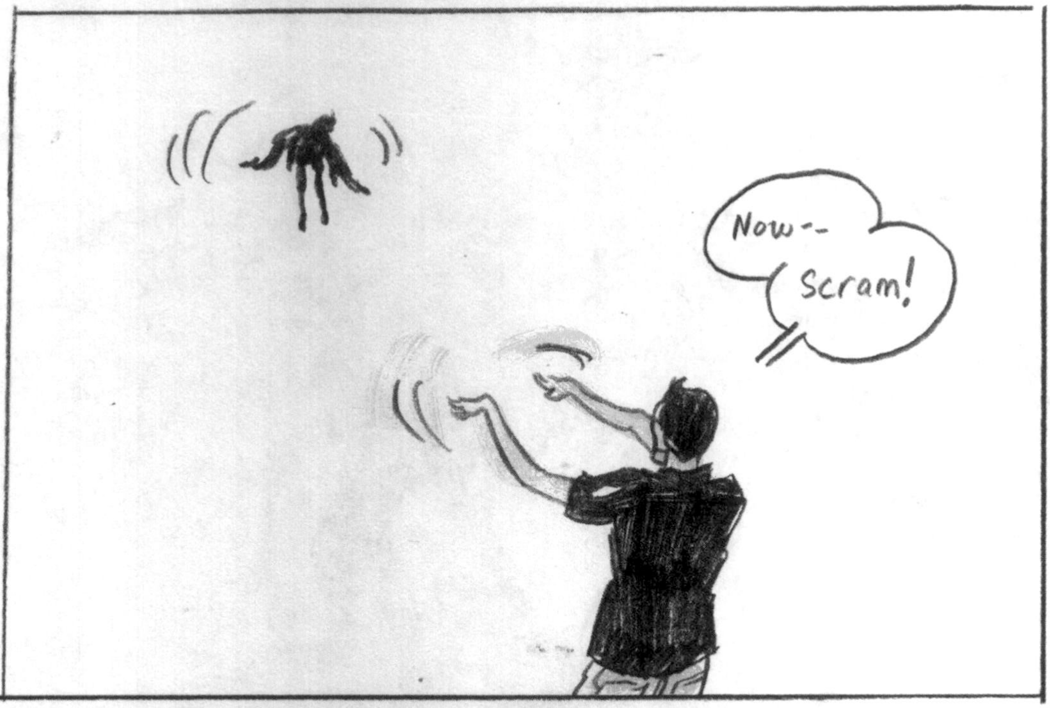
Now--
Scram!

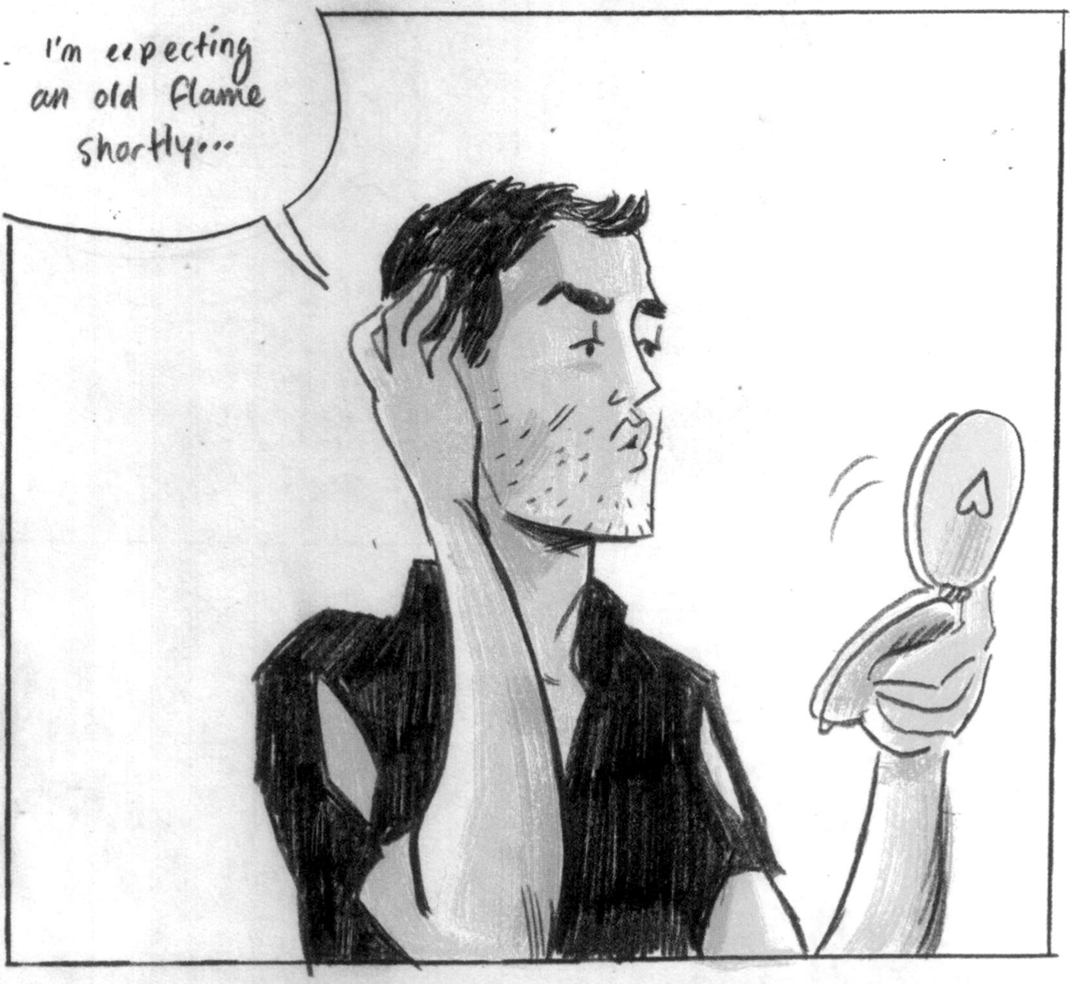
I'm expecting an old flame shortly...

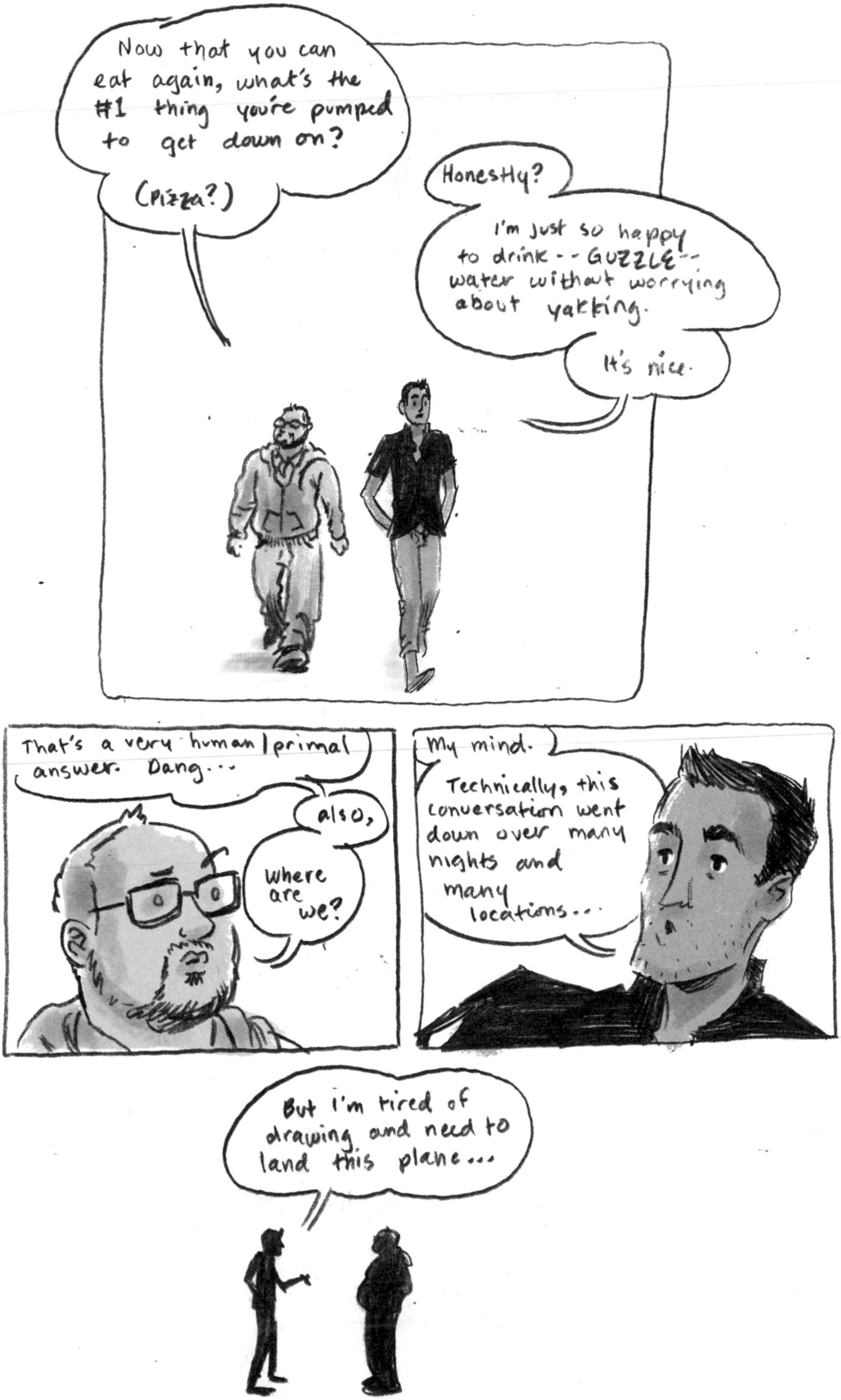
Now that you can eat again, what's the #1 thing you're pumped to get down on?
(PIZZA?)
Honestly?
I'm just so happy to drink --GUZZLE-- water without worrying about yakking.
It's nice.
That's a very human/primal answer. Dang...
also,
Where are we?
My mind.
Technically, this conversation went down over many nights and many locations...
But I'm tired of drawing and need to land this plane...

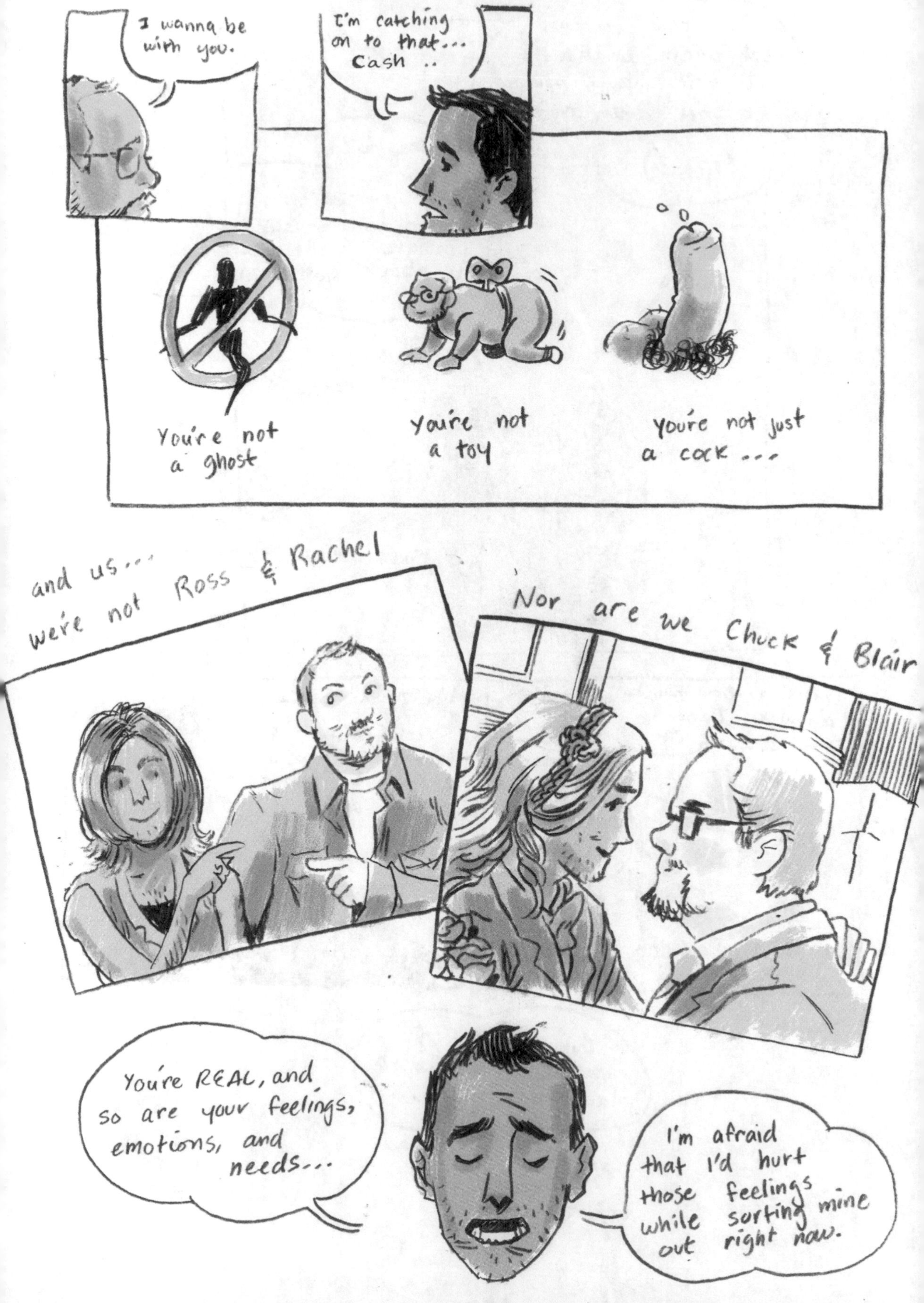
I wanna be with you.
I'm catching on to that... Cash ..
You're not a ghost
You're not a toy
You're not just a cock...
and us... we're not Ross & Rachel
Nor are we Chuck & Blair
You're REAL, and so are your feelings, emotions, and needs...
I'm afraid that I'd hurt those feelings while sorting mine out right now.

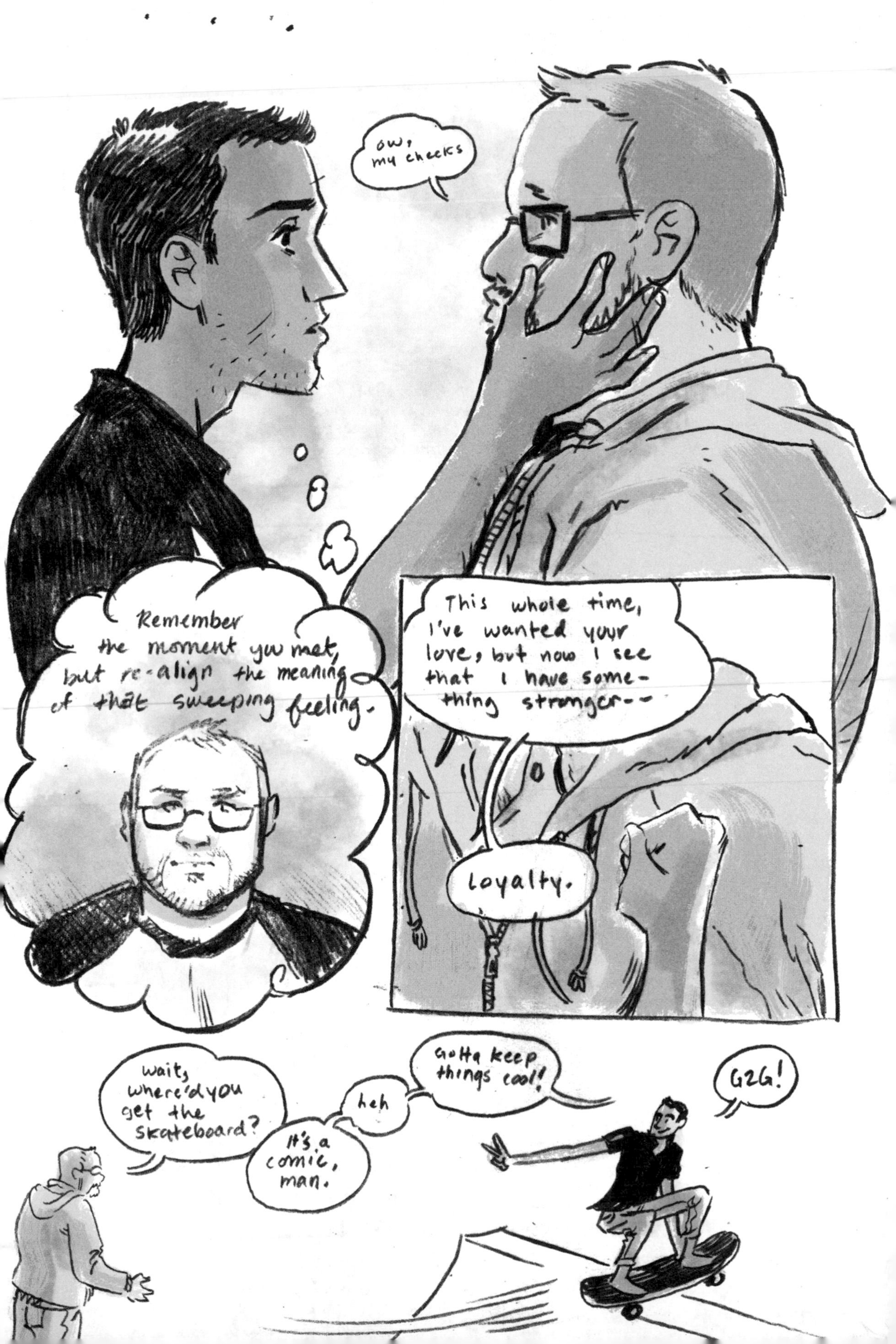
ow, my cheeks
Remember the moment you met, but re-align the meaning of that sweeping feeling.
This whole time, I've wanted your love, but now I see that I have some-thing stronger--
Loyalty.
Wait, where'd you get the skateboard?
heh
It's a comic, man.
Gotta keep things cool!
G2G!

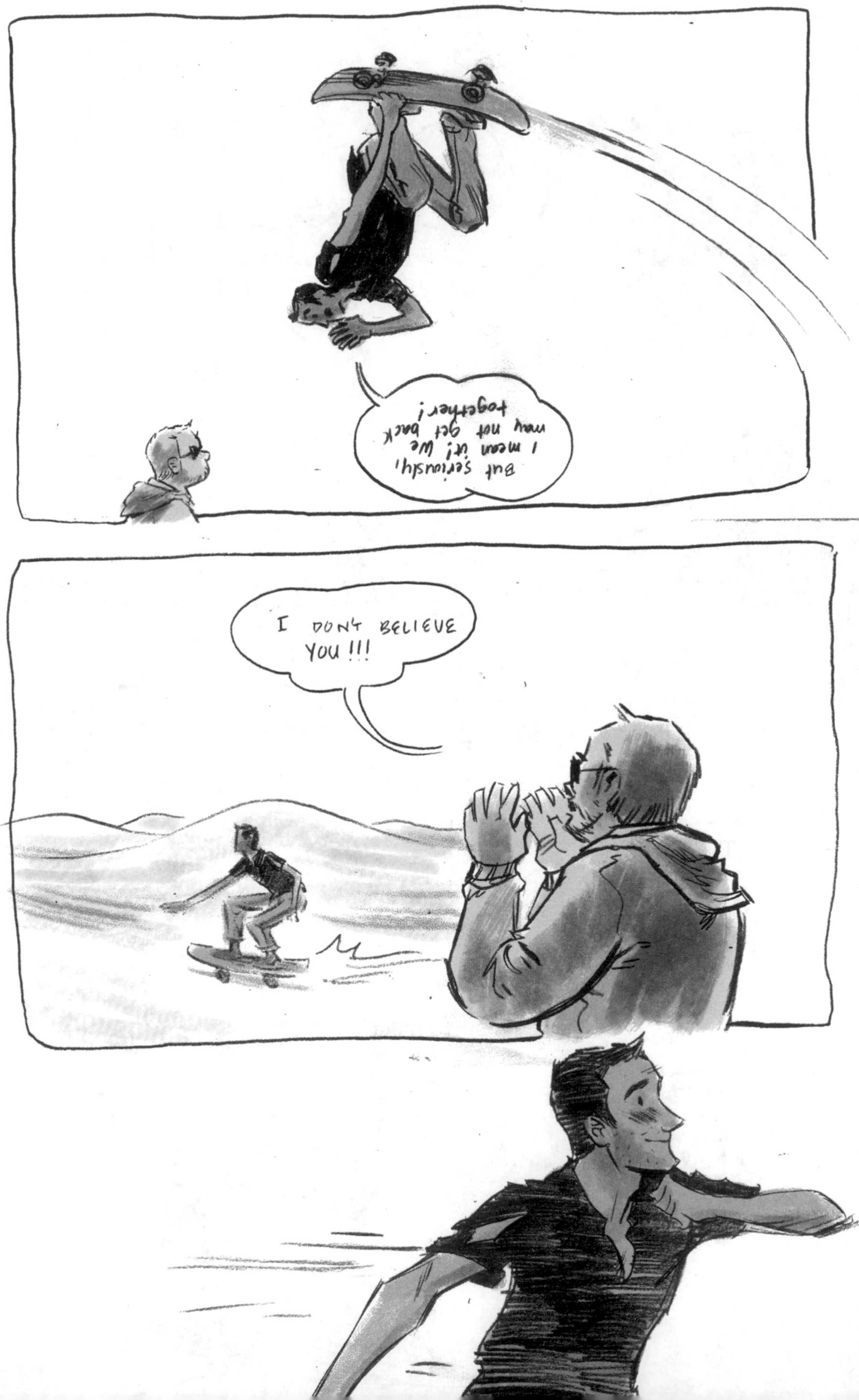
But seriously, I mean it! We may not get back together!
I DON'T BELIEVE YOU!!!

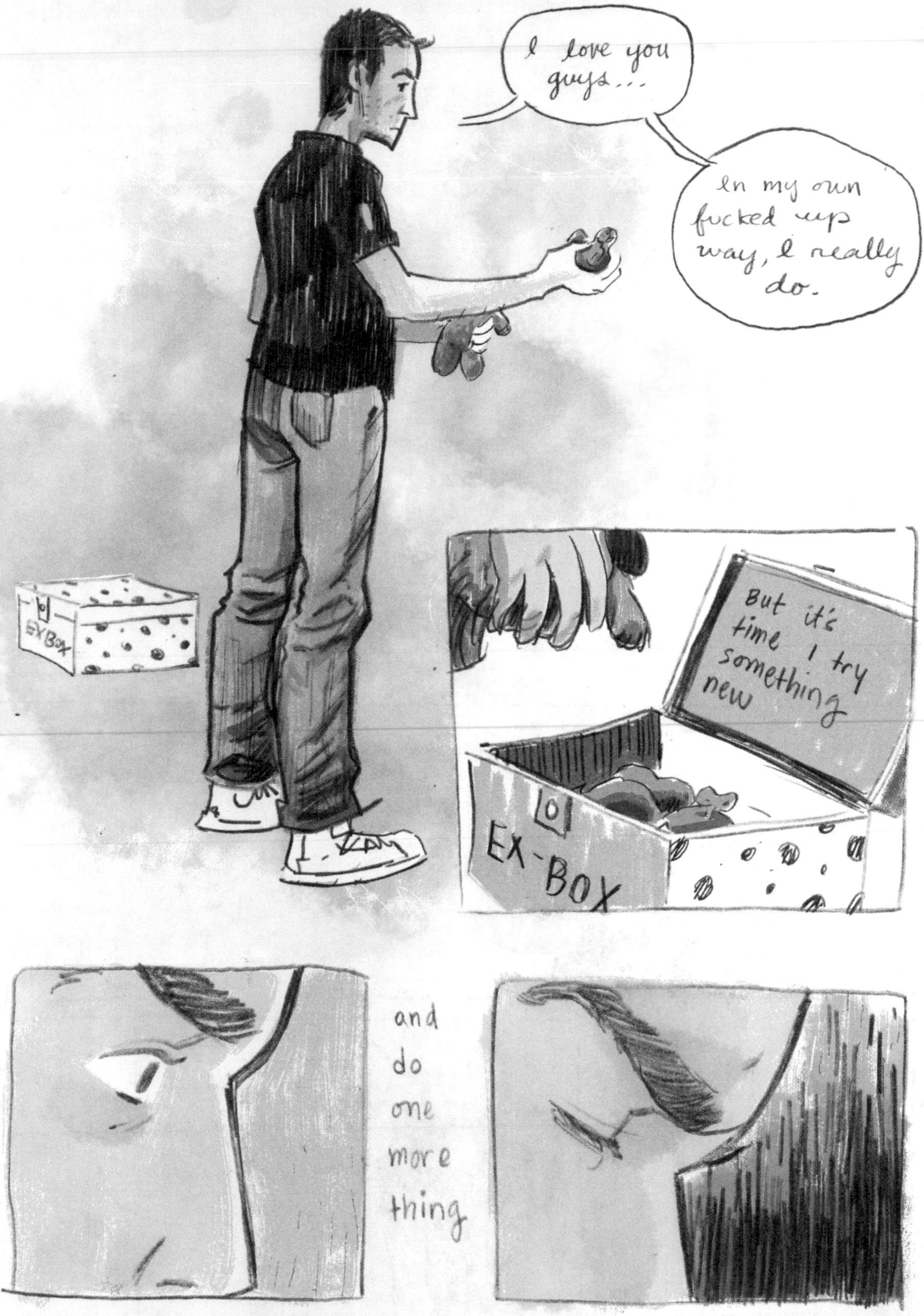
I love you guys...
In my own fucked up way, I really do.
EX Box
But it's time I try something new
EX-BOX
and do one more thing

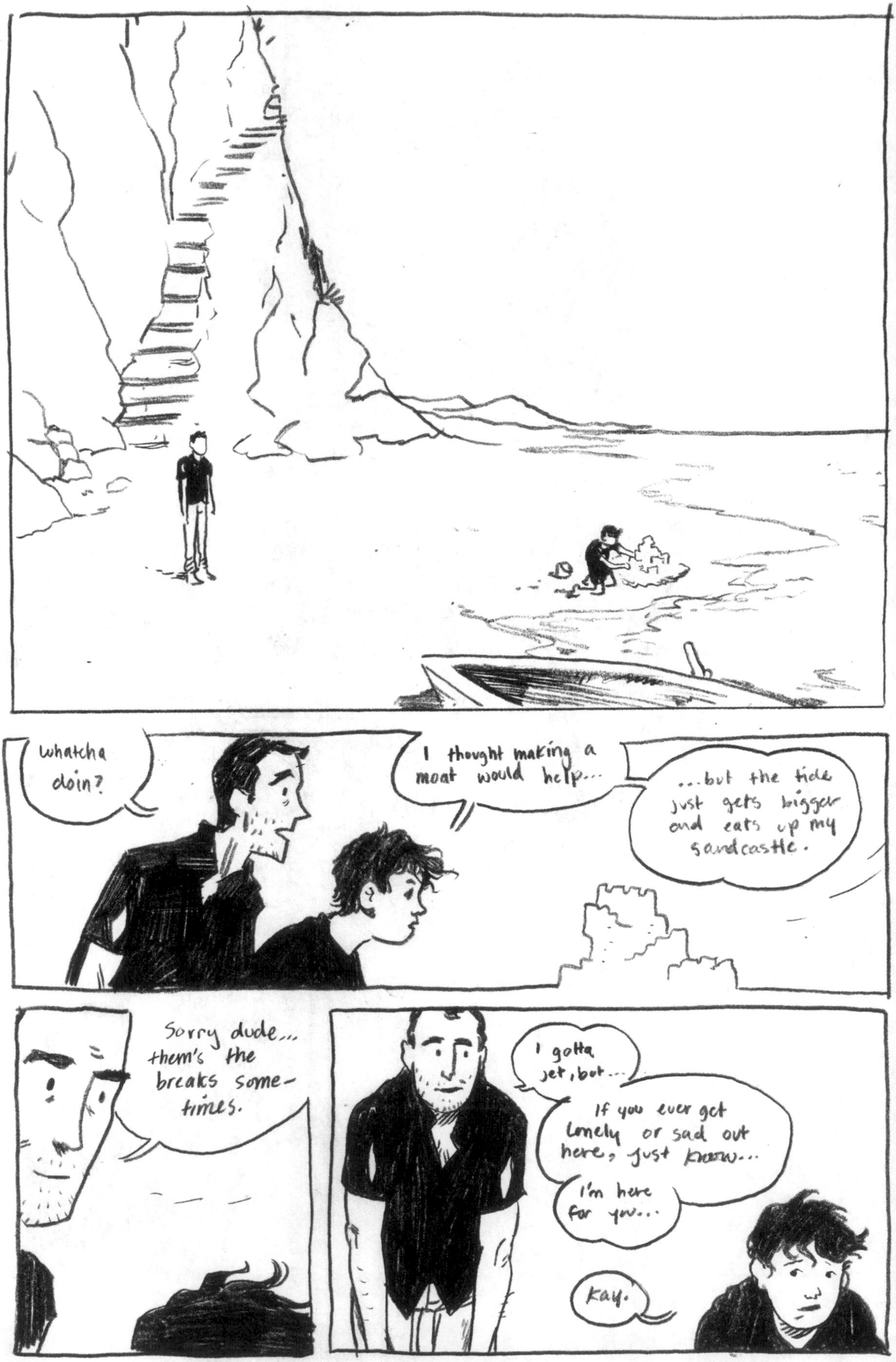
whatcha doin?
I thought making a moat would help...
...but the tide just gets bigger and eats up my sandcastle.
Sorry dude... them's the breaks sometimes.
I gotta jet, but...
If you ever get lonely or sad out here, just know...
I'm here for you...
Kay.

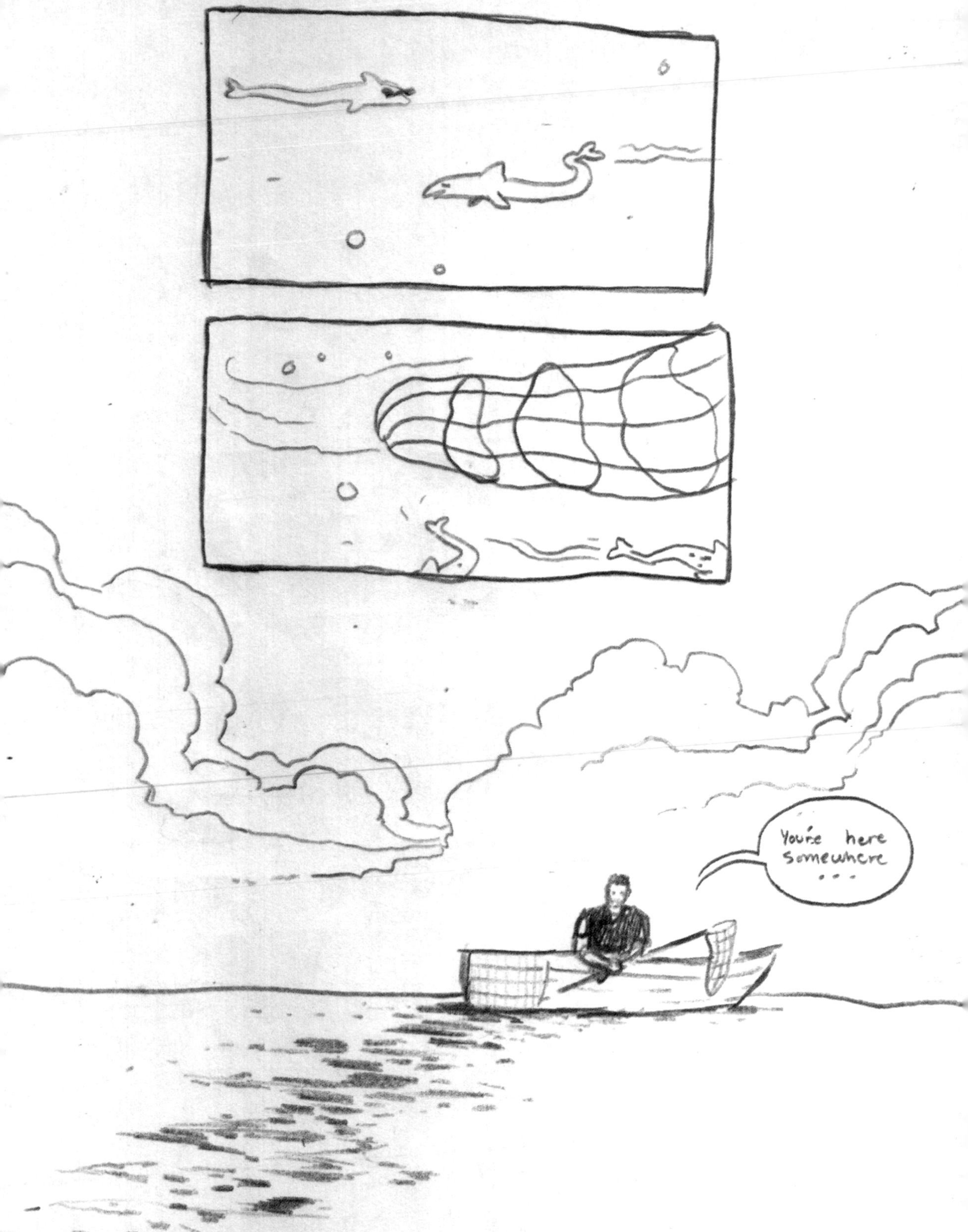
You're here somewhere ...

Acknowledgments

1st: Amber Benson & Jenny Lewis
        for guiding by example

2nd: Eric Stephenson & Erik Larsen
        for believing in me/this

3rd: Jenny D. Fine
        for stepping in

4th: Mikael Sebag
        for a decade of friendships
        and a week of assists

6th: Powry & Salomeh Grace
        for being the best family

7th: Robert, Ronnie & Brandon
        for being my bad girls

8th: Tim Or, Elena Megalos & Spencer Alcorn
        for knowing me

9th: Becky Cloonan, Brandon Graham &
     Riley Rossmo (and all comic creators)
        for being in the game

10th: Chris Register
        for believing in someone you
        don't always understand

♡S

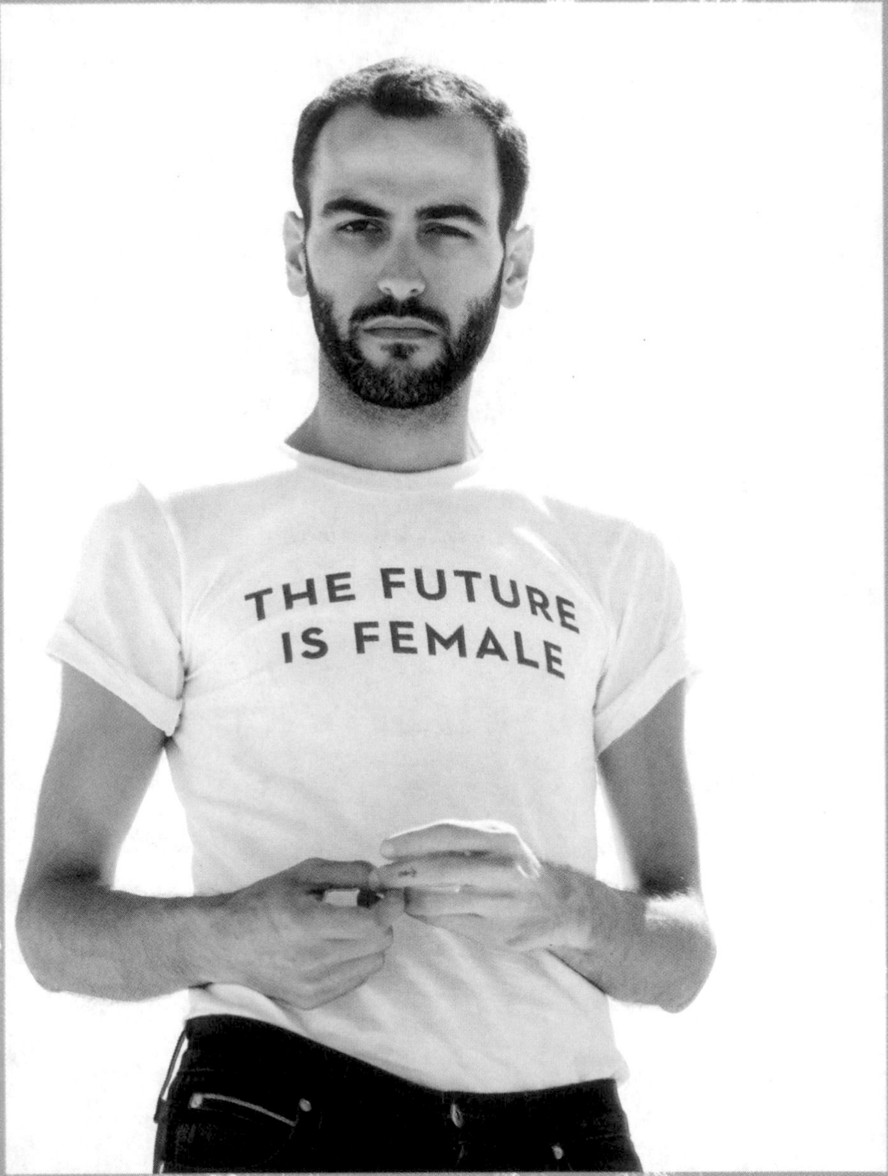
THE FUTURE
IS FEMALE

PHOTO BY NICHOLAS FREEMAN

SINA GRACE IS THE AUTHOR AND ILLUSTRATOR OF THE MEMOIR BOOKS *NOT MY BAG*, WHICH RECOUNTS A STORY OF RETAIL HELL, AND *SELF-OBSESSED*, WHICH HAS SINCE BEEN ADAPTED INTO A WEBSERIES. HE ACTS AS THE ARTIST FOR SHAUN STEVEN STRUBLE'S CULT HIT, *THE LI'L DEPRESSED BOY*, AND HANDLES ART CHORES ALONG WITH CO-WRITING THE FIGHTER GAME SEND-UP, *BURN THE ORPHANAGE*.

GRACE HAS ALSO DONE ILLUSTRATIONS FOR ALL-AGES READERS, INCLUDING *AMONG THE GHOSTS*, WRITTEN BY AMBER BENSON, AND *PENNY DORA & THE WISHING BOX*, WRITTEN BY MICHAEL STOCK. HE HAS WORKED WITH MANY MUSIC INDUSTRY GREATS, INCLUDING JENNY LEWIS, TEGAN & SARA, AND CHILDISH GAMBINO. FOR A TIME, HE ACTED AS EDITORIAL DIRECTOR FOR ROBERT KIRKMAN'S SKYBOUND IMPRINT AT IMAGE COMICS. TO DATE, HE'S WORKED FOR MARVEL COMICS, IDW, BOOM, DYNAMITE, VALIANT, AND MORE. HIS ESSAYS HAVE APPEARED ON SEVERAL WEBSITES, MOST NOTABLY THOUGHT CATALOG AND POPSUGAR.

HE'S CURRENTLY WRITING THE *ICEMAN* SERIES FOR MARVEL, AND LIVING IT UP IN LOS ANGELES, WHERE HE CAN BE FOUND IN COFFEE SHOPS DAYDREAMING ABOUT BOYS.